MW00615976

Praise for *Journey into t... ...*

"In crisp and clear prose, Hari-kirtana das offers an illuminating guide to the Bhagavad-gītā, a classic of India's spiritual wisdom. This guide makes the world of the Bhagavad-gītā – often confusing and trackless to the novice reader – accessible and easy to understand. Particularly useful is the 'prelude' to each chapter, which explains difficult concepts, defines unfamiliar terms, and offers key themes to reflect upon while reading the chapter. I recommend this book to any reader who is looking for a personal and heartfelt journey into the Bhagavad-gītā."

~ Dr. Ravi M. Gupta, Charles Redd Chair of Religious Studies, Utah State University

"Get ready to go on a life-changing adventure. Hari-kirtana das puts every piece of the puzzle in the right place for us to see the roadmap to spiritual success that's woven into the pages of the Bhagavad-gītā. This book is a great resource for yoga teachers, spiritual seekers, and anyone who wants to learn how to find lasting peace of mind."

~ Raghunath Cappo, author of *From Punk to Monk: A Memoir* and co-host of the Wisdom of the Sages podcast

"*Journey Into the Bhagavad-gītā* challenges us to see how every problem is ultimately a spiritual problem and why movement toward a new way of being begins with the transformation of our consciousness. Hari-kirtana's experiential approach to the Gītā's philosophy (which can sometimes be so complex for folks!) guides us across a bridge that leads to unity, lays a spiritual foundation for social justice, and hands us a key for unlocking our potential to live at our full power, together. Read this incredible book."

~ Justin Michael Williams, Grammy-nominated musician and author of *Stay Woke: A Meditation Guide for the Rest of Us*

"It is rare to find a commentary to a classical philosophical book that weaves together the meaning and key concepts and successfully integrates them into a practical life manual for modern times. Hari-kirtana das does that expertly and demonstrates how the timeless conversation between Krishna and Arjuna is a message of hope and victory in our personal battles today. *Journey Into the Bhagavad-gītā* is a most relevant and necessary guide for anyone looking to develop their personal expression of yoga and spirituality."

~ Divya Alter, Ayurvedic chef, culinary educator, author, and co-owner of Divya's

"I know what you are thinking . . . 'another Bhagavad-gītā translation?!' But there is a reason that th Gītā keeps getting translated over and over again: it still profoundly applies to the modern world. Hari's rendition is the one I have been waiting for and the best practical, real-world guide to the Bhagavad-gītā there is. You'll have a hard time putting it down. The language flows. The preludes to each chapter provide context so you won't get lost. But Part Three, on integrating the teachings into your life, is by far my favorite – with conversation starters, journaling exercises, personal experiments, and guided meditations. This book is great for anyone interested in the topic, but it is a must if you teach yoga and/or meditation."

~ Ann Swanson, author of *Science of Yoga* and *Meditation for the Real World*

"With *Journey Into the Bhagavad-gītā*, beloved yoga teacher Hari-kirtana das has added a valuable contribution to the growing library of contemporary presentations of the Gītā – particularly for those seeking to understand the book as a treatise on yoga philosophy. Perhaps not unlike its source text, this version is paradoxical in the most beautiful sense of that term. Here is an edition that is easily accessible and relatable, whatever a reader's familiarity with the Gītā might be, yet it doesn't sacrifice depth. It faithfully and respectfully draws from commentarial tradition, but offers us innovative ways to apply wisdom teachings to our everyday-lives and current contexts. It honors the cultural and religious paradigm that the Gītā arises out of, while emphasizing the text's universal, timeless message. In Hari-kirtana's sensitive and engaging treatment, the image of Krishna that emerges is one of a Divinity who is cosmically vast and incalculably powerful – and yet somehow also strikingly intimate, refreshingly approachable, and enchantingly beautiful."

~ Dr. Vineet Chander, Assistant Dean for Hindu Life
and Hindu Chaplain, Princeton University

"Dip into the refreshing, clarifying waters of the Gītā with the expert, gentle guidance of an experienced teacher. Hari-kirtana's many gems of insight and inspiration prove these ancient teachings remain relevant to our modern lives."

~ Pranada Comtois, author of *Wise-Love: Bhakti and the Search for the Soul of Consciousness*

"*Journey Into the Bhagavad-gītā* is a welcome addition to the ever-growing body of literature on this canonical text of India, and, indeed, of human spirituality in general. Hari-kirtana das channels his 40 years of devotional practice and study of the text into a commentary that is on the one hand grounded in tradition, but, on the other, firmly addressed to the modern reader. *Journey into the Bhagavad-gītā* harnesses the on-going relevance of the Gītā's truths that transcend place and time, and serves as an edition for practitioners who seek a traditional set of teachings that relevantly speaks to the perennial struggles of human existence."

~ Dr. Edwin Bryant, professor of Hindu Religion and Philosophy, Rutgers University

"Reading *Journey Into the Bhagavad-gītā* is a pleasure on every level. The book is satisfying intellectually, spiritually, and emotionally. The author is such an excellent wordsmith that his prose is as refreshing as poetry. Indeed, while the book is an easy and enlivening read that pleasantly flows, many of the phrases and sentences are so filled with meaning and wisdom that a reader will re-read just for the pure joy of doing so."

~ Urmila Edith Best, author of *Essence Seekers: A Quest Beyond the Forest of Enjoyment, The Great Mantra for Mystic Meditation: Opening the Lotus of Good Fortune*, and co-author of *Career Dharma: The Natural Art of Work*

"Hari-kirtana das speaks to a wide strata of Post-Enlightenment readers by unlocking the Pre-Enlightenment wisdom of the Gītā in a way that harmonizes the tensions of faith and reason."

~ Rukmini Walker, founder of the Urban Devi Collective

"*Journey Into The Bhagavad-gītā* is a wonderful and well-articulated explanation of the Gītā's many ethical, philosophical and theological concepts. Clearly structured for both those who are studying the Gītā for the first time and those who are deepening their understanding of these timeless teachings, it's a great contribution to the commentaries, study guides, and devotional literature that the Gītā has inspired for generations and across cultures. I recommend *Journey into the Bhagavad-gītā* for anyone teaching or learning the Gītā."

~ Kenneth N. Lee, Multifaith Chaplain Associate, Stanford University

Also by Hari-kirtana das:

In Search of the Highest Truth – Adventures in Yoga Philosophy

JOURNEY INTO THE BHAGAVAD GITA

JOURNEY INTO THE BHAGAVAD GITA

A Guide to Exploring
Timeless Principles of Transcendental Knowledge
and Integrating Them Into Your Life

HARI-KIRTANA DAS

JAGAT-MAṄGALA
PRESS
Washington, D.C.

Readers interested in the subject matter of this book are invited to correspond with the author via email: hari@hari-kirtana.com

Copyright © 2024 Hari-kirtana das (Howard Siegel). All rights reserved. No part of this document may be reproduced or transmitted in any form or by any means, electronic, mechanical, photocopying, recording, or otherwise, without prior written permission of the publisher.

Published by

JAGAT-MAṄGALA
PRESS

4000 Cathedral Avenue NW
Washington, DC 20016

ISBN-13 number: 978-0-9980773-1-4

LCCN number: 2023914842

Cover concept and illustration by K4V3R1

Creative direction by Jal Keli Das

Interior design by Mayapriya Long

DEDICATION

To

Śrīmān Ūrjasvāt dāsa

Prabhu, I just can't thank you enough.

"All journeys have secret destinations
of which the traveler is unaware."
~ Martin Buber

Contents

Preface

I was introduced to the Bhagavad-gītā when it appeared in the communal collection of books that routinely graced one of the tables in the cafeteria at Kennedy High School in Plainview, New York. The cafeteria doubled as an open study hall, and that particular table was the one where my friends could always be found. The books on the table were an anthology of the spiritual philosophies that floated through the psychedelic counter-culture of the early 1970s; books like *Be Here Now*, the *Tao Te Ching*, *Black Elk Speaks*, and *The Tibetan Book of the Dead*.

In due course of time, an edition of the Bhagavad-gītā made its way into the mix. A few of my friends were particularly enthusiastic about it, so I decided to read it, too.

I didn't get very far. The phraseology was archaic, the terminology was confusing, the cultural references were unfamiliar, I couldn't follow the dialogue . . . it was all pretty incomprehensible.

Except for one part: the part that said that I had always existed and that I would always exist. That part sounded familiar: one summer afternoon, when I was about 10 years old, I was sitting in our backyard with my uncle, who was telling me about Albert Einstein and trying to teach me some very basic principles of physics. One of those basic principles was the first law of thermodynamics: energy can be transformed but it can't be created or destroyed.

When I heard this I thought, "I'm a form of energy. Therefore, I can't be created or destroyed!"

This probably wasn't the take-away that my uncle had in mind, but the idea stuck. Finding validation for my epiphany in this ancient book of spiritual wisdom made me think that the Bhagavad-gītā was worth another try.

So, I tried to read it again. The only thing I got out of it on the second go round was the impression that the Bhagavad-gītā was a book about religion. I wasn't looking for religion. So, I let it go.

But the Bhagavad-gītā didn't let go of me. On the one hand, I'd kind of given up on it. On the other, I still felt an inexplicable attraction.

Eventually, my spiritual journey led me to take up full-time residence in a devotional yoga ashram. There, I encountered the Gītā once again. And, as they say, the third time was the charm.

Unlike before, when I was reading it on my own or with friends who didn't know any more than I did, I was now participating in a systematic group study under the guidance of more experienced and knowledgeable teachers. Just as significantly, the members of the spiritual community I'd joined were all committed to a spiritual practice and lifestyle based on the Gītā's teachings. This lent an experiential dynamic to our study: individual reading and group discussions were accompanied by complementary spiritual practices and a corresponding lifestyle.

This combination of contemplative study, meditation, and the practical application of the Gītā's teachings had a profoundly transformative effect: I began to feel a glimmer of the peace that goes with experiencing oneself as an infinitesimal part of an infinite and complete whole from which one can never truly be separated and upon whom one can always depend.

After five years of studying the Bhagavad-gītā as a lived experience in community with like-minded devotees, I left the monastic setting of the ashram but continued my practice of meditation and contemplative study for the better part of the next 40 years.

In 2007, I travelled to Vrindavan, a holy place of pilgrimage in northern India. I was walking near the bank of the sacred Yamuna River with two of my teachers when one of them said to me, "Harikirtana, you need to teach. It's in your nature. It would be good for you and you could do good for others. You should find a way to become a teacher."

I took his counsel as confirmation that I should act on an idea I'd already been thinking about. A few years earlier, I'd started practicing yoga in the modern postural sense of the word. I knew that I had a strong practice, I felt confident in my ability to lead classes, and it was clear to me that becoming a yoga teacher would give me a platform for teaching yoga philosophy, especially the transformative philosophy of the Bhagavad-gītā. My teacher's advice was the last push that I needed to make a firm commitment to becoming a yoga teacher.

By this time, I'd moved from New York to Washington, D.C., a city with a very vibrant yoga community of which I'd become an active member. As soon as I came home from India, I became a certified yoga instructor, started teaching at local studios, and began integrating the Gītā's teachings into my classes and workshops. It wasn't long before I found myself receiving invitations to be a guest teacher for Yoga Teacher Training programs throughout the Mid-Atlantic region.

But when students asked me which edition of the Gītā they should read, I found it difficult to recommend one that made its teachings accessible for contemporary readers, especially those who were encountering the Gītā for the first-time. Despite the availability of many excellent translations and the nearly mystical potency of the edition that inspired me to dedicate myself to the Gītā's teachings, each version of the Gītā that I was otherwise inclined to recommend required a caveat of one kind or another. In some editions the translator had sacrificed clarity for fidelity to the poetic structure of the original Sanskrit. In others, terse literalism accompanied by dense philosophical explanations overshadowed the beauty of the Gītā's poetry. Other authors used idiosyncratic phrasing that was hard for a novice to decipher, anachronistic analogies that might be off-putting to a modern audience, or old-fashioned "whilst thys" and "dost thous" that made the Gītā sound like a Shakespearean version of a Hindu Bible.

I also felt obliged to tell my students that many of the popular and presumably "more accessible" editions of the Gītā obscured or deflated the Gītā's message by injecting ideologically biased interpretations into their translations and commentaries or condescendingly mischaracterizing the Gītā as a second-rate presentation of a "perennial" philosophy.

Given the scarcity of editions that made the Gītā's teachings easily accessible and the multitude of misdirected editions that, at least in my opinion, didn't serve the best interests of the reader, I decided to follow the suggestion of many of my students and write my own book about the Gītā.

However, it didn't make much sense to write a book *about* the Bhagavad-gītā without including the Bhagavad-gītā itself. So, after eight years of presenting relatively short-form Gītā workshops, I embarked on a two-year series of live weekly online classes that covered the entire Bhagavad-gītā from beginning to end. In the process, I composed my own English renderings of the Gītā's verses as a part of my preparation for each class.

To do this, I surrounded myself with a wide variety of authoritative translations and commentaries in order to synthesize the best features of each translation in accordance with my understanding and realization of the speaker's intentions. I also listened to hundreds of hours of lectures given by over a dozen different scholar-practitioners whose knowledge and realization far exceeds my own in the hopes of incorporating as much of their wisdom into my project as possible.

One hundred and eight classes later, I completed my online course and, with it, my English renderings of the verses. From then until the time of this book's publication, I've revisited my presentation of the verses many times over to make sure that each verse has been rendered with the kind of accuracy, elegance, continuity, and clarity that I think a reader might experience if the Gītā had originally been spoken in contemporary American English. My hope is that I've composed the Gītā's verses in such a way as to make their teachings accessible for modern readers while simultaneously retaining both their lyrical beauty and their transcendental dimensions.

My attempt to present these teachings as I've heard and understood them serves a dual purpose. The first purpose is to purify my own heart. My life has been deeply enriched by the sustained proximity to these ancient teachings that writing this book required. And the act of writing and re-writing my understanding of these teachings has expanded my capacity to articulate the many ways in which the Gītā's ancient teachings remain relevant to life in the modern world.

The second purpose is to give you the opportunity to hear the very same thing that I heard from my teachers in such a way as to enable you to discover the transformative power of the Gītā for yourself. The reception of transcendental knowledge from a teacher who has heard it from their teacher and so on is the method that the Gītā itself recommends in order for it to be understood.

I have yet to hear a more sound, consistent, and beautiful explanation of the Gītā's philosophy than the one I've heard from my teachers. I feel as if I've received the most valuable of gifts by having placed myself at their feet. This book, however imperfect it may be, is my humble attempt to share that precious gift with you.

Introduction

Arjuna looks out across the vast field upon which the kings of the Kuru dynasty and their armies have assembled. He sees millions of warriors in battle formations with their weapons raised, ready to charge. On his side, he sees his brothers, friends, in-laws, and allies anxiously waiting for him to lead them into battle. On the other side, he sees his revered teacher, his beloved grandfather, his deceitful cousins and their envious co-conspirators, all ready to attack.

Just as the battle is about to begin, Arjuna is struck by a vision of what's to come: everyone on the battlefield will die. Win or lose, the world as he knows it will come to an end.

Arjuna's vision fills him with despair. He knows that his cause is just, but he also knows that the very act of fighting for that cause will end in devastation for his family and the destruction of his society. He wonders if abandoning the fight altogether would be better than engaging in a battle that can only end in either a senseless defeat or a pyrrhic victory. Even sacrificing his life seems preferable to waging war against those whom he regards as worthy of his worship. Incapacitated by confusion, he turns to his best friend, Kṛṣṇa, for guidance.

Kṛṣṇa validates Arjuna's assessment of the situation: the destruction Arjuna foresees is inevitable. But there's no way around the battle, only a way *through* the battle, and Kṛṣṇa can show him the way.

This is where the teachings of the Bhagavad-gītā begin.

The Bhagavad-gītā is a message of hope, but not the kind of hope we usually hope for. We usually hope for happiness. However, the "happiness" we usually hope for is attainable only in the fleeting moments when the world aligns with our desires. The Gītā offers us hope for a categorically different kind of happiness; a happiness that can be attained not by moving the world into alignment with our desires, but by aligning ourselves with changeless principles of universal harmony.

Generations of seekers from all walks of life have looked to the Bhagavad-gītā for practical knowledge and spiritual wisdom. Whether you live on Main Street or on the margins, the Gītā has something to offer you:

- For those who identify as spiritual but not religious, the Gītā offers a conception of Divinity that isn't bound by dogmatic doctrines, warped by authoritarian institutions, or undermined by corrupt human behavior.

- For those who feel unfulfilled, wounded, or abandoned by religion, the Gītā offers comprehensive answers to reasonable questions, deific opinions rather than paternal commandments, and the voice of a patient and compassionate God who welcomes everyone.

- For those who are interested in principles of leadership and personal growth, the Gītā offers guidance on how to analyze situations, understand people, make wise decisions, and act with integrity, even in exceptionally challenging circumstances.

- And for those who want to learn about yoga philosophy, the Bhagavad-gītā takes us far beyond the physical practices into the realms of metaphysics, mysticism, ethics, theology, and existential wonder.

The sublime dialogue of the Bhagavad-gītā is one of the most inspirational and challenging conversations in the history of literature. One reason why the Gītā may be especially challenging for a contemporary Western audience is that the conceptual foundation of the Gītā's worldview is radically different from those of a modern worldview and of most traditional religions. To understand and appreciate the value of the Gītā's worldview, the reader has to become familiar with a new set of philosophical concepts.

Another reason contemporary readers may struggle with the Gītā is that the dialogue contains numerous references to people, relationships, and events that extend beyond the Gītā's pages. Since these references are specific to the Vedic culture in which the Gītā appears, they're usually unfamiliar to a Western audience.

The last reason why the Gītā may be especially challenging for contemporary readers is that the only way to fully appreciate the Gītā's teachings is to try to live them rather than just read or think about them. The real key to unlocking the secrets of the Gītā's spiritual wisdom is a willingness to make oneself the subject of an experiment in a transformation of consciousness by acting on the basis of the Gītā's teachings.

My hope is that this book will allow you to approach these challenges with confidence and enthusiasm.

Part One is designed to help you recognize and appreciate the significance of the Gītā's transcendental synthesis of science and religion and become familiar with the Gītā's conceptual framework: its overarching theme, its metaphysical assumptions, its spiritual technologies, and its primary topic. This section also provides you with guidance on how to follow the dialogue and offers suggestions for contemplative reading that will help you develop a deep sense of connection to the text.

Part Two of this book is the Bhagavad-gītā itself: the conversation between Kṛṣṇa and Arjuna at the center of the battlefield. For the sake of setting the scene, I've added a summary of the events leading up to the battle that Arjuna is being called to fight. I've also included Preludes to each chapter of the Gītā that will help to demystify any culturally specific references and metaphors you might not be familiar with. These Preludes also describe how the chapters are connected to one another, provide an overview of the topics that will be discussed, and give you a heads up on which passages are especially significant.

Part Three of this book is designed to help you bridge the gap between the Gītā's spiritual ideas and the realities of life in the modern world. Here you'll find a series of short autobiographical stories, exploratory tools, and practical suggestions for incorporating the Gītā's teachings into your life.

The Gītā's authority as a vessel of transcendental knowledge rests not on its historicity but on the lived experience of those who follow its teachings. Accordingly, I've chosen to focus on how to dance with the contents of the dialogue rather than on how to trace the dialogue's historical development. This book is therefore neither a modern interpretation of an ancient teaching nor a quixotic attempt to reproduce a 5,000-year-old conversation verbatim; it's the continuation of a time-tested method for preserving Kṛṣṇa's message of hope to Arjuna and passing that message forward for the benefit of future generations. The continuity of community through cross-generational conversations is the secret to how the changeless principles at the heart of the Gītā's message have been preserved, transmitted, and appropriately adapted to changing times, places, and circumstances for thousands of years.

Unlike speculative interpretation and abstraction, conversations about the messages that spiritual wisdom texts contain are essential to the assimilation of sacred teachings. Sharing personal realizations in community with fellow truth-seekers plays an important role in developing a meaningful relationship with the text. In fact, the development of mutually supportive spiritual relationships is as much a goal of scriptural study as is one's own self-realization. Spiritual relationships are the foundation of spiritual communities that, in turn, provide the ground from which the cultural re-spiritualization of our entire human society may someday emerge.

....

As it is for Arjuna, so it is for us: there's no way around the battle, only a way *through* the battle. The question is not, "How will it end?" but rather, "How will we act?" The Bhagavad-gītā is an invitation to hear Kṛṣṇa's message, follow in Arjuna's footsteps, change the terms of the battle, and turn an inescapable tragedy into a glorious victory.

PART ONE

Challenges and Concepts

Reconstructing the Relationship Between Faith and Knowledge

"A quite specific astonishment stands at the beginning of every theological perception, inquiry, and thought."
~ Karl Barth

It's natural to engage with life's most difficult questions by looking at them through the lens of our own cultural frame of reference. Most of us tend to look at spiritual wisdom texts like the Bhagavad-gītā through that same lens. But the Gītā's underlying assumptions about the nature of reality and our relationship to it are fundamentally different from those of contemporary Western culture.

This makes the Gītā an exceptionally valuable resource for "outside the box" solutions to life's most difficult challenges. To access those solutions, we have to practice seeing the world through the lens that the Gītā offers us rather than reflexively looking at the Gītā through the lens that the culture and theories of our time prescribe.

This is easier said than done. Whether we realize it or not, most of us are deeply committed to the preservation of our existing worldview, which is precisely what spiritual wisdom texts like the Bhagavad-gītā are designed to deconstruct and replace.

The first deconstruction that entering the Gītā's worldview requires is actually a *re*construction; a radical renovation of the relationship between faith and knowledge.

In the West, we've become accustomed to a rigid separation between religion and science. So much so that we often feel obligated to choose between the sacred and the secular for lack of common ground. Conventional wisdom tells us that religion is what we *believe* and science is what we *know* – reinforcing the idea that faith and knowledge are two separate categories of experience.

This hasn't always been the case. Up to medieval times, Western civilization subscribed to a hierarchical conception of reality consisting of divine celestial life above, infernal damnation below, and mundane earthly life in between. The mundane and celestial worlds were connected by a metaphorical ladder by which denizens of the terrestrial plane could climb to a heavenly realm and, beyond that, to the kingdom of God. There was apparently no need for a ladder to connect the earthly realm to the hellish one; if you were going to Hell, you could just fall down into it.

In this worldview, ascension up the ladder was understood to be the goal of life. Learning how to climb the ladder was understood to be the goal of education; the function of knowledge was to serve the objectives of faith. Of course, much of what passed for knowledge back then was what we might think of today as religious dogma; consorting with natural science could get you burned at the stake.

As the "Age of Enlightenment" gradually elevated secular interests over religious ones, the ladder's mooring to the celestial world was dismantled. Unfastened from transcendence, the ladder fell on its side. The structure of the ladder remained, but its trajectory changed from one of vertical ascension to one of horizontal progression. In other words, the ladder went from being a stairway to heaven to being a measure of time, a recumbent catalog of the past that presumed to explain the present while pointing the way to the future.

This transposition of the ladder from vertical transcendence to horizontal temporalization marks the inauguration of the modern lens, a conceptual framework that presents a vision of the world in historical terms rather than in a spiritual context. It's at this point that faith and knowledge diverge into two mutually exclusive jurisdictions.

By contrast, the Gītā's Pre-Enlightenment cosmology corroborates the original position of the ladder along a vertical axis, but with some significant differences from the three-tiered model of medieval Christianity. The Gītā's map of reality is composed of two levels of existence, one material and one spiritual, and a "yoga ladder" that connects them to one another. Unlike contemporary postural yoga, the yoga ladder of the Bhagavad-gītā is an integrated system of theology, philosophy, and mystical technology that's specifically designed to facilitate a transformation of consciousness.

You can climb up to Heaven on this yoga ladder, but Heaven is not the destination that the Bhagavad-gītā recommends. Instead, the Gītā makes a clear distinction between a temporal heavenly realm that lies *within* the jurisdiction of the material world and an eternal transcendental realm that's *beyond* the jurisdiction of the material world. Its cosmology is therefore both a significant departure from the conventional "Heaven and Hell" dichotomy of popular Christianity and an elaboration on the conception of a Divine atmosphere beyond time and space that we find in the more contemplative theological philosophies of medieval European Christianity.

Unlike both the medieval and Enlightenment ladders, however, the yoga ladder of the Bhagavad-gītā fully embraces both the request for revelation that lies at the heart of religion and the quest for knowledge that lies at the heart of science. The fruit of this integration of religion and science is called "transcendental knowledge," a kind of knowledge that situates all that's accessible to the intellect within the context of a truth that lies beyond the reach of the intellect. The Gītā is both a dissertation on transcendental knowledge and a guide to developing an internal state of being that's conducive for experiencing that knowledge by direct perception.

....

The union of faith and knowledge in the Bhagavad-gītā is an underlying premise that can easily be missed by a Western reader. Becoming aware of our reflexive deference to a modern or postmodern frame of reference and loosening our grip on it for the sake of entertaining the possibility of an entirely different worldview is the first challenge we face on our journey into the Bhagavad-gītā. The second is to get a handle on the singular yet multifaceted organizing principle around which the Gītā's model of reality revolves.

The Overarching Theme of the Bhagavad-gītā

"Do the right thing. It will gratify some people and astonish the rest."

~ Mark Twain

One way to identify the central theme of a spiritual wisdom text is to look at the very first passage of that text and, more specifically, at the first word of the text. The Bhagavad-gītā telegraphs its overarching theme with its first word: *dharma.*

A second way to identify the central theme of a spiritual wisdom text is to look at how often and in what context key words appear throughout the text, especially how those words or phrases figure in the conclusion of the text. By looking at the first word of the Gītā's first verse and taking note of both Arjuna's concerns and Kṛṣṇa's priorities as we move through the dialogue, it becomes clear that the Bhagavad-gītā is, first and foremost, a book that answers the question, "What is the highest *dharma*?"

There are many ways in which the Sanskrit word *dharma* can be translated or understood. The meanings that follow are particularly significant insofar as the Bhagavad-gītā is concerned.

Dharma as the Organizing Principle of Cosmic Order

The root of the word *dharma* is *dhṛ*, which means "to support," indicating that which can't be taken away. *Dharma* can therefore be understood as that which gives ultimate support to one's existence.

The derivative *dhruva* indicates a pole or a fixed axis through which variable opposites are balanced. Therefore, *dharma* can also be understood to indicate the invariable constant around which life revolves, the organizing principle of cosmic order that supports all existence.

Dharma, in the sense of "divine law," is sometimes translated as "religion." People may therefore misunderstand *dharma* as a concept that belongs to a particular form of faith. A more accurate understanding of *dharma* as "divine law" is that it refers to universal and changeless principles of religion that are essential for the attainment of religious experience irrespective of which, if any, particular religion one subscribes to. In other words, *dharma* is an ordering principle rather than a restrictive doctrine. It therefore supports freedom of choice in how we express our faith.

Dharma can also be taken to indicate the essential nature of a person, place, or thing, the definitive inner reality that makes someone or something who or what they are. For example, the *dharma* of sugar is to be sweet. If you take sweetness away from sugar then it's no longer sugar. The *dharma* of water is to be wet. If you take wetness away from water then it's no longer water. *Dharma* manifests in the natural world as bees that make honey, cows that give milk, a sun that shines, fish that swim, rivers that flow, etc.

Just as each feature of cosmic order has an essential nature, cosmic order itself has an essential nature. In the Gītā's worldview, bringing ourselves into harmony with the essential nature of cosmic order is the way by which we can live peacefully in the world. Conversely, dissonant action relative to the essential nature of cosmic order brings about chaos and destruction.

Therefore, the function of *dharma* as a universal principle of divine law is to establish an objective standard of cosmic order and, with it, a shared sense of reality within which a healthy society can function. The project of discerning right from wrong is thus one of understanding how changeless ethical principles are properly applied to the variable details of moral decision-making in order to respond to any given situation in a way that's aligned with cosmic order.

As we'll soon see, Arjuna has lost track of what cosmic order is. And in the process, he's forgotten what his own essential nature is. As a result, he can't figure out how to respond to his situation in a way that's in harmony with cosmic order.

To figure it out, he needs to know the answers to three basic questions that the Bhagavad-gītā addresses:

1) What is the essential and definitive nature of a person?
2) What is the essential and definitive nature of the world?
3) What is the essential and definitive nature of the source of both the world and everyone in it?

Once Arjuna understands the answers to these three questions, he can play the hand he's been dealt from an empowered position of realized knowledge.

And so can we.

Dharma as an Objective Measure of Moral Excellence

The first verse of the Bhagavad-gītā is a question posed by Dhṛtarāṣṭra, the blind king, whose son, Duryodhana, is Arjuna's primary antagonist on the battlefield. Dhṛtarāṣṭra's question is summed up in the phrase *kim akurvata*: "What did they do?" or, "How did they act?" Dhṛtarāṣṭra is asking Sañjaya, his personal secretary and the narrator of the Gītā, to tell him how his sons, known as the Kauravas, and the sons of his deceased brother, known as the Pāṇḍavas, responded to having been brought to the battlefield by the will of providence to fight a fratricidal war that will decimate their family.

Aside from his literal significance as a facilitator of aggressions that have led up to the confrontation on the battlefield, Dhṛtarāṣṭra is metaphorically significant: he represents a person who knows right from wrong but selfishly chooses to do the wrong thing. Dhṛtarāṣṭra is clinging to a kingdom that rightfully belongs to his late brother's eldest son – Arjuna's older brother, Yudhiṣṭhira. Dhṛtarāṣṭra wants his own eldest son, Duryodhana, to inherit the throne. To this end, Dhṛtarāṣṭra gave his tacit support to a series of dastardly deeds through which Duryodhana and his allies had hoped to eliminate the Pāṇḍavas. All of their underhanded schemes failed, and now the two factions of the family will settle their differences with the weapons of war.

Dhṛtarāṣṭra is hoping that Sañjaya will describe a victory for his son, Duryodhana. At the outset, it appears as if Duryodhana has a clear military advantage. However, factors beyond numerical strength, martial virtuosity, and strategic superiority will influence the outcome of the battle. One such factor is that *dharma* is also understood to be synonymous with virtue or moral excellence. The setting for the battle, the "field of *dharma*" (*dharma-kṣetre*), favors morality over duplicity. This doesn't bode well for the duplicitous Duryodhana.

Fighting in Defense of *Dharma*

Dharma can also be translated as "duty" or "occupation" in the sense of having a responsibility to contribute to society in accordance with our natural aptitudes and inclinations. The Gītā stresses the importance of performing our "prescribed" duty (*sva-dharma*), irrespective of any apparent faults in its execution, imperfections in the outcome, or inconvenience imposed on the performer. For example, a soldier may not like doing what they've been called upon to do, the circumstances may be other than what they would have chosen, and they may even have to make the ultimate sacrifice in the course of responding to the call of duty, but tolerating hardships and making sacrifices for the sake of doing one's duty is considered virtuous. Members of the armed forces often have an understanding of duty that can't be fully appreciated by those without any firsthand experience of military culture.

Of course, not everyone is cut out to be a member of the armed services or to take positions of leadership. Some people are more naturally adept at engaging in commerce, others at working with their hands, others at scholarly occupations, and so on. The field of endeavor that takes us in the direction of *dharma* will differ from one person to the next. We move in the direction of universal *dharma* by following our personal *dharma*.

Whatever our natural occupation may be, knowing which naturally prescribed duty is right for us and sticking to it through thick and thin will, according to the Gītā, ultimately bring about the best possible result. Kṛṣṇa's emphasis on this point is made clear by virtue of its repetition, appearing first in Chapter 3, verse 35, and again in Chapter 18, verse 47.

Arjuna, a warrior by both natural aptitude and rigorous training, has a duty to fight in defense of righteousness. In other words, his *dharma* is to defend *dharma*. But, even though he repeatedly refers to *dharma* as he builds his argument against fighting, Arjuna has forgotten the essence of *dharma* and, therefore, can't figure out how to defend it. Understanding that dharmic action is the way to achieve the greatest good and trusting Kṛṣṇa to know which action would be the most dharmic, Arjuna asks Kṛṣṇa to tell him what he should do.

Arjuna's inability to see a dharmic way forward is understandable; it turns out that *dharma* itself has gone missing. In Chapter 4, verse 7, we learn that the recession of *dharma* from the world stage is one of the principal reasons for Kṛṣṇa's appearance. In this verse, the word *dharma* is used twice: once to indicate the retreat of *dharma* and again, in a negative form, to indicate the advance of the opposite of *dharma* (*adharma*).

In the next verse, Kṛṣṇa tells Arjuna that he, Kṛṣṇa, appears in the material world at regular intervals for the sake of re-establishing *dharma*. These two verses add emphasis to the position of *dharma* as the central theme around which the dialogue between Kṛṣṇa and Arjuna revolves.

The universal principle of *dharma* is a constant but our paths to living in harmony with *dharma* are variable. Just because fighting is the right way for Arjuna to move in the direction of *dharma* doesn't mean that fighting is everyone's *dharma*. We all have our own paths to *dharma* that are based on the kind of work that corresponds to our natural aptitudes and our personal definition of success. Fighting in defense of *dharma* corresponds to Arjuna's natural aptitude but, for Arjuna, "success" doesn't mean victory on the battlefield; it means serving the greatest good.

The Highest *Dharma*

Kṛṣṇa's conclusive instruction, Chapter 18, verse 66, serves as a final confirmation that *dharma* is the Gītā's overarching theme. Here, Kṛṣṇa advises Arjuna that all forms of *dharma* are subordinate to one supreme *dharma*: to become an instrument of Divine Will with full confidence that the Supreme Divinity will give complete protection to such a surrendered soul.

It's worth noting that this is not a command; it's an invitation. In fact, commands are conspicuous by their absence in the Bhagavad-gītā. As the dialogue advances, the progressively more direct and emphatic manner in which Kṛṣṇa offers his invitation is an indication of his emotional investment in Arjuna's wellbeing rather than a demonstration of power over Arjuna's destiny.

It's also important to recognize that Kṛṣṇa's invitation is also *not* a call to give up one religion in favor of another. Again, Kṛṣṇa is speaking about universal principles of religion rather than a particular religion. As we noted earlier, *dharma* does not denote "a religion," such as Hinduism, Christianity, Judaism, Islam, or any other specific form of faith; it denotes universal principles that point us in the direction of religious experience. Although the Bhagavad-gītā is widely regarded as the most famous Hindu scripture in the world, the Gītā predates the religious, ethnic, and national identity we know as Hinduism.

Following the teachings of the Gītā therefore doesn't mean converting to Hinduism if you don't already identify as Hindu, nor are Kṛṣṇa's teachings exclusively meant for followers of Hinduism. You can integrate Kṛṣṇa's teachings into whatever form of faith you follow or use Kṛṣṇa's teachings to develop your personal expression of faith. Religions are specific; religious experience is universal. The Bhagavad-gītā speaks to the universal nature of religious experience, which the Gītā regards as the ultimate fulfillment of knowledge.

....

The essential purpose of the Gītā's teachings is to point us in the direction of the highest *dharma*. Its directive methodology is a non-sectarian spiritual science. Having established the direction the Gītā is leading us in, we can turn our attention to the next challenge: becoming familiar with the topography of the Gītā's philosophy. The primary features of the Gītā's philosophical landscape are invisible by their very nature, but they can be seen, so to speak, if you know what to look for.

The Metaphysics of the Bhagavad-gītā

"We are more closely connected to the invisible than to the visible."
~ Novalis

Metaphysics is a type of philosophy that extends our investigation into the nature of reality beyond that which can be seen and measured. Whereas physics deals with physical realities, *meta*physics deals with more subtle aspects of reality, such as being and identity. The Bhagavad-gītā is a treatise on metaphysics: all of its underlying theories are concerned with features of reality that lie beyond the physical realm. And contrary to the modern assumption that metaphysical effects originate in physical causes, the Gītā proposes that the opposite is true: the shape and substance of metaphysical elements precede and determine the shape and substance of their corresponding physical structures.

Some metaphysical features of reality, such as thoughts and feelings, are self-evident. Although unseen, these particular metaphysical features of reality have a powerful hold on how we see the world and ourselves in it. This is why thoughts and feelings are what corporations, political factions, religious organizations, and the media target when they try to sell us manufactured conceptions of reality. Marketing is a metaphysical enterprise.

As for the realities we manufacture for ourselves, they're not so much Reality with a capital R as they are *personal conceptions* of reality. Born of a combination of external influences and an internal sense of identity, our personal truths are subjective conceptions of reality that exist in relationship to and, all too often, in conflict with other people's subjective conceptions of reality.

Which brings us to another reason why the Bhagavad-gītā is so challenging and so valuable: its conception of reality extends beyond relative subjective realities to include an Absolute Reality within which every relative reality resides. The metaphysical concepts that form the foundation of the Gītā's teachings are tools that help us to not only zoom out to see a more complete picture of reality but also to zoom in to get a better understanding of how we process our experiences on both personal and social levels.

However, the Gītā's metaphysical concepts are significantly different from those of both contemporary Western secularism and traditional Western monotheism. Understanding these different concepts is essential to developing the ability to see the world from the Gītā's perspective. The purpose of this chapter is to help you become familiar with these metaphysical concepts so that you can apply them in a practical way and see for yourself what they reveal.

The first four metaphysical features of reality that the Bhagavad-gītā speaks about are:

1. The eternal soul (*ātmā* or *jīva*)
2. The transmigration of the soul (*saṁsāra*)
3. The law of action and reaction (*karma*)
4. The three qualities of material nature (*tri-guṇa*)

These four features are interdependent; each would lose its meaning if any of the others were taken away. We'll look at each of these concepts individually and then see how they work together to create the fabric of our worldly experience according to the Gītā's conception of reality.

The Eternal Soul

Kṛṣṇa begins his instructions to Arjuna by making a clear and unequivocal distinction between consciousness and matter. He does so by establishing the presence of an eternal individual conscious self within every temporary material body. In Sanskrit, this eternal individual conscious self is called the *ātmā* or *jīva*. In the Bhagavad-gītā, the term *jīva* is used specifically to indicate an eternal soul who is currently experiencing temporal embodied life in the material world. The word *ātmā*, like the word *dharma*, has many meanings. In the Gītā, it's used to indicate the individual conscious self as well as, in different contexts, the mind, the body, and the Supreme Self.

It's important to recognize that the consciousness Kṛṣṇa speaks of when he introduces the distinction between spirit and matter clearly refers to individual consciousness differentiated from the material bodies within which we all reside. In other words, Kṛṣṇa validates our experience of individual existence by establishing individuality as a feature of *spiritual* reality, not just *material* reality. In the Gītā, Kṛṣṇa tells us that you, me, your friends and family, your dog, your cat, cows, monkeys, birds, fish, bugs – every sentient being in the world, irrespective of the body that they inhabit – is a unique spiritual entity, an irreducible unit of individual consciousness that has always existed and will always exist. This is the first element of knowledge in the Bhagavad-gītā: material bodies come and go but all individual conscious beings are eternal features of reality.

This is very different from the concept of Oneness, in which a singular undifferentiated "Self" resides in all bodies. In the Gītā, individual difference is as spiritually valid as undifferentiated Oneness. Both individual consciousness and Universal Consciousness are accounted for as essential features of the complete Absolute Reality. Kṛṣṇa will speak about the distinction between the many infinitesimal individual conscious beings and the one infinite universally conscious Being in greater detail as his conversation with Arjuna progresses.

For now, we can focus on how this concept of an eternal individual self is a profoundly radical idea; it means that the consciousness of the person who experiences embodied life never comes into nor goes out of being. Experiences come and go but the experiencer is forever. In other words, a *jīva* doesn't come into being at any point in time: each *jīva* has always been and will always be.

The idea that there has never been a time when we didn't exist is a radical departure from Western monotheistic accounts of how we come into being, such as the idea that the body and soul are simultaneously created at fertilization, or that both the body and soul are passed down from parents to offspring. In such conventional accounts of how we come to be, the eternality of the soul begins *after* conception – meaning that it is not truly "eternal" at all.

In the Gītā, Kṛṣṇa also tells us that the *jīva* is neither made of matter nor derived from it. As a result, the soul, though tethered to a body, is not dependent on the body for its existence. This distinction between the conscious person and the bodily machinery a person inhabits means that while our bodies may be subject to the passing of time, our consciousness is not. Each spiritual being is indestructible.

The Gītā's categorical distinction between spirit and matter offers a stark contrast to a naturalistic worldview. Kṛṣṇa's message is that spirit is *inherently* conscious and matter is not conscious, will never be conscious, and does not produce consciousness. This flies directly in the face of the modern creation story, which goes something like this:

> In the beginning, there was nothing. Or, perhaps there was something that was as close to nothing as something can be: an infinitesimal point of immensely condensed matter surrounded by . . . nothing.
>
> In any event, at some point *not* in time, since there was no time at the time, the infinitesimal point exploded . . . for no apparent reason. And although the natural function of an explosion is to disorganize whatever falls within its field of influence, the initial conditions of *this* explosion were such that the natural function of explosions was reversed: the matter within the field of the explosion, without direction or purpose, gradually progressed from a state of simple chaos to a state of complex organization. Over the course of billions of years, some particularly complex and highly organized forms developed the attribute of consciousness. Those particularly complex forms are us.

In this paradigm, our coming into being is defined by the development of physical bodies that exhibit something we take to be consciousness and our going out of being is defined by the breakdown of our physical bodies to the point that consciousness appears to be extinguished. When the brain dies, our consciousness comes to an end.

But although this version of reality presents itself as scientific, not every scientist embraces it. As Nobel laureate Max Planck, the father of quantum physics, put it, "We cannot get behind consciousness. Everything that we talk about, everything that we regard as existing, postulates consciousness."

The prevailing assumption of contemporary science, however, is that we *can* get behind consciousness, that consciousness isn't just tied to the body; it derives *from* the body. Apostles of the cyber-future characterize consciousness as nothing more than an emergent property of the brain and its metabolism, a collection of electro-chemical signals being transformed into hackable subjective experiences. Neuroscientists insist that they will eventually discover the biological origins of consciousness and integrate it into data-driven algorithms that are destined to become the new driving force of post-human evolution.

Beliefs like this can be so deeply ingrained in the mindsets of modern, intelligent, and educated people that we reflexively defer to them, even to the point of validating religious or spiritual beliefs in terms of such secular scientific explanations.

Re-orientating our mindset toward the Gītā's worldview doesn't necessarily mean that we reject everything about contemporary worldviews; it's merely a recognition of the limitations that a contemporary lens imposes on our view of the world. The modern lens, when applied to its appropriate realm of truth, addresses questions about how the material world works. The Gītā's realm of truth is primarily concerned with the underlying metaphysical questions about *why* the material world works the way it does. In so doing, the Gītā subsumes and transcends the modern lens by providing us with the means to understand the material world as something that exists within a spiritual context. And that context begins when we consider the possibility that we are spiritual beings having a material experience.

The Transmigration of the Soul

Have you ever noticed how we feel surprised when death arrives even when we know it's coming? We're told that death is a natural part of life. So why does something that's supposed to be natural feel so unnatural when it actually happens?

From the Gītā's perspective, this feeling means that we're onto something. According to the Bhagavad-gītā, the experience of death *is* unnatural for an eternal spiritual being; any reflexive anxiety we have about death is due to our misidentification of the body as the self and a corresponding ignorance of our true spiritual identity.

When this misidentification dominates our consciousness, we experience the very unnatural phenomenon we call "death."

If, on the other hand, we extend the meaning of "life" beyond the limits of a singular lifetime, thinking of our "life" as that of an eternal spiritual being experiencing innumerable material lives, then we might think about death quite differently.

The Bhagavad-gītā presents death as the departure of the eternal spirit soul from the temporary material body, not as the cessation of our existence or the dissipation of individual consciousness into the totality of matter. More specifically, the Gītā defines death as the transition of the eternal individual soul from one temporary material body to another. This coming and going from one body to another in a perpetual cycle of birth and death is called the transmigration of the soul; in Sanskrit, *saṁsāra.*

Transmigration is not quite the same thing as reincarnation. Though they're often regarded as synonymous, the concept of reincarnation implies that an individual's personality is inseparable from their eternal, changeless soul. In other words, when someone dies, they would be reborn in a different body but would have the same personality traits as they had in their previous lifetime. As that person grew up, they would recognize themselves as the same person they were before.

The Gītā's description of transmigration is slightly different. While the Gītā does take some continuity of personal psychology across multiple lives into account, genuine recollections of past life experiences would be the exception rather than the rule. This is because, just as it views the soul as distinct from the body, the Gītā views the eternal spirit soul as being wholly independent from the many temporary personalities it acquires over the course of innumerable lifetimes.

It's important to note that this perpetual cycle of birth and death in the material world can be broken. Becoming aware of our entrapment in the cycle of repeated birth and death is the first step toward liberation from it.

From the viewpoint of those who grieve for the deceased, death appears to be cessation of the departed's existence. From the viewpoint of the Bhagavad-gītā, death is the departure of the soul from the material body in accordance with a karmically-determined lifespan. Shortly thereafter, that same soul will arrive in a new body, the shape, substance, and duration of which will, once again, be karmically set as a reaction to past actions.

The Law of Action and Reaction

Assuming that what the Bhagavad-gītā tells us about how our futures extend well beyond a single lifetime is true, we should consider the possibility, or even the probability, that what we do in this life will have consequences that reverberate well beyond it. In the Gītā, the obligation to experience reactions to our actions is known as the law of *karma*.

Karma is probably the most misunderstood concept to make its way from Eastern spiritual philosophy to Western conversational vernacular. And the reason is simple: *karma* is complicated.

To put it as simply as possible, *karma* is an action that generates a reaction. Both the action and the reaction can be referred to as *karma*. Every action, be it a mental action (thought), a verbal action (word), or a physical action (deed) generates a reaction of one kind or another: positive actions produce positive reactions, negative actions produce negative reactions, hence good *karma* and bad *karma*.

There's also potential *karma*; an internal action that doesn't directly generate an external karmic reaction but has the potential to trigger a karmically-charged chain of events. For example, thoughts generate a subtle karmic reaction insofar as the "vibrations" we send out to the universe are concerned. Positive or constructive thoughts can produce uplifting words and beneficial deeds that generate correspondingly positive karmic reactions.

Although negative or destructive thoughts have the same kind of potential, we don't get "punished" for thought crimes. Thoughts hold the potential for karmic reactions in the same way that seeds hold the potential for fruits. Sweet seeds produce sweet fruits, bitter seeds produce bitter fruits. You can push back against a thought so that the seed never sprouts, no action is taken, and no reaction is incurred. But once a thought makes its way out into the world in the form of a word or deed, then, good or bad, a bell has been rung that can't be un-rung.

This brings up the question of who's to say what's good or bad, or what's right and what's wrong. The Gītā's reply is that an objective standard of right and wrong is hardwired into the cosmic order of the material world. This is one of the meanings and functions of *dharma*: righteous action. Just as each feature of cosmic order has an essential nature, cosmic order itself has an essential nature. Bringing ourselves into harmony with the essential nature of cosmic order is the way to live peacefully in the world. Conversely, dissonant action relative to the essential nature of cosmic order prompts the universe to react with a discordant response.

Karma can therefore be good or bad but, either way, *karma* is always temporary: we act, we get a reaction, the end. Once our good *karma* is used up, we're right back where we started. Once our bad *karma* comes to an end, we get a chance to try again. *Karma* itself is essentially neutral; it's a natural law, not a divine judgement or a "blame the victim" rationalization.

Karma, however neutral it may be, is also problematic. The law of *karma* mandates that everything we do, every action we take, must generate a reaction. And we're always doing things! Every action plants a karmic seed, but that seed may not come to fruition within the timeframe of a single lifetime. It would appear that everything we do perpetuates our entrapment in material existence: the *jīva* seems to be inextricably locked into *saṁsāra* on account of *karma*.

Fortunately, the situation is not quite that dire: it *is* possible to act without generating a karmic reaction. How the *jīva* can put an end to *karma* and achieve liberation from *saṁsāra* is one of the most significant questions that the Bhagavad-gītā answers.

In order to understand the answer, we need to understand why we act one way instead of acting another, like one thing and dislike another, gravitate toward this and distance ourselves from that. There is another metaphysical feature of reality that's influencing our thoughts, feelings, decisions, and actions, usually without our being aware of it.

The Three Qualities of Material Nature

In the Gītā's metaphysics, there are three qualities or modes of being that influence every aspect of our mental, emotional, and physical experience: luminance (*sattva*), passion (*rajas*), and darkness (*tamas*).

These three qualities, known in Sanskrit as *tri-guṇa*, act like primary colors that are perpetually blending together to create every hue, tint, and shade of every person, place, and thing in the material world. The dynamic interactions of these three subtle forces provide both the essence and the substance of who we appear to be, both to ourselves and to one another. Hence, the three qualities, referred to collectively as "material nature," are active modes of being that have a profound influence on how we see, act in, and respond to the world.

In addition to being dynamic, material nature is also hierarchical; the three qualities are vertically stacked, with darkness on the bottom, passion in the middle, and luminance at the top. The purpose of the ethical directives and personal observances of *yoga* is to progressively lift the practitioner's consciousness out from under the influence of darkness and passion and up into the mode of illumination.

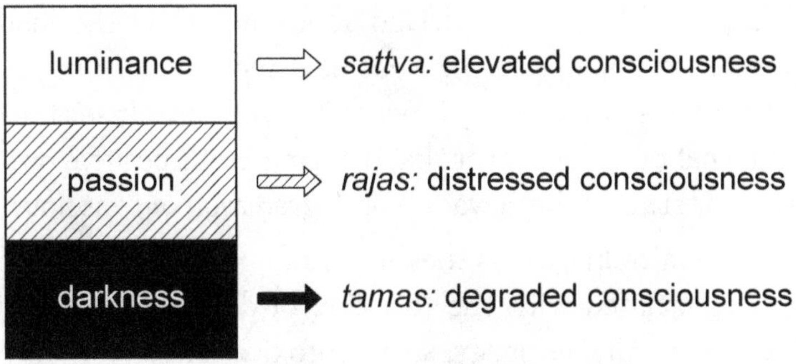

Luminance, also known as the "mode of goodness," arises from purity. Associated with the function of preservation, it's characterized by kindness, generosity, clarity of thought, contentment, compassion, the desire for knowledge, and detachment from material dualities such as loss and gain. Orienting ourselves toward the mode of luminance results in the elevation of consciousness, accuracy of perception, wisdom, and happiness.

It's important to note that luminance is not the same thing as intelligence; a very simple person can be situated in the mode of luminance. It's also not a balance of the lower modes of passion and darkness; according to the Gītā's presentation of *tri-guṇa*, equanimity is understood to be a characteristic of the mode of illumination that's not found in the lower modes, balanced or otherwise.

Passion, also known as the "mode of activity," arises from hankering. Associated with the functions of creation and transformation, it's characterized by intense and relentless striving, a profound attachment to the results of our efforts, and a subsequent distortion of intelligence. Acting under the influence of the mode of passion results in greed, anxiety, misery, and stalled spiritual progress.

The material mode of passion isn't synonymous with enthusiasm. Enthusiasm is a function of the mode of passion that can also be applied to activities in either the mode of luminance or the mode darkness; qualities can be nested inside of one another. When nested inside of the mode of luminance, action in the mode of passion can produce a positive result. Conversely, a negative result can be expected for passion-driven action nested in the mode of darkness. For example, creating a business and transforming expertise and hard work into money is neutral in and of itself; it's the why, how, and what of the endeavor that determines it's positive or negative value in terms of the elevation or degradation of consciousness.

Darkness, also known as the "mode of ignorance," arises from delusion. Associated with the function of destruction, it's characterized by apathy, lethargy, sleep, intoxication, anger, entropy, and insanity. It results in misperception, foolishness, unprovoked violence, and the degradation of consciousness.

Though stupefying, being influenced by the mode of darkness is not the same thing as being stupid. The quality of darkness induces an inversion of perception that makes the unreal seem real, actuates an unshakeable faith in the reality of that which is unreal, and stirs up an inclination to impose this misperception on others, violently if necessary. This is not the same thing as an absence of intelligence. On the contrary, we see high levels of intelligence operating in the mode of darkness all the time: a great deal of human intelligence goes into devising strategies of domination and technologies of destruction that are based on warped conceptions of reality.

The Connecting Thread of the Gītā's Metaphysics

In the Gītā's theoretical framework, *ātmā*, *saṁsāra*, *karma*, and *tri-guṇa* make up the foundation of a spiritual hypothesis that can be expressed as follows:

1. We are eternal spiritual beings, not these temporary material bodies.
2. We are currently subject to an ongoing cycle of repeated births and deaths in different material bodies.
3. The kind of body we take birth in and the quality of our experience in any given lifetime is determined by our

own actions; we create our future lives through our own thoughts, words, and deeds.

4. The psychology and physiology of any given material body that we acquire as a result of our past actions is composed of a combination of the qualities of material nature that corresponds with the destiny we have created for ourselves.

However, each statement in this theory implies a fifth metaphysical element upon which the entire hypothesis depends. In order for previous births to be prior, current bodies to be temporal, and future lives to be forthcoming, *ātmā*, *saṁsāra*, *karma*, and *tri-guṇa* all have to be connected by something: *kāla*. Time.

A manifestation of divine power operating within the material realm, time is the relentless undertow that creates the experience of temporal life by pulling the *ātmā* ever farther out into the endless ocean of *tri-guṇa*, *karma*, and *saṁsāra*, where every action generates a reaction that finds its fruition in the form of a future birth.

Karma provides the blueprint for how our lives will play out. Material nature provides the substance of our lived experience. When you put the blueprint and the substance together with an eternal spiritual being perpetually transmigrating through time from one life form to another, you get the spiritual self under the influence of material nature.

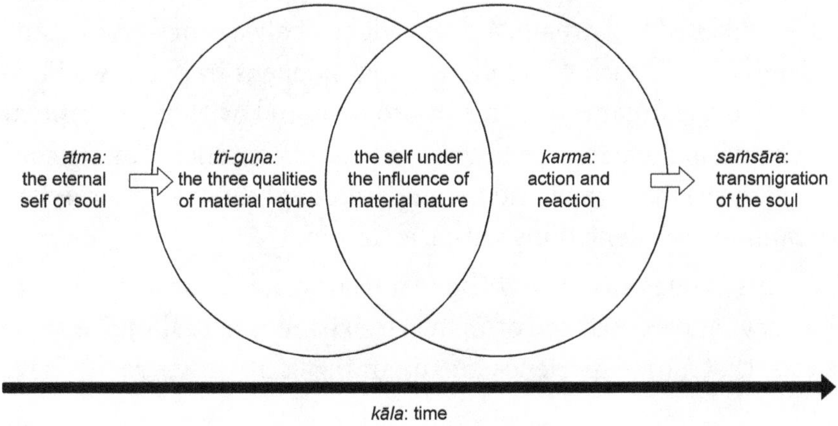

Summary

The *ātmā,* or *jīva*, is the eternal individual soul whose presence is symptomized by consciousness. *Saṁsāra* is the transmigration of the soul through a perpetual cycle of repeated birth and death. *Karma* is the law of action and reaction that provides the blueprint for the soul's experience in any given lifetime. The substance of that experience is supplied by *tri-guṇa*, the three qualities of material nature. *Kāla*, time, acts as the tracks that the train of material existence is running on.

Now here's the really tricky part: the Gītā unequivocally declares that the spirit soul in contact with material nature *appears* to be performing actions but that all of the actions the spirit soul appears to be performing are actually being carried out by whatever qualities of material nature a soul has come to identify and interact with (Chapter 3, verse 27).

It's important to note that the Gītā is *not* saying that we're just automatons. It's saying that, while our free will is far more limited than we'd like to believe, our consciousness *is* actively engaged with material nature and, as a consequence, we can choose to *disengage* from material nature. Our freedom to choose how we'll act, particularly in response to a revelation of transcendental knowledge, is essential to the ultimate meaning of the Gītā's message.

The experience of the self under the influence of material nature is likened to a dream. A dream doesn't always make sense and we don't have much control over what happens in it, but we identify with the dream while it's in progress and, within the context of the dream, we're able to respond to its contents. Our journey through the material world is comparable to that of a person who's dreaming and identifying with the dream.

This is one reason why the material world is considered to be illusory: our experience of material existence is real in the same sense that our experience of dreaming is real: we really have dreams, and our dreams seem real while we're having them, but we regard our waking state to be a far more substantive experience of reality than our dreaming state. The Bhagavad-gītā is, in one sense, a handbook for developing the skill of lucid dreaming: moving through the dreamlike material world in a state of awakened spiritual consciousness.

In the Gītā, Kṛṣṇa wastes no time in advising Arjuna to establish himself in spiritual consciousness. Of course, that's easy for Kṛṣṇa to say since he's speaking to Arjuna from a transcendental position, appearing within the realm of material nature without any possibility of being influenced by material nature. In fact, Kṛṣṇa describes the three qualities of material nature as his own "divine power of illusion" that's nearly impossible to overcome.

There is, however, a way to do it.

....

In the course of showing Arjuna how to transcend the influence of material nature, Kṛṣṇa will speak about eight different topics and drive the conversation back and forth along three levels of experience. Knowing what topics are being discussed and the structure of the conversation is another key to being able to follow the dialogue. And being able to follow the dialogue will make it much easier to access the information that the dialogue contains.

The Topics and Structure of the Bhagavad-gītā

"But if you study the logistics and heuristics of the mystics you will find that their minds rarely move in a line."
~ Brian Eno

The dialogue of the Bhagavad-gītā takes a non-linear path through an extraordinary landscape, the contours of which redefine the boundaries of reality. Knowing what topics will be discussed and how the dialogue is structured will make it a lot easier to navigate your way across the Gītā's literary landscape.

In the Gītā's first chapter, Arjuna realizes that, win or lose, the results of the battle will be catastrophic. He's torn as to what he should do. Fighting is what's expected of him. After all, he's a warrior. But, warrior or not, he can think of four reasons why he shouldn't fight:

1. Compassion for the combatants
2. Unhappiness even if he wins
3. Social instability as inevitable collateral damage
4. Fear of bad karmic reactions

Arjuna's confusion is traditionally considered to be the fifth reason why he's unable to summon the determination to fight.

Here's a brief elaboration on each of Arjuna's reasons:

1. Compassion for the combatants: Arjuna is kind-hearted by nature. He isn't motivated to kill his enemies or to cause the deaths of his friends, teachers, and family members no matter what he might gain from doing so.

2. Unhappiness even if he wins: Arjuna will not be able to enjoy whatever power, wealth, and fame victory might bring if it will have cost the lives of everyone on the battlefield.

3. Social instability as inevitable collateral damage: Arjuna assumes that the deaths of those who are responsible for upholding dharmic values will result in a breakdown of family cohesion and undermine social stability.

4. Fear of bad karmic reactions: Arjuna is all too aware that killing is sinful, to say nothing of how sinful it is to kill members of one's own family for personal gain.

5. Indecision: Arjuna has become paralyzed by confusion. Not knowing what to do and in no condition to do anything, the foremost of warriors does the unthinkable: he drops his weapons, sits down, and, from the depths of unfathomable despair, declares that he won't fight.

In his paralyzed state, Arjuna asks Kṛṣṇa for guidance. In response, Kṛṣṇa addresses each of Arjuna's reasons for not fighting by way of a philosophical argument that's based on a comprehensive explanation of five core topics:

1. The infinitesimal individual self
2. The Infinite Supreme Self
3. Material nature
4. The law of action and reaction
5. Time

Three additional topics can be broken out from these five topics:

6. The infinitesimal individual self under the influence of material nature
7. The characteristics of the material world
8. Yoga

Here's a brief elaboration on each of these topics:

1. The infinitesimal individual self, as noted earlier, refers to an *ātmā* (or *jīva*): an individual spiritual entity, the presence of which is symptomized by consciousness. You, me, and every other sentient being in the world, irrespective of the body that we inhabit, is understood to be an irreducible and indestructible living unit of consciousness.

2. The Infinite Supreme Self refers to the one *ātmā* who is categorically different from all other *ātmā*-s by virtue of being the omniscient, omnipotent, omnipresent, independent, and inconceivable source and ultimate substance of everyone and everything. In other words, God, or the one *ātmā* who, unlike all other *ātmā*-s, is uniquely qualified to hold the position of God.

3. Material nature refers to the aforementioned divine energy comprised of three perpetually interactive qualities (*sattva*, *rajas*, and *tamas*) that combine to provide the metaphysical substance of the physical world.

4. The law of action and reaction refers to *karma*: actions that generate pleasant or unpleasant reactions according to how those actions align or misalign with an objective standard of cosmic order.

5. Time (*kāla*) refers to the phenomenon of past, present, and future that establishes the relationship between embodied souls and material nature. Conspicuous by its absence in the spiritual realm of pure consciousness, unstoppable time is the foremost representative of divine power in the material world.

6. The infinitesimal individual self under the influence of material nature refers to the characteristics we acquire when we become conditioned by a particular combination of the three qualities of material nature and misidentify ourselves as being those transient material characteristics rather than as being what we really are: eternal, pure, and inherently joyful spiritual beings.

7. The characteristics of the material world refers to the intrinsic features of the world of our experience, which is composed of the three qualities of material nature and animated by their interactions.

8. Yoga refers to the practical technology by which the theories of knowledge put forward in the Bhagavad-gītā can be tested and verified by direct perception.

If at any point you feel as if you've lost track of where the conversation between Kṛṣṇa and Arjuna has gone, you can refer back to this list to see which topic or combination of topics are being discussed in order to get back on track.

When Arjuna turns to Kṛṣṇa for guidance, Kṛṣṇa immediately attempts to re-orient Arjuna's perspective by changing the level of the conversation. In other words, Kṛṣṇa doesn't accept the underlying premise of Arjuna's argument, which is that there must be some way for everyone to live happily ever after.

But Kṛṣṇa's attempts at reorientation don't stick right away; Arjuna can't map Kṛṣṇa's perspective onto his own frame of reference. As a result, Arjuna remains confused by Kṛṣṇa's instructions for the first several chapters. He can't reconcile what he's hearing with what he thinks he already knows. Arjuna's initial inability to see what Kṛṣṇa is trying to show him speaks to our own predicament of being limited to looking at the world through the lens of our own biases.

So if you get to chapters 4 or 5 of the Bhagavad-gītā and you think you're not getting it yet, don't worry: Arjuna doesn't get it yet, either.

The twists and turns of the dialogue in the Bhagavad-gītā can be difficult to follow because the conversation proceeds in a somewhat elliptical pattern, where topics that are covered on a rudimentary level in earlier chapters are revisited and expanded upon in later chapters. However, this non-linear dialogue moves back and forth along a fixed structure that connects two categories of *dharma*: conditional *dharma* and constitutional *dharma*. Understanding the distinction between these two kinds of *dharma* and learning to recognize the structure along which the dialogue moves will make it easier to follow the conversation.

Plot, character, and conflict are the three basic elements that form the structure of a story. The Bhagavad-gītā integrates these three basic elements into a three-tiered story structure that's based on a hierarchical concept of reality consisting of two levels of experience and an intermediate level that connects them. Here's what that looks like:

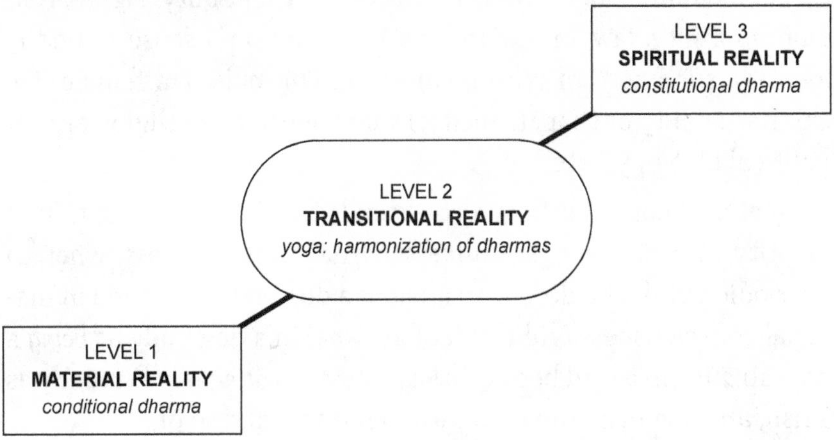

The dialogue between the characters, Kṛṣṇa and Arjuna, moves up and down this structure as Kṛṣṇa tries to help Arjuna resolve his inner conflict. The plot, however, is driven in a resolutely upward trajectory, using the middle level as a bridge to cross from the bottom level of reality to the top level. Each elliptical movement of the dialogue drives the plot further upward along the structure to progressively higher levels of knowledge about each level of reality.

You can recognize each level of reality by its different values and the different states of being that are associated with each of them. Here's a brief description of the values and states of being that are associated with each level:

Level 1: Material Reality or the experience of 'conditional' *dharma*

Material reality consists of temporal, worldly life experienced through the lens of material consciousness. Material consciousness is the state of being wherein our perception is filtered through and limited by the experiential bandwidth of our material body, mind, and senses.

Our sense of *dharma* is conditioned by material consciousness; consciousness under the influence of the three qualities of material nature. Hence, life on the level of material reality is characterized by personal and social conceptions of vocation, duty, rights, religion, morality, law, order, and justice based on a sense of bodily identity, such as "I'm White, I'm Black, I'm male, I'm female, I'm this nationality or that ethnicity, I subscribe to this religion or that political ideology," etc.

Material consciousness also extends this bodily conception of identity to other beings. Unlike spiritual consciousness, wherein we would think of a dog as an *ātmā* in a dog body, someone in material consciousness will think of an *ātmā* in a dog body as *being* a dog, an *ātmā* in a bird body as *being* a bird, an *ātmā* in a fish body as a fish, an *ātmā* in a human body as a human, and so on.

Worldly happiness and prosperity are the primary values of material consciousness, the former usually being seen as dependent on the latter. Actions are deemed to be right or wrong based on their likely outcome and attachment to the results of those actions is considered perfectly normal. In material consciousness, to "live long and prosper" is understood to be the logical goal of life.

At some point, however, those caught up in material reality or conditional *dharma* may begin to think that life is meant for a higher purpose than the pursuit of material enjoyment - in which case, they may feel drawn to approach the next level of experience.

Level 2: Transitional Reality or the path of *yoga*

Transitional reality, or the path of yoga, is the bridge between the experience of material reality and the experience of spiritual reality. The path of yoga is one of progressive detachment from worldly life and movement toward liberation from the constraints of material consciousness.

The values of yoga favor the attainment of equanimity in both happiness and distress over the attainment of worldly prosperity. A yoga practitioner strives to develop equal-mindedness toward all beings irrespective of the body that they inhabit, and attachment to the pursuit of transcendental knowledge becomes stronger than attachment to the pursuit of material desires.

Whereas action in material consciousness is dictated by our conditional *dharma*, action in yogic consciousness is guided by five principles of transitional *dharma*: austerity, purity, mercy, truthfulness, and surrender to the Supreme Person. These five principles support the harmonization of our conditional *dharma* with our constitutional *dharma*.

To get a better sense of how someone on the path of yoga would practically apply these principles, here's a brief description of each:

1. **Austerity** has two meanings. The first is to minimize material comforts to just what's needed in order to live peacefully. The second is to intentionally step out of our comfort zones for the sake of personal growth.
2. **Purity** means to maintain bodily and environmental cleanliness. It also means saintliness of character or freedom from corruption.

3. **Mercy** means being compassionate to all sentient beings and offering kindness even to those who are themselves unkind.
4. **Truthfulness** means being honest, living with integrity, and acting in alignment with the highest truth we can conceive of.
5. **Surrender to the Supreme Person** means making ourselves available for service to the highest truth we can conceive of, allowing ourselves to become instruments of divine will, accepting the will of providence insofar as the results of our actions are concerned, and having faith that, whatever happens, we're always being brought closer to God.

Transitional reality is characterized by a state of being wherein we think of ourselves and others as eternal spiritual beings having temporary material experiences rather than as being the temporary material bodies that we inhabit. The ethics of transitional reality bend in the direction of principles rather than outcomes and those who are in transitional consciousness proceed under the assumption that an action that conforms to universal principles of righteousness will ultimately bring about the best possible outcome.

As we cross the bridge of yoga, the third level of experience comes into view.

Level 3: Spiritual Reality or constitutional *dharma*

Spiritual reality is the level of reality in which we experience ourselves in our natural, liberated state of spiritual existence. Having crossed the bridge of yoga, theoretical spirituality is transformed into experiential spirituality. We experience ourselves as being integrally connected to all other beings through the agency of the infinite and complete whole of which we are all infinitesimal parts. This state of being is therefore characterized by feelings of intense compassion for all beings, a sense of being intimately connected to everyone and everything, an awareness of the omnipresence of Universal Consciousness, and a feeling of intimate connection to the Supreme Divinity.

Our sense of the world is determined by the level of reality we're experiencing. If we're on the level of material reality then we'll be convinced that we are the bodies that we inhabit, that what happens to our bodies happens to us, and that the goal of life is to enjoy life for as long as possible. If we're on the transitional level of reality, then we'll have reasonable faith that we're embodied spirit souls having a temporary material experience and the goal of life is to transcend material consciousness. And if we're on the level of spiritual reality then we'll see the Supreme Being everywhere and see everything in connection with the Supreme Being.

Someone whose frame of reference is limited to material reality can't access the higher levels of yoga and spiritual reality. This is Arjuna's starting point: he's thinking solely in terms of material reality and therefore trying to sort out his dilemma based on the values of conditional *dharma.*

By contrast, Kṛṣṇa's frame of reference is the complete set of all three levels of reality. He's not limited to the same set of assumptions or values that Arjuna is limited to. Kṛṣṇa's immediate response to Arjuna's arguments against fighting is to re-frame the entire discussion by introducing a higher level of reality, spiritual reality, as the context within which material reality operates. And he introduces yoga, the intermediate level of reality, as the means by which our conditional *dharma* can be harmonized with our constitutional *dharma.*

Seeing his friend incapacitated by despair, Kṛṣṇa meets Arjuna where he's at in order to guide him toward progressively higher levels of consciousness. In doing so, Kṛṣṇa dispels Arjuna's doubts about how he should act. The elevation of Arjuna's consciousness gives him access to a broader vision of reality. And that broader vision provides the impetus for Arjuna's transformational journey from fear and confusion to courage and conviction.

....

The elliptical movement of the Gītā's dialogue along its three-tiered conception of reality serves to unite the terrestrial with the transcendental. The unifying technology, yoga, can be seen as having four distinct paths and as four steps on one integrated path. While each path is sufficient unto itself for achieving liberation, there are levels of realization *beyond* liberation. And the ultimate fulfillment of three of the paths of yoga is dependent on the fourth. How the four paths of yoga can be both independent and hierarchical can be understood when we take a closer look at each step on the ladder that connects material reality to spiritual reality.

The Yoga Ladder

"Any sufficiently advanced technology is indistinguishable from magic."
~ Arthur C. Clarke

As with any science, the transcendental science of self-realization that Kṛṣṇa is teaching in the Bhagavad-gītā includes a technology that's designed to test its hypotheses. That technology is yoga. In the Bhagavad-gītā, the word "yoga" has a double-meaning that extends the idea of yoga far beyond the perimeter of a physical practice: the extrication of consciousness from the influence of illusion and the union of infinitesimal individual consciousness with infinite Universal Consciousness.

There are four main paths of yoga in the Bhagavad-gītā:

1. *karma-yoga*; the yoga of action
2. *jñāna-yoga*; the yoga of knowledge
3. *dhyāna-yoga*; the yoga of meditation
4. *bhakti-yoga*; the yoga of devotion

The traditional understanding is that there are three major divisions of the Bhagavad-gītā that correspond to three of these four paths of yoga: *karma-yoga*, *bhakti-yoga*, and *jñāna-yoga*. The central position of *bhakti* within the three major divisions is said to be comparable to a crown jewel flanked by accent stones.

The idea of a fourth distinct path of *yoga* being integrated into the first major division of the Gītā and acting as a segue into the second major division is a relatively recent elucidative development. This fourth path, *dhyāna-yoga*, is also commonly referred to as *raja-yoga* or *aṣṭāṅga-yoga*, the latter designation not to be confused with the modern style of postural yoga that goes by the same name.

Kṛṣṇa speaks about each path of yoga in the following order:

- In the first major division of the Gītā (chapters 1-6), Kṛṣṇa will introduce the principles of *karma-yoga* after he establishes basic principles of discernment (*sāṅkhya*) by which we can distinguish spirit from matter.
- Next, Kṛṣṇa will expand the scope of *karma-yoga* by introducing elements of *jñāna-yoga* to illustrate how action should be informed by knowledge.
- Then, in chapters 5-8, Kṛṣṇa will transition from the outward-facing path of action (*karma-yoga*) to the inward-turning path of mysticism and meditation (*dhyāna-yoga*). This transition straddles the first two major divisions.
- The second major division (chapters 7-12) focuses on *bhakti-yoga*, the *yoga* of devotion.
- The third major division (chapters 13-18), focuses on *jñāna-yoga*, and in Chapter 18 Kṛṣṇa concludes with a summary of the entire Gītā.

Each path of yoga in the Bhagavad-gītā can be thought of as the purification of a different aspect of our lives:

- *karma-yoga* is the purification of our daily activities.
- *jñāna-yoga* is the purification of our intellect.

- *dhyāna-yoga* is the purification of the mind.
- *bhakti-yoga* is the purification of the heart.

All four paths share the same metaphysical assumptions that we've already discussed. They also share a common element of practice: self-discipline. Those who have mastered each path share similar symptoms, such as freedom from material desires, fearlessness, and contentment.

Each path of yoga can be seen as both a self-contained system unto itself and as a component part of an integrated and progressive system. To understand the progressive aspect of the four paths, it's helpful to visualize them as a ladder, as I've done in the diagram below.

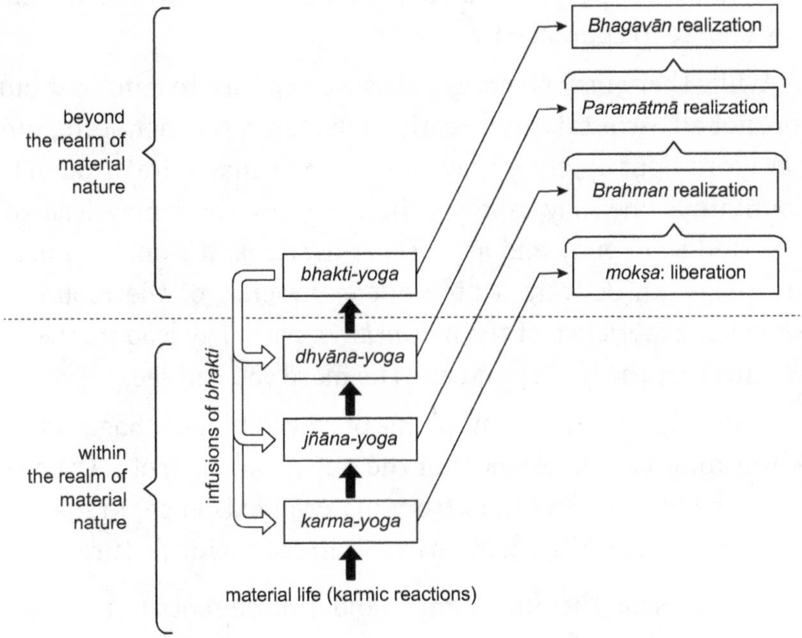

Each rung delivers the practitioner to a different level of realization that corresponds to progressively higher states of being. And each progressively higher state of being includes the levels of realization beneath it. As is the case with elevation in general, the higher we go, the more we can see. In this case, what we can see is an expanding view of reality from progressively higher spiritual perspectives.

A popular assumption in contemporary spirituality is summed up by the phrase "Many paths, one Truth." The Gītā both confirms and modifies this truism by describing the one Truth as having different features, each of which being associated with a different path. From the Gītā's point of view, all roads lead to Rome, but the train to St. Louis doesn't go to Chicago.

The idea of one Truth with multiple features is a paradox that invites the question, "Are some features higher than other features?" In the Gītā, we'll see that the answer is a qualified "yes." The one Truth can be understood on multiple levels according to the mood of the person who's approaching the Truth and the path they choose to approach by.

While there may be many paths we can take to climb a mountain, not all paths take us directly to the top of the mountain; some may go straight up, some may zig-zag, some may spiral around the mountain, some may take you half-way up, some may lead to a cave, and some may end at a scenic overlook. It's one mountain, but each path delivers a different experience of the mountain. Whatever experience of the mountain a path may lead to, the fact remains that the higher you are, the more you can see.

Similarly, the different paths of yoga in the Bhagavad-gītā deliver different experiences of the one Absolute Truth. Over and above the idea of liberation from material existence, Kṛṣṇa talks about the Absolute Truth in terms of three specific features:

1. *Brahman*: the impersonal and undifferentiated spiritual substance of reality *in toto*.
2. *Paramātmā*: the all-pervading and ever-present expansion of Universal Consciousness.
3. *Bhagavān*: the personal and all-inclusive form of the complete Absolute Truth.

In a sense, there's no difference between the three features of the Absolute Truth because the Absolute Truth is singular by definition. And yet, these features are not all the same. This paradox is one of the inconceivable mysteries of the Bhagavad-gītā: the complete Absolute Truth has a variety of features, but this variety doesn't compromise the singularity of the Absolute Truth.

To get a better understanding of the Gītā's paradoxical synthesis of variety and singularity, let's take a closer look at each of the four paths of yoga.

karma-yoga

Karma-yoga is the art and science of transcendental action; action that doesn't generate a reaction.

In the Bhagavad-gītā, Kṛṣṇa describes three different kinds of action: moral action, immoral action, and transcendental action. Moral action is action in harmony with cosmic order that generates a correspondingly harmonious reaction, otherwise known as "good *karma*." Immoral action is action in disharmony with cosmic order that generates a correspondingly dissonant reaction, otherwise known as "bad *karma*." In each case, such actions are considered to be mundane on the assumption that they're undertaken for the sake of attaining a material objective.

As far as the Bhagavad-gītā is concerned, "bad *karma*" is bad and "good *karma*" is . . . also bad. The whole idea of a transactional relationship with cosmic order wherein we make deposits and withdrawals and try to maximize our dividends without getting hit with penalties is derided in the Gītā as an ideology for the unintelligent. Our motivation for action may be selfish or altruistic, but either way, if we act with the intention of fulfilling a material desire then we generate a corresponding material reaction that perpetuates our entanglement in material existence.

The Gītā isn't a handbook for gaming the karmic system to our advantage nor does it promote the ethical pursuit of karmic profits; it promotes putting an end to *karma* altogether.

The means to that end is transcendental action, otherwise known as *karma-yoga*: action that transcends cosmic order and therefore doesn't produce any reaction at all. Practicing *karma-yoga* allows us to act without adding any new reactions to our existing backlog of reactions-in-waiting and gives us an opportunity to empty out the stockpile of reactions we've accrued over the course of a gazillion previous lives. The result of emptying out our karmic backlog is freedom from the obligation to experience any further karmic reactions, otherwise known as *moksa* or liberation.

The key to practicing *karma-yoga* isn't found in what we do; it's found in why we do it and who we do it for. *Karma-yoga* is all about progressively changing our motivation for action and letting go of our attachment to the outcomes of our actions. What we do may change or it may not. We may get the result we hope for, or we may not. Either way, the substance of an action is subordinate to the transformation of our motivation from selfish to selfless and to the principle of detachment from the results.

As we move deeper into the art and science of *karma-yoga*, Kṛṣṇa introduces *jñāna-yoga*, the yoga of knowledge, as an enlightened context for the performance of *karma-yoga*. A persuasive argument could be made that the end product of *karma-yoga*, *moksa*, is synonymous with the end product of *jñāna-yoga*: realization of *Brahman*. Although this equivalence isn't explicitly stated in the Bhagavad-gītā and the goal of freedom from material bondage isn't exactly the same aspiration as the desire to experience the spiritual unity of reality, we can still think of liberation and *Brahman* realization as a package deal. In any event, when action without attachment is informed by knowledge, the *yogī* makes further progress up the yoga ladder to a higher level of spiritual realization.

jñāna-yoga

Jñāna-yoga, the yoga of knowledge, is the science of seeing the unseen spiritual context within which the material world operates. This path of yoga recognizes two kinds of knowledge: book knowledge and realized knowledge. Book knowledge, or theoretical information, is referred to in the Gītā as *jñāna*. Realized knowledge, or experiential wisdom, is referred to as *vijñāna*, the latter being acquired by acting on the basis of the former. In other words, realized knowledge arises from the practical application of book knowledge.

As we saw with the word *dharma*, Sanskrit words can have multiple meanings. As a result, Sanskrit verses often contain multiple layers of meaning and a word that means one thing in one verse may mean something very different when that same word appears in another verse. For example, *jñāna* and *vijñāna* can also be understood to mean material knowledge and spiritual knowledge respectively.

The practice of *jñāna-yoga* consists primarily of renunciation, austerity, meditation, and the study of *Vedānta*, which refers to the philosophical conclusions of the Upaniṣads. The usual objective of *jñāna-yoga* is the realization of *Brahman*, the first of the three features of the Absolute Truth that was noted above. *Brahman*, can be thought of in two ways, which is a little ironic since *Brahman* is nondual by definition. Those two ways are:

1. The undifferentiated spiritual foundation of all existence.
2. The spiritual quality of existence that's shared by all sentient beings.

Just as *jñāna-yoga* informs *karma-yoga* by providing an enlightened context for the performance of our daily activities, *jñāna-yoga* also informs the next path of *yoga*, *dhyāna-yoga*, by providing an enlightened context for the performance of meditation.

dhyāna-yoga

Also known as *rāja-yoga* ("king yoga") and *aṣṭāṅga-yoga* ("the yoga of eightfold mysticism"), *dhyāna-yoga* is the purification of the mind by means of meditation. This form of *yoga*, which is also systematically presented in Patañjali's Yoga-sūtras, is extremely difficult to perform; it requires the practitioner to disengage from the world, maintain strict control of the senses, observe celibacy, direct their awareness inward, control the movements of the life force within the body through disciplined control of the breath, and meditate continuously on the Supreme Self.

The Supreme Self, known in Sanskrit as the *Paramātmā*, is the second of the three features of the Absolute Truth. Present everywhere all the time and fully cognizant of everything in all respects, the *Paramātmā* is the one Soul of all souls. Whereas we are only aware of our own experiences, the "paramount" *ātmā* or "Super-Soul" is fully aware of everyone's experiences.

The objective of *dhyāna-yoga* is the realization of this *Paramātmā*, the localized aspect of Universal Consciousness who resides within the heart. Whereas *Brahman* is an impersonal feature of the Absolute Truth that corresponds to the attribute of eternality, *Paramātmā* is a personal feature of the Absolute Truth that adds the attributes of omnipresence and omniscience to eternality. Cognition and agency are characteristics of person-ness and the *Paramātmā* has both. Hence, the *Paramātmā* is a personal feature of the Absolute Truth.

Throughout the Gītā, Kṛṣṇa will often refer to "the Lord" or speak of the *Paramātmā* as if the *Paramātmā* were someone other than himself. Elsewhere, he directly confirms that he is the *Paramātmā*. Therefore, we can understand that Kṛṣṇa, who is externally appearing before Arjuna in his own personal form and simultaneously residing within Arjuna's heart in his expanded form as the *Paramātmā*, the innermost friend of all living beings, usually speaks about himself in the third person when referencing his *Paramātmā* feature.

This brings us to the third feature of the Absolute Truth, *Bhagavān*, the form of the Absolute Truth that facilitates the highest levels of personal relationship, which is only revealed to those who have perfected the fourth path of yoga, *bhakti-yoga*.

bhakti-yoga

Bhakti-yoga is the purification of the heart through active expressions of love for *Bhagavān*: the one person who, being categorically different from all other people, is the original cause of all subsequent causes and effects. In other words, *Bhagavān* is the one person who is uniquely qualified to occupy the position of God.

Contrary to popular misconceptions, *bhakti* is not just the sentiment of devotion nor is it just the principle of devotion without any particular object of devotion. The term *bhakti* specifically indicates devotional service performed as an active expression of love for the Supreme Person or for the purpose of developing such love.

The practice of *bhakti-yoga* is the scientific method by which we gradually develop a heightened sense of God's omnipresence, a deeper appreciation of God's beauty, and a deeper awareness of God's love. The goal of *bhakti-yoga* is to realize the full potential of our personal relationship with the Supreme Person. The perfection of *bhakti-yoga* is spontaneous love for God; the offering of love for the sake of love. *Bhakti-yoga* is both the means to an end and an end in and of itself; the cultivation of love in practice evolves into the experience of love in perfection, but the methods by which love is expressed remain the same.

Kṛṣṇa repeatedly recommends the practice of *bhakti-yoga* throughout the Gītā, so much so that we see the interjection of *bhakti* into each of the other paths of yoga. *Karma-yoga*, *jñāna-yoga*, and *dhyāna-yoga* don't just culminate in *bhakti-yoga*; they each require an element of *bhakti-yoga* in order to reach their own fulfillment.

In addition to being the straw that stirs the drink of all the other paths, *bhakti-yoga*, as it's described in the Gītā, is categorically different from the other paths in three significant ways:

1. The practice of *bhakti-yoga* takes place on the level of liberation; even if the practitioner isn't liberated (yet), the devotional activity the practitioner engages in is spiritual by definition. The power of *bhakti-yoga* to accelerate the liberation of the practitioner is derived from the spiritual nature of *bhakti* itself.
2. The practice of *bhakti-yoga* brings about all of the results that can be achieved by following the other three paths.
3. The highest level of spiritual realization can only be attained by the practice of *bhakti-yoga*.

This highest level of realization, according to Kṛṣṇa, is realization of Kṛṣṇa's own personal form, otherwise known as *Bhagavān* realization. Throughout the Gītā, Kṛṣṇa makes it abundantly clear that, as far as he's concerned, there's no truth higher than himself.

Kṛṣṇa's position as *Bhagavān* is established by the phrase that precedes his vocalizations in the Gītā: *śrī-bhagavān uvāca*, which may be translated in numerous ways, such as "the Blessed Lord said" or "the Beloved Lord said."

We should take note that the phrase that precedes Kṛṣṇa's voice in the Gītā is not just *bhagavān uvāca*, it's '*<u>śrī</u>-bhagavān uvāca*.' The word '*śrī*' is very significant: beyond being an honorific that indicates beauty or opulence, '*Śrī*' is the name of the Goddess of Fortune, the feminine aspect of Ultimate Divinity and the source of Kṛṣṇa's magnificence.

Śrī is the *śakti* of *bhakti*, the personification of the power of devotion. This is another of the Gītā's secrets hiding in plain sight:

the feminine aspect of divinity is also present on the battlefield, hidden within the form of Kṛṣṇa, yet shining forth as Kṛṣṇa's splendor in the same way that the core of the Sun is the hidden source of sunshine.

Therefore, a *bhakti-yogī* develops a devotional relationship with Kṛṣṇa, the male aspect of divinity, by seeking the grace of the bestower of devotion: the female aspect of divinity. Again, the Absolute Truth is singular by definition and yet the Absolute Truth has differentiated attributes because both duality and non-duality must be present in the Absolute Truth in order for the Absolute Truth to be complete.

In this case, the one Absolute Truth is understood to consist of two aspects that are both beyond gender and the epitome of gender. Because the Absolute Truth is complete, all gender identities, along with the male and female archetypes, originate in the Absolute Truth. Therefore, the Absolute Truth is all-inclusive: anyone can practice *bhakti-yoga* and enter into a relationship of love with the personal feature of the complete Absolute Truth.

....

The highest rung on the ladder, *bhakti-yoga*, doesn't invalidate our experience of individuality by declaring that we are all One. Instead, it affirms our individuality as a spiritual feature of reality and proposes a natural relationship between all individual souls and the one transcendental Soul who is the ultimate source and substance of Absolute Reality.

The Concept of Kṛṣṇa

"God is neither Hindu nor Muslim nor Christian. He's God. And we are also not Hindu or Muslim or Christian. This is our bodily designation. We are all pure, part and parcel of the Supreme."
~ A.C. Bhaktivedanta Swami Prabhupāda

Most Western readers encounter Kṛṣṇa for the first time in the pages of the Bhagavad-gītā. However, Kṛṣṇa also appears in other Vedic literature, most prominently in the Śrīmad-Bhāgavatam, also known as the Bhāgavata Purāṇa. The Śrīmad-Bhāgavatam is a theological elucidation of Vedānta philosophy, the crescendo of which is a biography of Kṛṣṇa that includes the following story:

Once, when Kṛṣṇa was a little boy, his playmates thought it would be fun to get him in trouble by telling Kṛṣṇa's mother that he had been eating dirt. Upon hearing the other boys tattling on her son, Kṛṣṇa's mother, Yaśodā, picked Kṛṣṇa up and asked him, "Why have you been eating dirt?"

Kṛṣṇa replied, "I have never eaten dirt; my friends are making it up. You can look in my mouth and see."

Yaśodā took Kṛṣṇa up on his offer: "All right then, open your mouth so I can see." Kṛṣṇa dutifully complied.

When she looked in her son's mouth, Yaśodā was astonished: she saw the entire cosmic manifestation, both physical and metaphysical, including all moving and non-moving entities and all of the luminaries and planetary systems in all directions of outer space. She could see mountains, islands, oceans, all the features of the surface of the earth and the elements of which they were made. She saw the interactions of the three qualities of material nature, the mind, senses, intelligence, and desires of all beings, the reactions to all actions and the calculations of time for the duration of all lifespans.

And she saw herself, at her home in the rural countryside, looking into the mouth of her beloved child, Kṛṣṇa.

Dumfounded, Yaśodā questioned whether what she was seeing was a dream, an illusion, or a figment of her imagination. She finally concluded that her son possessed mystic powers that were the source of her vision.

Then, for a moment, she could understand the illusory nature of material existence and her position as an eternal servant of the Supreme Lord, to whom she immediately offered prayers of surrender and petitions for protection of her little boy.

But what she couldn't quite grasp was that her little boy *was* the Supreme Lord to whom she was praying and that she was already serving the Supreme Lord by playing the role of his mother.

Even though Kṛṣṇa momentarily revealed his divine nature to her, the intensity of her maternal affection overwhelmed any sense that her child was actually the inconceivable source and substance of everything she saw when he opened his mouth.

In an instant, the vision was gone and forgotten, replaced by feelings of increased affection for her little son, who hid the truth about his position as the Supreme Lord so as not to interfere with Yaśodā's feelings of maternal devotion.

Such intimate feelings of lighthearted friendship and parental affection are only possible in connection with God when God chooses to indulge in playfulness rather than in demonstrations of power, when a devotee's spontaneous love for God overrides the impulse to worship God from a respectful distance, and when the power and majesty of the Supreme Divinity are eclipsed in the heart of the devotee by the incomparable beauty of the Supreme Divinity.

The concept of Kṛṣṇa is one that emphasizes the divine form and transcendental personality of God. It's a concept that supports the possibility of interpersonal love between God and God's devotee such that intimate or even casual proximity to God becomes possible.

Interpersonal love requires three things in order for it to be experienced: a lover, a beloved, and love itself. Love by itself, absent an object of love or a subject of love, has no meaning. Love cannot live in a vacuum. The lover, the beloved, and love itself must all be present and must all be real in order for the experience of love to be real.

The concept of Kṛṣṇa presents us with a conception of God as a real person who desires to have a meaningful personal relationship with each of us. The Gītā's ultimate message only makes sense, and its full force can only be felt, if the speaker of the Bhagavad-gītā, Kṛṣṇa, is understood to be a living expression of God's innermost personality.

All too often, this key point is undermined by commentators who present the Gītā in purely allegorical terms. By presenting Kṛṣṇa as a stand-in for Arjuna's higher self or as a material representation of a monistic state of being or as anything but a real, albeit a categorically different kind of, person, the beloved, Kṛṣṇa, is cast into the realm of the unreal. And where the beloved goes, love and the lover follow.

It's easy to understand why it's so tempting to allegorize Kṛṣṇa. For starters, to do otherwise would allow for the possibility that the Gītā is an invitation to enter into a relationship with God. Relationships require us to acknowledge one another, to be responsive to one another, and to be accountable to one another. A relationship with God asks us to acknowledge and lean into a relationship with someone who is infinitely more powerful and complete than we could ever be.

Another reason to allegorize Kṛṣṇa is our aversion to the idea of a Supreme Being who advocates violence under any circumstance. On one level, Kṛṣṇa's purpose in speaking the Gītā is to convince Arjuna that he should fight. Thoughtful people generally take a dim view of a God who advocates for the eradication of those he disfavors. Given the long history of wars and atrocities perpetrated in the name of religion, it makes sense to have misgivings about a God who argues in favor of fighting on the basis of "religious principles."

Confining Kṛṣṇa to the realm of metaphor allows us to avoid the inherent risks of a relationship with a Supreme Being, sidestep the problem of ascertaining the nature of divine ethics, and stay in step with the modern consensus. The problem with confining Kṛṣṇa to the realm of metaphor, however, is that we confine ourselves to a much smaller realm of possibility than if we experimented with the idea that the Bhagavad-gītā is precisely what it says it is: a divine revelation spoken by a real Supreme Being whose motivation for speaking it is love for the listener.

During the course of his Ivy League education, one of my teachers met a professor of religion who presented him with an interesting alternative to conventional thinking about the question of whether or not God exists. The professor said, "The basic question of theology is not 'does God exist?' It's 'is God available?' because if God's available then the question of God's existence is already answered and if God's not available then God might as well not exist."

You can't get much more available than standing alongside your best friend as he faces the biggest battle of his life, listening patiently and compassionately when his knees start to buckle, and offering the kind of wisdom and unconditional love that will give him the strength and courage he needs to meet the challenge he's facing.

A real God who takes the initiative to personally show up at the moment of his devotee's greatest need is certainly a higher conception of God than an unreal God who only shows up as a literary device or a meditational prop. If God is that being who is more perfect than any other being we can conceive of, then a God who exists is surely more perfect than a God who doesn't.

The concept of Kṛṣṇa in the Bhagavad-gītā is one of a Supreme Being who's emphatically available and who, therefore, emphatically exists.

But is Kṛṣṇa a person? To answer this, we first have to consider what it means to be a person. The Bhagavad-gītā, and the entire Vedic wisdom tradition of which it's a part, doesn't think about person-ness as a social construct that's subject to legal definitions; it thinks of person-ness as an intrinsic attribute of all conscious beings. Therefore, to be a person means, first and foremost, to be conscious. To be conscious means to have senses that connect the person who's conscious to whatever they're conscious of. Next, to be a person means to have agency. The function of agency also requires senses: senses through which someone can act upon and react to whatever they're conscious of. The coherent organization of senses through which a person experiences and responds to the world requires a form: a body.

Bodies are boundaries with an inside and an outside. Bodies move through space. To have a body means to exist in an environment: a world. A world implies activity, namely, the activities of other living beings. A person is defined by their relationships with other people. Relationships are defined by names, forms, qualities, and actions.

One could argue that all this "person" and "people" stuff might apply to us but couldn't possibly apply to a Supreme Being, that the Supreme Being must be featureless because features are limiting; to have one feature is to negate the presence of other features. A Supreme Being would have to be beyond all such limiting factors as names, forms, qualities, actions, and relationships in order to be Supreme.

The concept of Kṛṣṇa rises above such an either-or argument: Kṛṣṇa is a Supreme Being who's both formless *and* has limitless forms *and* has one Unlimited Form.

Some might say that forms are limited by definition. If we assume that all forms are material, that might be so. But who says that "form" means "material form"? The opposite of "material form" isn't "formless," it's "spiritual form." And a Supreme Being whose spiritual form is paradoxically unlimited is surely greater than a Supreme Being with no form at all.

The same goes for names. I have a name. In fact, I have several names. People call me by different names according to the nature of their relationship with me. I'll bet the same goes for you. We all have names. If we have several names then it's reasonable to think that the Supreme Being has so many names that we could recite them forever and there would still be more. If the Supreme Being is the original cause of everything then the Supreme Being is also the original cause of names; language, rather than being a product of human evolution, would find its origins in transcendence.

In other words, the concept of Kṛṣṇa is one of an Absolute Truth that is both complete and limitless, that includes everything and excludes nothing. Therefore, the attribute of person-ness must also be present in the complete Absolute Truth; it's impossible for us to have an attribute that Kṛṣṇa doesn't have.

Which brings us to an aspect of Kṛṣṇa's completeness that's often overlooked or misunderstood: Kṛṣṇa's completeness includes us. We aren't Kṛṣṇa but Kṛṣṇa is us; our senses are extensions of Kṛṣṇa's senses.

Quantitatively, Kṛṣṇa is the complete actuality of infinite existence and we are infinitesimal parts of that existence. Qualitatively, we share the same spiritual nature as Kṛṣṇa, which includes the attribute of individual personhood; our person-ness is derived from the person-ness of the Absolute Truth.

Let's accept, just for the sake of argument, that Kṛṣṇa *is* a real person. What kind of person is he? We can find out by taking a closer look at his relationship with Arjuna.

One of the first things we can note is that, for the most part, Kṛṣṇa accompanies Arjuna incognito: just as Kṛṣṇa hid his full majesty from his mother in the story from the Śrīmad-Bhāgavatam, he hides his full majesty from Arjuna in order to relate to Arjuna as a well-wishing friend rather than as an all-powerful, all-knowing God. Arjuna *knows* that Kṛṣṇa is God but Kṛṣṇa's position as God isn't the main factor in their relationship. Arjuna isn't turning to Kṛṣṇa because Kṛṣṇa is God; he's turning to Kṛṣṇa because Kṛṣṇa is his friend. He trusts Kṛṣṇa.

Arjuna's knowledge of Kṛṣṇa's divinity is significant but secondary. So secondary, in fact, that Arjuna accepts Kṛṣṇa's offer to be his chariot driver. Ask yourself: how comfortable would you feel letting God be your personal chauffeur? Sure, the wisdom of God can appear through the voice of your driver, but I'm talking about the idea of God personally showing up to take you to the airport or drive you home from the grocery store. Most of us would probably feel some level of discomfort. And yet, Kṛṣṇa obediently drives Arjuna's chariot wherever Arjuna commands him to. Why would Kṛṣṇa do this? Out of love for his friend.

Kṛṣṇa drives Arjuna's chariot to the center of the battlefield. Upon arriving there, Arjuna's heart breaks as he foresees the deaths of his family and friends. At this point, Arjuna asks Kṛṣṇa for guidance and the relationship changes from one of fraternal camaraderie to that of teacher and student.

What Kṛṣṇa does next might be very surprising for anyone who was raised in or around the Abrahamic religious traditions: rather than carving commandments in stone, Kṛṣṇa offers Arjuna his opinions. And Kṛṣṇa's opinion is that Arjuna should fight rather than leave the battlefield.

This leads us to the second reason why it's so tempting to allegorize Kṛṣṇa rather than think of him as a real person who is really speaking on a real battlefield where real people are really going to die: we're scared to death of a God who encourages violence in the name of religion. And rightly so. As Blaise Pascal put it, "Men never do evil so completely and cheerfully as when they do it from religious conviction." So, when Kṛṣṇa tells Arjuna to fight, we're like, "Hey, wait – no! No fighting!" We don't want a God who picks sides and encourages fighting! Especially when we ourselves are working to cultivate compassion and peace.

But aren't some things worth fighting for? Even dying for? Dr. Martin Luther King, Jr., the architect of the American civil rights movement's strategy of non-violent protest, said, "A man who does not have something for which he is willing to die is not fit to live." Kṛṣṇa thinks Arjuna's cause is worth fighting for. And Kṛṣṇa's admonishment of Arjuna for capitulating to misplaced compassion seems to fly in the face of the more familiar commandment "Thou shalt not kill."

What can easily confuse the reader is that Kṛṣṇa will later confirm non-violence (*ahiṁsā*) as a fundamental principle of spiritually-informed ethics. So if non-violence is a symptom of knowledge then why is violence the right path for Arjuna? This question is the ethical paradox at the heart of the Bhagavad-gītā.

Unraveling this ethical paradox begins with the understanding that sometimes, irrespective of what our natural aptitudes and inclinations may be, the will of providence gives us no choice but to fight for something or someone. In such cases, fighting a defensive battle, even in the form of physical combat, doesn't violate the principle of non-violence. This is confirmed by traditional commentaries on the Bhagavad-gītā and the modern model of just war theory, which traces its origins to the writings of Saint Augustine and has informed the development of international law since the 17th century.

The principles of just war theory, insofar as reasons to wage a defensive war are concerned, are that if all other options have been exhausted, the fighter is authorized to fight on behalf of their community rather than being a self-appointed vigilante, the purpose of the battle is to right an injurious wrong, there's a realistic chance of winning, a higher standard of justice will follow a victorious campaign, the forcefulness of the defense is proportionate to the offensive threat, and non-combatants will not be targeted, then fighting is justified. In the case of the battle that Arjuna is being called to fight, each of these qualifications have been met.

Kṛṣṇa is not advocating for the initiation of a holy war. The Gītā does not provide a rationalization for religiously motivated terrorism nor does it support violence in the name of nationalistic tribalism. The evil-minded sons of Dhṛtarāṣṭra are not heretics; they're bad guys. Arjuna is being called to become an instrument of divine will, to fight in defense of *dharma*. Kṛṣṇa is guiding Arjuna toward his specific path to harmonizing his conditional *dharma* with his constitutional *dharma*.

When Kṛṣṇa personally appears for the sake of re-establishing principles of *dharma*, he does so in a manner that's suitable for the time and place he drops in on. In the Gītā, the specific when-and-where of the dialogue is significant but it's also a variable detail. The most important when-and-where of the Gītā's teachings is the here-and-now of our lived experience. Far from being an inflexible one-size-fits-all doctrine, Kṛṣṇa's teachings are eternal principles that, with the help of a qualified teacher, we can learn to apply to the variable details of our lived experience.

My *parama-guru*, A.C. Bhaktivedanta Swami Prabhupāda, who came to America from India in the mid-1960s, was a brilliant innovator who preserved the spiritual culture he personally embodied while simultaneously making appropriate adjustments according to time, place, and circumstance. Those adjustments are what ensured that the culture he was transplanting would be transmitted to future generations.

One key to the success of his adjustments was his gift for coming up with catchy English phrases to comprehensively communicate complex ideas that otherwise would have remained locked in impenetrable philosophical jargon or encased in obscure Sanskrit literature. One of his catchiest and most ingenious phrases was the one he used to explain Kṛṣṇa's identity: "The Supreme Personality of Godhead."

The word "Godhead" refers to the source of the qualities that make God the kind of being that we call "God." In Christianity, the Godhead refers to the unity of the Holy Trinity: the Father, the Son, and the Holy Spirit. Some forms of Christian mysticism propose that God is absolutely unknowable, that substantive contact with transcendence necessitates going beyond any conception of a describable or personal God, including beyond the Trinity, to a "God beyond God," a divine emptiness that can only be defined by what it's not rather than what it is.

This is a conception of transcendence that echoes the voidism and impersonalism found in the philosophical conclusions of Buddhism, Absolute Non-dualism, and, perhaps surprisingly, a significant portion of Christian theology, from medieval times to the present.

Yet here, in the phrase "Supreme Personality of Godhead," we find the proposition that the Godhead, the categorically singular Being who is the source of all being, who is beyond being, and who is being itself, has a knowable personality that finds its expression in a transcendentally spiritual form.

The proposition that God is ultimately and irreducibly a person closes the gap between the material world of our experience and the transcendental world beyond our experience because a personal God is a God who's available; an impersonal "God beyond God" is a God who's not.

The concept of Kṛṣṇa is one of a Supreme Being who is both impersonal *and* personal, who is formless *and* has limitless forms *and* has one unlimited transcendental form, who is beyond the limits of language *and* has innumerable names, who is eternally changeless *and* perpetually changing, who is simultaneously one with everything and yet different from everything, who is both a being *and* being itself.

It's no wonder that Kṛṣṇa's mother was amazed when she looked in his mouth.

But we needn't be amazed at how Kṛṣṇa presents himself as a Supreme Person who invites questions, holds space for our doubts, embraces critical thinking, accepts our conflicts, complexity, courage, and concerns, loves us just the way we are, and invites us to dance with him in the safest of spaces; his own spiritual atmosphere.

....

Kṛṣṇa's personal spiritual atmosphere and the exchanges of love that take place there are endowed with particular moods. Taking a contemplative approach to reading the Bhagavad-gītā is a great way to tap into Kṛṣṇa's mood as he speaks to Arjuna and, by extension, to us. We can develop a relationship with Kṛṣṇa by developing a relationship with the Gītā. Developing a relationship with the Gītā is also a science, with techniques that can help us enter into the feeling of the Gītā's philosophy.

Tips for Contemplative Reading

"There is an irreducible opposition between the deep transcendent self that awakens only in contemplation, and the superficial, external self which we commonly identify with the first person singular."

~ Thomas Merton

Taking a contemplative approach to reading the Bhagavad-gītā is one of the best ways to access its transformative potential. The goal of this kind of reading is to allow the Gītā to affect you on an emotional level while simultaneously letting the text take you into its world with your capacity for critical thinking intact.

Contemplative reading is a combination of attitude and technique that will help you enter into a meaningful relationship with this ancient wisdom text. It's a way of spending time with the messenger, listening carefully to the message, and then letting it penetrate deeply into the core of your consciousness. It's reading for the sake of absorbing yourself in the flow and feeling of the dialogue rather than reading for the sake of collecting information.

Here are some tips on how to do it:

Choose a time and place. Find a quiet location where you can focus your attention and set aside a specific block of time, ideally one when your mind will be fresh and energized. If possible, read in the same place at the same time every day. By consistently practicing contemplative reading in the same place at the same time, you'll gradually create a sacred time-space that quickly propels you into the text every time you step into it.

Set an intention. Before you start reading, take a moment to set an intention of reading with an attitude of humility, receptivity, attentiveness, and gratitude. This is a great way to acknowledge the value of the text and set yourself up to be able to read with rapt attention.

Keep a journal or a notebook nearby. Write by hand, not on a keyboard or a device; this makes a big difference in how deeply you internalize your thoughts and feelings. Then, absorb yourself in the text until a word or a phrase captures your attention. Repeat the word or phrase that captured your attention a few times, either out loud or in your mind. As soon as you notice that you've stopped repeating and started thinking, start writing.

Let your writing flow with your thoughts. Feel free to write in fragments. Don't worry about writing complete sentences. Remember, when writing in "stream of consciousness" mode, you don't have to be coherent. Just let it flow. You can always go back and edit what you've written later.

Keep writing until your writing stops by itself. When you've gotten your thoughts on paper, hang with what you've written for just one more moment to fully assimilate the thoughts that the text inspired you to contemplate. See if what you've written inspires you to go even deeper and write some more. Stay in this moment of inspiration until you feel a sense of completeness about what you've written.

When you feel that you've gone as far and as deep as you can go for the moment, express your gratitude for the insights you've been given and then continue to read until another passage captures your attention. Wash, rinse, repeat.

Consider both the literal meaning and the metaphorical significance of the text. There are two ways to interpret a sacred text: directly and indirectly. A direct interpretation applies when the meaning of the text is self-evident. In other words, if the text is unambiguous then we take it to mean exactly what it says. As a philosophical term, "self-evident" means that it doesn't require further proof; the meaning of the statement is obvious.

An indirect interpretation is one in which the text or passage is assumed to be allegorical or representational, even when statements in the text don't require any interpretation in order to ascertain their meaning. Gandhi's metaphorical interpretation of the Gītā, wherein the battlefield represents the body and the battle represents an internal psychological conflict rather than an external historical event, is a prime example of an indirect interpretation.

Indirect interpretations may feel more intellectually satisfying than direct interpretations. However, they're prone to be plagued by internal contradictions that require convoluted philosophical contortions to arrive at anything resembling a coherent conclusion. And though they may tickle the fancy of those who are predisposed to mental speculation, they're limited to the boundaries of the interpreter's sensibilities.

Of particular note where the Gītā is concerned, indirect interpretations often serve as evasive maneuvers meant to justify avoidance of self-evident meanings, especially when the self-evident meaning involves submission to a Supreme Deity. Indirect interpretations often circumvent this inconvenient assault on the ego by erasing the distinction between the speaker and the spoken to.

There is value to be found in both kinds of interpretations as long as we recognize when each kind of interpretation should be applied. A verse may have both a self-evident meaning and a metaphorical one. Contemplative reading allows us to take the time to consider both literal and figurative meanings that we may find in any given passage. It also gives us time to make distinctions between verses that explicitly use a metaphor for the sake of illustrating a philosophical point and verses where the literal meaning *is* the point.

Listen for the message of the speaker. Although this may seem obvious, it's worth mentioning because, unconsciously or otherwise, we are prone to giving priority to our own perspective rather than the perspective of the author, especially when the author is calling on us to challenge our own previously held beliefs.

It can be tempting to interpret a spiritual wisdom text in ways that validate our own "personal truths" rather than to accept propositions that directly challenge the ground on which our personal truths are based. Our minds, like good guard dogs, leap to the defense of the ego whenever the mind thinks the ego is being attacked. Our ego is where our adherence to a familiar conception of reality resides. Personal growth is hard precisely because it requires us to let go of what's familiar and step out of our comfort zones.

If we interpret a traditional wisdom text with the intention of validating our own opinions or lifestyle, then our egos will undermine our reception of the real message and sabotage its transformative potential. By contrast, contemplative reading is reading with a receptive attitude that welcomes the message of the author. Once we open ourselves up to hearing what the author is trying to tell us, then we can decide if what we're hearing resonates with us or not.

Resist the temptation to cherry-pick. It can be tempting to accept the parts of the text that we like and reject the parts we don't. We can usually justify cherry-picking by dismissing inconvenient verses as cultural anachronisms or by turning them into metaphors or by inventing a more favorable interpretation.

The problem with cherry-picking the verses we like and casting the ones we dislike aside is that, by doing so, we elevate our own attachments and aversions above the authority of the text. Our attachments and aversions are the Tweedledum and Tweedledee of our egos, and our egos are precisely what spiritual wisdom texts are meant to help free us from. By elevating our personal preferences over the counsel of the text, we make ourselves the ultimate authority on the topic we're supposedly studying, which effectively disconnects us from the line of transmission through which the teachings are being given to us.

Instead of dismissing, allegorizing, or re-interpreting a disconcerting passage according to conventional wisdom or your own personal biases, try asking yourself, "How might this be true?" If you come up empty, then put the passage aside and see if it comes back to reveal itself in the future. The important thing to remember when considering the plausibility of a questionable passage is that the Gītā never asks for blind faith; it encourages reasonable faith.

Focus on what the text emphasizes. Hermeneutics is the art and science of interpretation and explanation, particularly as it applies to understanding sacred wisdom texts and philosophical literature. Hermeneutics is closely related to exegesis; the branch of theology that defines how we determine the meaning of a scriptural passage or the entirety of a scripture.

We can use some simple rules of hermeneutics to help us recognize what the Bhagavad-gītā is emphasizing and, by extension, where we should direct most of our attention. The easiest way to identify the focal points of the Gītā is to look for these four things:

1. What's first
2. What's last
3. What's in the middle
4. What gets the most ink

Here are three other rules of hermeneutics for you to consider:

1. **A correct interpretation of any given scriptural passage will always be consistent with the rest of the scripture,** which is to say that it won't contain or result in any internal contradictions. In addition, a correct interpretation of the scripture as a whole will always be consistent with other scriptures that appear within the same tradition. The Bhagavad-gītā appears in the Vedic tradition. Scriptural evidence is one of the elements of Vedic epistemology, the means by which the Vedic tradition distinguishes a justifiable belief from mere opinion. Therefore, it's quite common to see editions of the Gītā where the commentator refers to passages from other Vedic texts, such as the Upaniṣads, as evidence to support their interpretation or philosophical conclusion.
2. **The meaning of a word, a phrase, a sentence, or a paragraph must be derived from the context in which it appears.** This is another reason not to cherry-pick verses: in many cases, the meaning of a verse can't be found if we ignore the verses that surround it. The Gītā's verses are generally grouped together around a particular topic. For example, early in the second chapter of the Bhagavad-gītā we'll hear a very counter-intuitive proposition: that a wise person doesn't lament for anyone, either living or dead. You could speculate about what this verse means and why it may or may not be true but if you want to know Kṛṣṇa's reasoning behind this counter-intuitive proposition, all you have to do is read the next verse.

3. **The goal of scriptural interpretation is to reveal the self-evident meaning, not to invent a hidden or secret truth, or to come up with a unique interpretation of one's own design.** There's a big difference between *inventing* a hidden truth and *discovering* a hidden truth. The Gītā's truths are hidden only to the extent that we lack the ability to recognize them when we see them. Discovering them is really just a matter of developing the ability to recognize that which is plainly visible. The rules of hermeneutics, which are meant to help us develop this ability, encourage us to accept the simplest or most direct explanation of a passage as the correct one unless a figurative meaning is required in order to make sense of it.

Finally, re-visit the Gītā. The Bhagavad-gītā isn't the kind of book that you read just once. Six months or a year after you've read the Gītā all the way through and discovered the ways in which you can integrate its teachings into your life, repeat the process of contemplative reading from start to finish. When you return to the Gītā, return to the notes you took during your previous reading, too. Re-reading your notes as you re-read the Gītā will show you how your consciousness is changing. Each time I return to the Gītā, passages that I've read dozens of times inspire new insights and deeper realizations. This phenomenon never ceases to amaze me. There is simply no end to the depth of the Gītā's teachings.

....

The techniques of contemplative reading provide us with practical ways to develop a deep and meaningful relationship with the Bhagavad-gītā. Another way to deepen our relationship with the Gītā is to chant the verses in the language of its original composition: Sanskrit. Even if you can't read the original Sanskrit, you can still chant the verses thanks to what's known as transliterated Sanskrit: Sanskrit rendered in the Roman alphabet. With this in mind, I've paired the English renditions of each verse with its corresponding transliterated Sanskrit and provided you with a pronunciation guide.

A Guide to Sanskrit Pronunciation

The Sanskrit words that appear in this book have been rendered in the Roman alphabet in accordance with the academically recognized system for Sanskrit transliteration called the International Alphabet for Sanskrit Transliteration (IAST). This system enables accurate voicing of Sanskrit words through the use of diacritics to indicate how each letter is pronounced.

In Sanskrit, each letter is pronounced, including twin-paired letters such as the two *t*s in the word *sattva* (*suht-tvuh*). However, it's common for a vowel at the end of a word to be treated as silent, especially by people whose native language is Hindi, Bengali, or one of the many other languages spoken on the Indian subcontinent. I've heard different Sanskrit scholars from different parts of India pronounce the same words with different inflections according to their respective regional influences. This is not particularly significant insofar as word meanings is concerned.

Each letter is pronounced only one way. For example, if you want an *s* sound you use an *s*, if you want a *k* sound you use a *k*, and if you want a *c* sound, well... *s* and *k* already have the two usual options covered so the letter *c* is used to indicate a *ch* sound, as in *chocolate* (as opposed to *Chanukah*). With transliterated Sanskrit, you will never run into the kind of pronunciation conundrums posed by English words like *psychosis* (heaven help adults who have to learn English as a second language).

All sounds in Sanskrit are articulated using one of five locations: the juncture of the mouth and throat, the palate, the cerebrum, the root of the upper teeth, and the lips. The sounds associated with each location are technically referred to as being guttural, palatal, cerebral, dental or labial. The proper articulation of Sanskrit words, phrases, mantras, or verses requires the use of the full length of your mouth from back to front rather than primarily around the teeth and lips as is common for English.

Vowels come in short and long forms, as indicated by the absence or presence of a bar across the top of the vowel. Two exceptions to this rule are the vowels *e* and *o*, which are always long and, as such, have no bar above them to differentiate them from a short form. Sometimes the diacritics indicate that a letter that would normally be a consonant in the Roman alphabet is a vowel in transliterated Sanskrit. Two Sanskrit vowels are "gliding vowels," also known as diphthongs, meaning that the sounds of those vowels have two parts. In such cases, which are relatively rare, two letters of the Roman alphabet are used to indicate a single Sanskrit vowel.

Vowels are pronounced as follows:

a as in wh*a*t

ā as in entour*a*ge

i as in b*i*n

ī as in sw*ee*t

u as in f*oo*t

ū as in l*oo*p

e as in bet

ai as in *weigh-in* (the *a* sound in *weigh* and the *i* sound in *in* are both sounded)

o as in holy

au as in cow

ṛ as in b*r*im

ṝ as in *ree*d with the tip of the tongue bouncing off of the roof of the mouth instead of the top teeth bouncing off of the lower lip (rarely used.)

There are also four semi-vowels and two sort-of vowels. The four semi-vowels are:

ya as in *ya* think?

ra as in *ru*mble with the tip of the tongue bouncing off of the roof of the mouth instead of the top teeth bouncing off of the lower lip

la as in *la*ment

va as in *vo*lume

The two sort-of vowels are *ṁ* and *ḥ*.

The *ṁ* is a simultaneous closure of the lips in front and the nasal passages in the back of as if you were wrapping your mouth around a small walnut. Say *bong* and then close your lips to get the right sound (but don't inhale).

The *ḥ* is an aspiration and then an echo of the preceding vowel but only when the *ḥ* appears at the end of a word that appears at the end of a line. For example, the word *śāntiḥ* is pronounced as *shahnti-hih* and the word *namaḥ* is pronounced as *nama-hah* when they appear at the end of a sequence of words. In the case of a long vowel preceding the *ḥ*, the echo is a short version of the same vowel. When *ḥ* appears in the middle of a word or at the end of a word in the middle of a phrase the echo is negligible so you just add a little air to the sound. For example, in the mantra *oṃ śāntiḥ śāntiḥ śāntiḥ*, the echo only occurs on the third and final *śāntiḥ*.

An *h* without the dot under it is a simple aspiration, as in *ha ha ha.*

Consonants are even more conspicuous in their being sounded differently according to the origination point of the letter. The consonants listed below flow through the mouth as follows:

- The back of your tongue up against the back of your mouth (guttural)
- Your tongue flattened up against the back roof of your mouth (palatal)
- The underside of the tip of your tongue pressed to the middle roof of your mouth (cerebral)
- The tip of your tongue against your teeth (dental)
- Your lips pressed together (labial)

Note that consonants are described using two letters rather than one, the second letter being a short *a*. Also, please note that more than one variation of a letter may appear, with different diacritical marks to indicate differences in pronunciation. The difference in the pronunciation of the consonant is not necessarily related to the *a* that follows it in the transliterated presentation. Therefore, the pronunciation examples that follow may seem a little counter-intuitive at first glance.

The first set of consonants include:

ka as in *ka*bob

ca as in *ch*ocolate

ṭa as in P*t*olemy (You may think I'm just being clever, but try the next one and see the difference.)

ta as in *t*ingle (Notice the difference in your tongue's position when the letter *t* is followed by a short *i* sound instead of a short *a* or *o* sound?)

pa as in *pa*paya

A variant of these consonants puts an *h* after them. Since you pronounce every letter, this indicates that you will add some air to the sound at the end of that consonant.

Once again, going from the back of your mouth to the front:

kha as in The Wrath of *Kh*an

cha as in *ch*ai with a little extra air in the *h*

ṭha as in *tah*ini, with the underside of the tip of your tongue pressed to the middle roof of your mouth.

tha as in *tah*ini, with the tip of your tongue against your teeth

pha as in *puff*

The next set of consonants is a softened, rounder version of their predecessors:

ga as in *gu*mmy bear

ja as in *jo*b

ḍa as in *duh*, with the underside of the tip of your tongue pressed to the middle roof of your mouth

da as in *duh*, with the tip of your tongue against your teeth

ba as in *bu*tterfly

And again, from back to front:

gha as in the name of the country *Gha*na

jha as in *jo*cular

ḍha as in *do*ck, with the underside of the tip of your tongue pressed to the middle roof of your mouth

ḍha as in *do*ck, with the tip of your tongue against your teeth

bha as in *bo*p

The last set, again, from back to front:

ṅa as in hun*g*ry

ña as in the Spanish word se*ñ*or

ṇa as in start to say the letter *r* and then say *n* instead

na as in *n*evermore

ma as in *mama*

The last three sounds are called sibilants:

ś as in *sh* from the back of the mouth (like low-pitched Pink Noise)

ṣ as in *sh* from the middle of the mouth (like high-pitched White Noise)

s as in *s*ame (a regular *s* sound)

An idiosyncrasy: the combination *jñ,* as in the word *jñāna* (theoretical knowledge) is commonly pronounced using a hard-ish *g* sound, as in *going*, rather than a soft *j* sound, as in *joy*, when it's paired with the *nyuh* sound of the *ñ*. The result is that *jñāna* tends to sound more like *ngyaahnuh.*

....

A final element that will support your entering into the feeling of the Bhagavad-gītā is to understand the significance of the different Sanskrit names that Kṛṣṇa and Arjuna use for one another throughout the course of their conversation. You can practice your Sanskrit pronunciation by looking at how these different names are composed and learn more about what they mean in the guide that follows.

A Guide to Kṛṣṇa's and Arjuna's Various Names

Throughout the dialogue of the Bhagavad-gītā, Kṛṣṇa and Arjuna call one another by various names according to the particular feelings or concerns that they're expressing to one another. Sañjaya, the narrator of the Gītā, also uses various names, words, and phrases to refer to both Kṛṣṇa and Arjuna as he relays both the literal and emotional contents of the conversation to the blind king, Dhṛtarāṣṭra. On a few occasions during the course of his narration, Sañjaya will also refer to Dhṛtarāṣṭra by honorific names to indicate Dhṛtarāṣṭra's royal standing or the ancestry he shares with Arjuna.

Kṛṣṇa will often call Arjuna names like *mahā-bāhu* ("mighty-armed") and *dhanañ-jaya* ("winner of wealth") and Arjuna will call Kṛṣṇa names like *janārdana* ("source of inspiration") and *mādhava* ("source of all good fortune"). Each of these different names are significant because they amplify the sense of urgency, indicate the level or nature of a particular inquiry, highlight the significance of an ancestral heritage, or convey the nature of the relationship between Kṛṣṇa and Arjuna.

These alternative names may also have multiple meanings, which sometimes adds a multi-dimensional aspect to the verses in which an alternative name appears. In cases where the meanings of a name are exceptionally diverse, I've only included the meanings that are most important to gaining a deeper appreciation for the sentiments being expressed in those particular verses.

I've also included the meanings of these names in the English renderings of the verses whenever they appear for the first time in the dialogue to illustrate why those particular names are contextually significant and to make it easier for you remember what they mean when they appear again later in the text.

Here is a list of the various names for Kṛṣṇa and Arjuna, along with their meanings, in alphabetical order.

Kṛṣṇa:

Acyuta: infallible

Ādi-kartṛ: original creator

Ādya: original or primal

Ananta: unlimited

Ananta-rūpa: infinite form

Aprameya: immeasurable

Apratima-prabhāva: possessor of immeasurable power

Deva-deva: God of gods

Deva-vara: revered by all subordinate divinities or demigods

Deveśa: Lord of all subordinate divinities or demigods

Govinda: the source of pleasure for the senses; one who gives pleasure to the cows (the personality of Kṛṣṇa, especially in his youth, is closely associated with cows)

Hari: he who removes darkness and sorrow from the hearts of his devotees

Hṛṣīkeśa: the Lord who directs the senses; the ultimate controller of everyone's senses

Jagan-nivāsa: abode of the universe

Janārdana: source of inspiration; protector of all living beings

Keśava: slayer of a demon named Keśī, who personified baseless pride or egoism due to illusion; one whose hair is long, fragrant, and beautiful; a synonym for Viṣṇu

Keśi-niṣūdana: slayer of false pride; eradicator of doubts (similar to Keśava; killer of the Keśī demon)

Mādhava: indicative of Kṛṣṇa's unique, honey-like sweetness; referring to Kṛṣṇa's position as the source of good fortune or as Viṣṇu, the husband of the Goddess of Fortune

Madhusūdana: slayer of a demon named Madhu, who personified the illusion of material happiness

Mahā-bāhu: mighty-armed (Kṛṣṇa also calls Arjuna by this same name)

Mahātman: great Self

Parameśvara: Supreme Lord

Prabhu: Lord or master

Puruṣa: supreme or original person

Puruṣottama: ultimate or supreme person

Sahasra-bāhu: thousand-armed

Vārṣṇeya: descendent of Vṛṣṇi

Vāsudeva: son of Vasudeva (the name of Kṛṣṇa's "father"); all-pervading

Viṣṇu: the personality or form of God through which God manifests omnipresence, omniscience, and unlimited power; the maintainer of everyone and everything; the majestic form of God

Viśva-mūrti: universal form

Viśveśvara: Lord of the universe

Yādava: descendent of the Yādu dynasty

Yogeśvara: master of mystic yoga

Yogin: supreme mystic

Arjuna:

Anagha: sinless

Bhārata: descendant of King Bhārata (also used by Sañjaya as a name for King Dhṛtarāṣṭra; an indication of the family lineage shared by both sides).

Bharatarṣabha: best of the descendants of King Bhārata

Bharata-sattama: best of the descendants of King Bhārata (similar to *Bharatarṣabha*)

Dhanañ-jaya: winner of wealth; conqueror of riches

Dhanur-dharaḥ: holder of the bow and arrow

Guḍākeśa: conqueror of sleep; one who overcomes ignorance

Kaunteya: son of Kuntī (Arjuna's mother, Queen Kuntī, is also Kṛṣṇa's paternal aunt; Kṛṣṇa and Arjuna are cousins as well as friends)

Kirīṭī: one whose head is adorned with a symbol of sovereignty

Kuru-nandana: beloved son of the Kuru dynasty

Kuru-pravīra: most valiant of the Kuru warriors

Kuru-sattama: best of the Kuru dynasty

Kuru-śreṣṭha: best of the Kuru dynasty (synonymous with *Kuru-sattama*)

Mahā-bāhu: mighty-armed

Pāṇḍava: son of Pāṇḍu

Paran-tapaḥ: he who sets fire to his enemies; subduer of enemies

Pārtha: son of Pṛthā (Arjuna's mother, Queen Kuntī, is also known as Pṛthā; her birth name. She became known as Kuntī after she was adopted by her uncle, Kuntibhoja)

Savyasācī: masterful archer; someone who can fight equally well with either hand

....

In most cases, the names Arjuna uses when he addresses Kṛṣṇa are his way of telling Kṛṣṇa, "I have faith that you can dispel my doubts and confusion, that you can guide me on the right path." When Kṛṣṇa calls Arjuna by various names, it's Kṛṣṇa's way of telling Arjuna, "You can do this, you can rise to the occasion, you have the qualities you need to be successful," and so on. Now, as they observe the two armies from the center of the battlefield, Kṛṣṇa, feeling especially compassionate toward his friend, is anxious to dispel the incapacitating darkness that has flooded Arjuna's heart in his moment of crisis.

PART TWO

Bhagavad-gītā
The Song of the Blessed Lord

Prologue: Setting the Scene

"Everything is complicated; if that were not so, life and poetry and everything else would be a bore."
~ Wallace Stevens

Arjuna doesn't want to kill his grandfather. Nevertheless, he has to try. Not that it'll be easy: Bhīṣma, Arjuna's grandfather, is all but invincible. In fact, it seems far more likely that an act of divine intervention will be required to prevent Bhīṣma, the preeminent warrior on the battlefield, from killing Arjuna.

Years of family conflict have come to a head. Now, legions of soldiers have assembled on a vast battlefield to fight a war that will determine which side of the family will rule an empire.

Arjuna wants no part of it. Although he's a warrior of incomparable skill, all he wants is for everyone to live happily ever after. Fate, however, has other ideas. Now, Arjuna finds himself entangled in a complex web of politics and personal vendettas that are about to culminate in a devastating war.

Must it be this way? How did it come to this? Who are all of these people and what chain of events brought them all to this battlefield?

If it feels like you're jumping into the middle of a drama-already-in-progress when you open the Gītā, it's because you are. The events leading up to this battle are described in an epic eighteen-book story called the *Mahābhārata*. The Bhagavad-gītā appears as an episode in the *Mahābhārata*'s sixth book. Scholars are at odds over whether or not the Bhagavad-gītā was originally part of the *Mahābhārata* or a later addition. Extensive attempts to authoritatively re-construct the original epic have failed to conclusively support either position.

The *Mahābhārata* is a tale of complicated relationships, supernatural adventures, diabolical plots, narrow escapes, and demands for justice that have led up to this pivotal moment when Arjuna and his brothers must fight a final, decisive battle against their lifelong foes. Just as this moment arrives, the action stops and the Bhagavad-gītā begins. The entire drama of the *Mahābhārata* serves as an elaborately orchestrated setting for the Gītā's teachings.

The first showstopper that most first-time readers encounter in the Bhagavad-gītā is the cornucopia of unfamiliar names that march through the first twenty-eight verses: Dhṛtarāṣṭra, Sañjaya, Duryodhana, Yuyudhāna, Virāṭa, Drupada, Dhṛṣṭaketu, Cekitāna, Purujit, Kuntibhojas, Śaibya, Bhīṣma, Karṇa, Kṛpa, Aśvatthāmā, Vikarṇa, the son of Somadatta, Bhīma, Yudhiṣṭhira . . . even the conch shells that the combatants are blowing have names!

For one who's familiar with *Mahābhārata*, the recitation of the names of the warriors assembled on the battlefield in the Gītā's opening chapter serves as the culmination of the intrigues, adventures, and conflicts that have brought the story to its dramatic crescendo and acts as an intensifying prelude to the conversation between Kṛṣṇa and Arjuna that's about to take place. Arjuna has a relationship with all of the combatants that Duryodhana, his cousin and principal opponent, names in the Gītā's opening soliloquy. In some cases, those relationships are life-long and familial. Arjuna is not about to do battle with strangers; his beloved grandfather and his revered martial arts teacher, among many others for whom he has affection, are politically obligated to fight for the opposing army. The recitation of the names of the principal combatants gives us an indication of just how heartbreaking the situation is for Arjuna.

But if you haven't read the *Mahābhārata*, you may think, "How am I going to keep track of all these people? I can't even pronounce these names, much less remember them!" I've heard many Western readers say they've tried to read the Gītā, but never got past the first chapter because they thought that they'd never be able to keep track of who's who.

Here's the most important thing you need to know about all the warriors whose names we hear at the beginning of the Bhagavad-gītā: they all disappear from the pages of the Gītā after the first chapter. There's no need to remember or keep track of them. Although hearing their names amplifies the reasons for Arjuna's despair at the outset of the Gītā, they have limited significance for the reader who's interested in understanding the philosophy of the Bhagavad-gītā rather than in following the story that surrounds it.

Beyond the opening verses of the first chapter, the Gītā consists almost entirely of a two-man dialogue. Sañjaya, who's relating the events unfolding on the distant battlefield to the blind King Dhṛtarāṣṭra, appears from time to time to remind us that we're reading a narration of the conversation between Kṛṣṇa and Arjuna, but everyone else to whom we're introduced in the first chapter will stand aside for the duration of the Gītā.

. . . .

This leaves us with the challenge of understanding who's fighting and why. Knowing something about the Gītā's backstory can deepen our sense of emotional connection to the story and expand our potential range of insight into its teachings.

So, with this in mind . . .

When Arjuna's grandfather, Bhīṣma, was a young man, he took two vows: that he would never ascend to the throne of his father, Santanu, the king of the Kuru dynasty, and that he would live a life of absolute celibacy. His vow ensured that not only would he relinquish his position as next in line for the throne but that he would never have children who would claim the right to royal succession.

He took these vows because his father had fallen in love with a woman named Satyavatī and wished to marry her. However, Satyavatī's father insisted that, as a condition of marriage, his daughter's children would inherent the throne despite her not being born of the ruling class. Ordinarily, Bhīṣma and his progeny would be next in the line of succession. However, Bhīṣma had yet to marry and, consequently, had no children. Hence, Bhīṣma, whose only interest was in his father's happiness, took his vows to prove to Satyavatī's father that his conditions would be met.

Santanu had never asked Bhīṣma to take such vows and was surprised to learn of them. Realizing that Bhīṣma would never go back on his word, Santanu accepted Bhīṣma's vows and married Satyavatī.

King Santanu and his new queen, Satyavatī, had two sons, one of whom passed away shortly after Santanu himself died. In the absence of King Santanu, it was up to Bhīṣma to make arrangements for the remaining son to marry in order to ensure that the family line would continue.

To fulfill his obligation, Bhīṣma arranged for three sisters of a royal family to marry his remaining younger half-brother . . . by kidnapping them. Abduction was considered a socially acceptable "arrangement" for royal marriages in Bhīṣma's time and it was common practice for brides-to-be to arrange their own abductions for the sake of assuring that they would be wed to the groom of their choice.

In this case, however, prior consent was neither sought nor

given. So, not surprisingly, one of the princesses, Ambā, rejected Bhīṣma's arrangement and returned to the palace from which she had been seized. The other two sisters, Ambikā and Ambālikā, willingly agreed to marry the surviving son of King Santanu and Queen Satyavatī.

As fate would have it, however, the surviving son didn't survive long enough for an heir to be conceived. According to tradition, it would normally have been Bhīṣma's responsibility to accept the throne and engage with his younger brother's wives in such a way as to ensure the continuation of the dynasty. Satyavatī tried to convince Bhīṣma to renounce his vows but, even though the original purpose of his vows had already been served, Bhīṣma refused to renounce them as a matter of principle.

This left Satyavatī with no choice but to reveal a long-kept secret:

Satyavatī was born in a humble family and, in her youth, she participated in the family business of ferrying people across the river. On one such crossing, her lone passenger was a great sage. Feeling the pull of both Satyavatī's feminine charms and the call of destiny, the sage told Satyavatī that if she would fulfill his desire for intimacy with her, he, by his mystic power, would make love to her and yet leave her virginity intact.

The sage further claimed that he would give Satyavatī a son who would be born to her that very day and would grow to adulthood immediately. Satyavatī accepted the sage's word and, after magically surrounding the boat with fog so that their liaison would not be seen, the sage made love to Satyavatī.

Upon landing on an island in the river, Satyavatī immediately gave birth to a son who miraculously grew into manhood right before her eyes. The mysterious son thanked his dumbfounded mother for giving birth to him and said, "I have a mission to fulfill and must go to the mountains. If you ever need me, just sit facing north and meditate on me; I will come."

Satyavatī's son became known as Vyāsa, the scribe of all Vedic knowledge. According to the accepted standards of succession back-up plans, Vyāsa was technically qualified to unite with his late half-brother's wives for the sake of producing an heir. Satyavatī told Bhīṣma that she could call upon Vyāsa to fulfill the need for a surrogate father.

Bhīṣma approved of Satyavatī's plan, and so she went to a suitable place, took a northward-facing seat, and fixed her mind on Vyāsa.

Vyāsa kept his promise and soon arrived at the palace. Because he was a renounced *yogī* living a life of severe austerity in the mountain forests, he looked like a wild man; his hair was long and matted, his body was encrusted with dirt, and he smelled . . . bad.

That night, when Vyāsa entered Ambikā's bedchamber, she was so horrified by Vyāsa's appearance that she couldn't bring herself to look at him. Knowing that the continuation of the family dynasty was at stake, she reluctantly submitted to her duty but kept her eyes tightly shut for the entire time.

Afterwards, Vyāsa told Ambikā that she would have a son who would be as prideful as he was powerful, but that he would be born blind due to her having kept her eyes closed during his conception. The son's name would be Dhṛtarāṣṭra.

The next morning, Ambālikā heard about Vyāsa's prophecy. Wanting her own child to have the gift of sight, she was determined to keep her eyes open when Vyāsa came to her that night. But Vyāsa's appearance was so unnerving that, when she saw him, the blood rushed from her skin and she turned a ghostly white.

Afterwards, Vyāsa told Ambālikā that she would have a son who was noble and kind, but whose complexion would be unusually pale. The son's name would be Pāṇḍu.

. . . .

Nine months later, Dhṛtarāṣṭra was born shortly before the birth of Pāṇḍu. But despite being born first, Dhṛtarāṣṭra could not inherit the throne because he was born blind. Therefore, the line of succession would run through Dhṛtarāṣṭra's younger brother, Pāṇḍu.

In due course of time, Pāṇḍu married two beautiful princesses, Kuntī and Mādrī. However, before he could conceive a child with either of them, he accidently caused the death of a great mystic who, with his dying breath, cursed Pāṇḍu to die the next time he attempted to enjoy the pleasures of lovemaking. Thus, Pāṇḍu could no longer attempt to conceive an heir without losing his life.

This left Kuntī with no choice but to reveal another long-kept secret:

When she was a very young woman, Kuntī's family played host to a powerful and notoriously incorrigible sage. Kuntī's family, aware of her expertise at providing hospitality, relied on her to see to the sage's needs without incurring his dissatisfaction.

The usually incorrigible sage was, in fact, so satisfied with Kuntī's humble and attentive service that he gave her an extraordinary gift: a mantra with which Kuntī could call any demigod to beget a child with her.

When Kuntī told Pāṇḍu about the sage's gift, Pāṇḍu enthusiastically encouraged her to use the mantra to call selected demigods to act as surrogate fathers. Kuntī called Yamarāja, the god of justice, who fathered Kuntī's first born child, Yudhiṣṭhira. Yudhiṣṭhira was destined to become famous for his unfailing adherence to principles of righteousness.

The next year, Kuntī called upon Vāyu, the god of the wind. Their union resulted in the birth of Kuntī's second son, Bhīma, who was destined to become famous for his extraordinary physical strength. Then she called upon Indra, the god of the heavenly planets. Indra fathered Arjuna, who was to become famous as the most accomplished of archers.

Kuntī let her co-wife, Mādrī, use the mantra and, after calling the great celestial physicians, known as the Aśvinī-kumāras, gentle twins named Nakula and Sahadeva were born.

Although the five sons of Kuntī and Mādrī were fathered by gods of various celestial realms, they were still recognized as the sons of Pāṇḍu and became known as the Pāṇḍavas. For some years thereafter, Pāṇḍu, his wives, and the five young Pāṇḍava princes lived happily in the forest.

One beautiful spring day, Pāṇḍu was overcome by the desire to enjoy the intimate company of his wife, Mādrī. Ignoring Mādrī's warnings, Pāṇḍu's caresses and kisses evoked the curse that was leveled at him years ago, and he died, just as the sage had promised.

Pāṇḍu's wives erected a funeral pyre and, as Pāṇḍu's body was consumed by the flames, Mādrī voluntarily entered the fire to follow Pāṇḍu into their next lives. Kuntī was left by herself to care for their five young boys.

....

Kuntī and her five sons returned to the family palace, whereupon Dhṛtarāṣṭra found himself reluctantly obliged to acknowledge that his younger brother's eldest son was the rightful heir to the kingdom. Dhṛtarāṣṭra had also married and his wife had also given birth to sons, who became known as the Kauravas. The eldest son, Duryodhana was envious of his cousins, the Pāṇḍavas, and grew to consider them his life-long enemies.

As the sons of Pāṇḍu and the sons of Dhṛtarāṣṭra grew up together in the palace of the Kuru dynasty, Dhṛtarāṣṭra quietly encouraged his son's ambition to usurp the throne from Yudhiṣṭhira, the eldest of the Pāṇḍava princes.

Duryodhana, his brothers, and their allies did everything they could to dispose of the Pāṇḍavas. Their plans culminated in an assassination attempt that appeared to succeed because the Pāṇḍavas, after narrowly escaping, went into hiding.

Many months later, the Pāṇḍava brothers went, incognito, to a contest that would determine who would win the hand of Draupadī, the daughter of King Drupada. Draupadī, who had wished to marry Arjuna since she was very young, knew that the Pāṇḍavas had survived the assassination attempt and specifically designed the contest so that only Arjuna could win. Upon Arjuna's doing so, the truth that the Pāṇḍavas were still alive was revealed.

Realizing that the assassination attempt had failed, Dhṛtarāṣṭra reluctantly proposed a compromise that would keep the peace by splitting the kingdom between his son, Duryodhana, and his late brother's son, Yudhiṣṭhira. Anxious for peace, Yudhiṣṭhira and his brothers accepted the compromise and went on to build a beautiful city crowned by a spectacular palace from which they ruled a prosperous nation-state.

The success of Yudhiṣṭhira and his brothers infuriated Duryodhana. More determined than ever to undermine the Pāṇḍavas and claim the entire kingdom as his own, Duryodhana enlisted the help of co-conspirators who lured Yudhiṣṭhira into a rigged gambling match.

Duryodhana's plan worked: Yudhiṣṭhira was goaded into making progressively higher bets until he lost everything. In the end, the Pāṇḍavas were obliged to surrender their half of the kingdom and accept twelve years of exile.

When the time of their exile expired, the Pāṇḍavas returned but Duryodhana refused to relinquish his claim on the entirety of the kingdom. Kṛṣṇa, who had been surreptitiously helping the Pāṇḍavas through their various travails, tried to negotiate a peaceful settlement with Duryodhana. Duryodhana, more entrenched than ever, doubled down on his claim to the kingdom and vowed that he wouldn't even give the Pāṇḍavas enough land into which they could drive the point of a pin. With all diplomatic options exhausted, war was inevitable.

Kṛṣṇa was a prince in his own right and had a superb army at his command. When both Duryodhana and Arjuna approached Kṛṣṇa in the hopes of getting Kṛṣṇa's support, Kṛṣṇa told them that he would command his army to participate in the battle but that he would not personally engage in the fighting.

Kṛṣṇa then gave Arjuna a choice: he could have Kṛṣṇa's army or he could have Kṛṣṇa himself. Arjuna chose to let Duryodhana have Kṛṣṇa's army so that he could have his friend, Kṛṣṇa, accompany him on the battlefield. In lieu of personally taking up arms, Arjuna asked Kṛṣṇa to be his chariot driver. Kṛṣṇa gladly agreed to Arjuna's request.

Duryodhana came away with Kṛṣṇa's excellent army and, with it, the illusion that he had gotten the better end of the deal. Duryodhana, his heart polluted by envy, didn't understand who Kṛṣṇa really was.

The blood feud instigated by Duryodhana and enabled by his father, Dhṛtarāṣṭra, had finally come to a head. The opposing armies, each swelling with millions of fearsome warriors, assembled on the vast plain known as Kurukṣetra for a final fight to the death.

CHAPTER ONE

viṣāda-yoga THE YOGA OF DESPAIR

Prelude

Millions of hands grip millions of weapons as millions of warriors, bristling in a rush of adrenaline, press into the balls of their feet, ready to hurl themselves into mortal combat. The fate of an empire is about to be decided. Everyone is in position. The battle is about to begin.

It's at this precise moment, when all eyes are on the battlefield and everyone's attention is fixed on what's about to happen, that the wondrous and sacred dialogue of the Bhagavad-gītā begins.

The Pāṇḍava army is both outnumbered and outclassed by the Kaurava army. Nevertheless, numerous omens – the location of the battlefield (the field of *dharma*), the blowing of their conch shells (announcing the presence of Viṣṇu), and the image of Hanumān emblazoned on the flag atop Arjuna's chariot (indicating that the invincible devotee of Lord Rāma was also present) – all suggest that it will be the Pāṇḍavas who prevail.

Despite so many indications that he is destined to be victorious, Arjuna hesitates. Rather than signaling for the battle to commence, he asks his charioteer, Kṛṣṇa, to place his chariot between the two armies so that he can see all those who have come to the battlefield ready to fight.

Kṛṣṇa purposely places the chariot directly in front of those in the opposing army whom Arjuna loves and respects the most. Upon seeing them, it becomes clear to Arjuna that the only possible outcome of the battle, no matter who wins, will be a catastrophe of unfathomable magnitude. Overwhelmed by compassion and grief, Arjuna has an emotional breakdown and loses his will to fight.

Things to look for:

- In verse 1, the first spoken word, *dharma*, tells us that the Bhagavad-gītā is a book about how to respond to the will of providence.
- In verse 3, Duryodhana is using diplomatic sarcasm as a way to intensify his martial arts teacher's fighting spirit. Duryodhana's teacher, Droṇa, also trained the warrior who is now the chief strategist of the Pāṇḍava's army. And he did so even though this student was the son of his enemy, Drupada. Now "the son of Drupada" will use everything he learned to try to defeat his own teacher. Duryodhana is therefore giving his teacher a cleverly calculated back-handed compliment as a way to motivate him to fight as hard as he can.

  The fact that Droṇa was also Arjuna's martial arts teacher is also very significant.
- In verse 7, the phrase "twice-born" is a reference to Duryodhana's teacher's standing as a *brāhmaṇa*, the highest division of the Vedic social order. In Vedic culture, teachers

are considered to be the highest and most valuable members of society. The term "twice-born" specifically indicates someone who has experienced both a physical birth and a second birth in the form of spiritual initiation by a qualified guru.

- In verses 14 through 16, Kṛṣṇa and the Pāṇḍavas signal their readiness for battle by blowing their conch shells. Curiously, each conch shell is referred to by name. At the time of the battle at Kurukṣetra, it was customary for a warrior's weapons and accoutrements to be given names that signified a particular potential, pastime, or quality. The significant quality shared by Kṛṣṇa's and the Pāṇḍava's conch shells is that of being "divine," as indicated by the Sanskrit word *divyau*. This differentiates the conch shells of Kṛṣṇa and the Pāṇḍavas from those of the Kauravas and serves as a further indication that the Pāṇḍavas would ultimately be victorious.
- In verse 30, as Arjuna feels himself falling into a state of despair, he calls Kṛṣṇa by the name "Keśava," which means "killer of the demon of false pride." This is a subtle indication that Arjuna's despair is a symptom of his having fallen under the influence of false egoism; a misconceived sense of identity. The effect that an illusory conception of identity has on a person and the means to extricate oneself from such an illusion will be a key topic throughout the Bhagavad-gītā.
- In verses 28 through 46, Arjuna expresses his doubts about the wisdom of proceeding with the battle. His arguments against fighting are based on four principles: compassion, enjoyment, saintliness, and social stability.
- In verse 41, as Arjuna is making his principled arguments, he makes a reference to ritualistic offerings to one's ancestors.

He uses the phrase "fall down" (*patanti*), which indicates a descent into unfortunate circumstances, otherwise known as "bad *karma*." According to Arjuna's cultural frame of reference, families have the ability and a responsibility to invoke "good *karma*" for their ancestors by periodically performing rituals that help their forebearers maintain a position that's favorable for material enjoyment. If such rituals cease to be performed, those same forebearers will "fall down" from the favorable position that the rituals had helped them to maintain.

1.1

dhṛtarāṣṭra uvāca
dharma-kṣetre kuru-kṣetre - samavetā yuyutsavaḥ
māmakāḥ pāṇḍavāś caiva - kim akurvata sañjaya

Dhṛtarāṣṭra said: O Sañjaya, when my sons and the sons of Pāṇḍu assembled on the field of righteousness at Kurukṣetra with their respective armies, determined to fight, what did they do?

1.2

sañjaya uvāca
dṛṣṭvā tu pāṇḍavānīkaṁ - vyūḍhaṁ duryodhanas tadā
ācāryam upasaṅgamya - rājā vacanam abravīt

Sañjaya said: After seeing the army of the sons of Pāṇḍu deployed in battle formation, Duryodhana [Dhṛtarāṣṭra's eldest son] approached his teacher and spoke the following words:

1.3

paśyaitāṁ pāṇḍu-putrāṇām - ācārya mahatīṁ camūm
vyūḍhāṁ drupada-putreṇa - tava śiṣyeṇa dhīmatā

O my teacher, behold the great army of the Pāṇḍavas, so skillfully arranged by your disciple, the son of Drupada.

1.4

atra śūrā maheṣv-āsā - bhīmārjuna-samā yudhi
yuyudhāno virāṭaś ca - drupadaś ca mahā-rathaḥ

Here are their heroes, mighty archers equal in skill to Bhima and Arjuna: Yuyudhāna, Virāṭa and the great chariot warrior, Drupada, . . .

1.5

dhṛṣṭaketuś cekitānaḥ - kāśirājaś ca vīryavān
purujit kuntibhojaś ca - śaibyaś ca nara-puṅgavaḥ

Dhṛṣṭaketu, Cekitāna, and the powerful King of Kāśi; Purujit, Kuntibhoja, and Śaibya, the foremost of men, . . .

1.6

yudhāmanyuś ca vikrānta - uttamaujāś ca vīryavān
saubhadro draupadeyāś ca - sarva eva mahā-rathāḥ

the mighty Yudhāmanyu, the valiant Uttamaujā, the son of Subhadrā and the sons of Draupadī, all great chariot fighters.

1.7

asmākaṁ tu viśiṣṭā ye - tān nibodha dvijottama
nāyakā mama sainyasya - saṁjñārthaṁ tān bravīmi te

O best of the twice-born, know as well the highly qualified leaders of my forces; I will tell you about them.

1.8

bhavān bhīṣmaś ca karṇaś ca - kṛpaś ca samitiṁ-jayaḥ
aśvatthāmā vikarṇaś ca - saumadattis tathaiva ca

There is your good self, Bhīṣma, Karṇa and Kṛpa, as well as Aśvatthāmā, Vikarṇa, and the son of Somadatta, who are sure to be victorious in battle.

1.9

anye ca bahavaḥ śūrā - mad-arthe tyakta-jīvitāḥ
nānā-śastra-praharaṇāḥ - sarve yuddha-viśāradāḥ

Many other heroes are prepared to forfeit their lives for my sake. Well-equipped with various weapons, they are all expert warriors.

1.10

aparyāptaṁ tad asmākaṁ - balaṁ bhīṣmābhirakṣitam
paryāptaṁ tv idam eteṣāṁ - balaṁ bhīmābhirakṣitam

Perfectly shielded by Bhīṣma, our strength is immeasurable; the strength of the Pāṇḍavas, though carefully guarded by Bhīma, is limited.

1.11

ayaneṣu ca sarveṣu - yathā-bhāgam avasthitāḥ
bhīṣmam evābhirakṣantu - bhavantaḥ sarva eva hi

[Turning to address all of his military leaders] All of you, without exception, must be certain to arrange your battle formations in such a way as to give full support to Bhīṣma.

1.12

tasya sañjanayan harṣaṁ - kuru-vṛddhaḥ pitāmahaḥ
siṁha-nādaṁ vinadyoccaiḥ - śaṅkhaṁ dadhmau pratāpavān

[Sañjaya continued:] To the delight of Duryodhana, the valiant grandsire of the Kuru dynasty [Bhīṣma] roared like a lion and triumphantly blew his conch shell.

1.13

tataḥ śaṅkhāś ca bheryaś ca - paṇavānaka-gomukhāḥ
sahasaivābhyahanyanta - sa śabdas tumulo 'bhavat

Then conch shells and kettledrums, cymbals and other drums, trumpets and various horns were all suddenly sounded together in a tumultuous uproar.

1.14

tataḥ śvetair hayair yukte - mahati syandane sthitau
mādhavaḥ pāṇḍavaś caiva - divyau śaṅkhau pradadhmatuḥ

On the other side, Mādhava [Kṛṣṇa] and the son of Pāṇḍu [Arjuna], standing on a magnificent chariot drawn by white horses, blew their divine conch shells.

1.15

pāñcajanyaṁ hṛṣīkeśo - devadattaṁ dhanañ-jayaḥ
pauṇḍraṁ dadhmau mahā-śaṅkhaṁ - bhīma-karmā vṛkodaraḥ

The Lord of the senses [Kṛṣṇa] blew his conch shell, called Pāñcajanya; the winner of wealth [Arjuna] blew his conch shell called Devadatta; the voracious eater [Bhīma], whose acts of strength are terrifying to behold, blew his great conch called Pauṇḍra.

1.16

anantavijayaṁ raja - kuntī-putro yudhiṣṭhira
nakulaḥ sahadevaś ca - sughoṣa-maṇipuṣpakau

The son of Queen Kuntī, King Yudhiṣṭhira, blew his conch called Ananta-vijaya; Nakula and Sahadeva blew their conches called Sughoṣa and Maṇipuṣpaka.

1.17

kāśyaś ca parameṣv-āsaḥ - śikhaṇḍī ca mahā-rathaḥ
dhṛṣṭadyumno virāṭaś ca - sātyakiś cāparājitaḥ

The great archer, the King of Kāśī, the great warrior Śikhaṇḍī, their princely allies Dhṛṣṭadyumna and Virāṭa, and the unconquerable Sātyaki; . . .

1.18

drupado draupadeyāś ca - sarvaśaḥ pṛthivī-pate
saubhadraś ca mahā-bāhuḥ - śaṅkhān dadhmuḥ pṛthak pṛthak

King Drupada, the sons of Draupadī, and many others, O Lord of the earth, such as the mighty-armed son of Subhadrā, each in turn blew their respective conch shells.

1.19

sa ghoṣo dhārtarāṣṭrāṇāṁ - hṛdayāni vyadārayat
nabhaś ca pṛthivīṁ caiva - tumulo 'bhyanunādayan

Reverberating throughout the sky and across the surface of the earth, the uproarious sound shattered the hearts of the sons of Dhṛtarāṣṭra.

1.20

atha vyavasthitān dṛṣṭvā - dhārtarāṣṭrān kapi-dhvajaḥ
pravṛtte śastra-sampāte - dhanur udyamya pāṇḍavaḥ
hṛṣīkeśaṁ tadā vākyam - idam āha mahī-pate

Upon seeing the military formation of the sons of Dhṛtarāṣṭra from his chariot, which was decorated with the banner of Hanumān, Arjuna, the son of Pāṇḍu, raised his bow in preparation to fire his weapons. Then, O lord of the earth, Arjuna addressed Kṛṣṇa, the Lord of the senses, with these words:

1.21-22

arjuna uvāca
senayor ubhayor madhye - rathaṁ sthāpaya me 'cyuta
yāvad etān nirīkṣe 'haṁ - yoddhu-kāmān avasthitān
kair mayā saha yoddhavyam - asmin raṇa-samudyame

Arjuna said: O infallible one, please place my chariot between the two armies so that I may see those who have assembled here, eager to do battle, with whom I must fight in this great trial of arms.

1.23

yotsyamānān avekṣe 'haṁ - ya ete 'tra samāgatāḥ
dhārtarāṣṭrasya durbuddher - yuddhe priya-cikīrṣavaḥ

Let me see those who have come here to fight for the sake of pleasing the evil-minded son of Dhṛtarāṣṭra.

1.24

sañjaya uvāca
evam ukto hṛṣīkeśo - guḍākeśena bhārata
senayor ubhayor madhye - sthāpayitvā rathottamam

Sañjaya said: O descendant of Bhārata [Dhṛtarāṣṭra], the Lord of the senses [Kṛṣṇa], having been thus addressed by the conqueror of sleep [Arjuna], placed the finest of chariots between the two armies.

1.25

bhīṣma-droṇa-pramukhataḥ - sarveṣāṁ ca mahī-kṣitām
uvāca pārtha paśyaitān - samavetān kurūn iti

Facing Bhīṣma [Arjuna's grandfather], Droṇa [Arjuna's teacher] and all the other rulers of the world, he [Kṛṣṇa] said, "O son of Pṛthā, behold all the members of the Kuru dynasty who have assembled here."

1.26

tatrāpaśyat sthitān pārthaḥ - pitṝn atha pitāmahān
ācāryān mātulān bhrātṝn - putrān pautrān sakhīṁs tathā
śvaśurān suhṛdaś caiva - senayor ubhayor api

There, in the midst of both armies, Arjuna, the son of Pṛthā, saw fathers and grandfathers, teachers, maternal uncles, brothers, sons and grandsons, as well as friends, fathers-in-law, and well-wishers.

1.27

tān samīkṣya sa kaunteyaḥ - sarvān bandhūn avasthitān
kṛpayā parayāviṣṭo - viṣīdann idam abravīt

Upon seeing his friends and relatives in battle formation, the son of Kuntī was overwhelmed by intense feelings of compassion and, in despair, spoke the following words:

1.28

arjuna uvāca
dṛṣṭvemaṁ sva-janaṁ kṛṣṇa - yuyutsuṁ samupasthitam
sīdanti mama gātrāṇi - mukhaṁ ca pariśuṣyati

Arjuna said: My dear Kṛṣṇa, seeing my friends and relatives assembled here, eager to fight, I feel the strength of my limbs deserting me; my body is quivering and my mouth is drying up.

1.29

vepathuś ca śarīre me - roma-harṣaś ca jāyate
gāṇḍīvaṁ sraṁsate hastāt - tvak caiva paridahyate

Shaking uncontrollably, I feel my hair standing on end, my bow slipping from my hand, and my skin burning.

1.30

na ca śaknomy avasthātuṁ - bhramatīva ca me manaḥ
nimittāni ca paśyāmi - viparītāni keśava

Seeing only horror to come, my mind is reeling. O Keśava, killer of the demon of false pride, I feel myself collapsing as I become lost to myself.

1.31

na ca śreyo 'nupaśyāmi - hatvā sva-janam āhave
na kāṅkṣe vijayaṁ kṛṣṇa - na ca rājyaṁ sukhāni ca

I do not see how any good can come from my being the agent of death to my own friends and relatives. Nor, dear Kṛṣṇa, can I aspire to any subsequent victory, kingdom, or the pleasures that winning a kingdom would offer.

1.32-33

kiṁ no rājyena govinda - kiṁ bhogair jīvitena vā
yeṣām arthe kāṅkṣitaṁ no - rājyaṁ bhogāḥ sukhāni ca

ta ime 'vasthitā yuddhe - prāṇāṁs tyaktvā dhanāni ca
ācāryāḥ pitaraḥ putrās - tathaiva ca pitāmahāḥ

O Govinda, O fountainhead of pleasure for the senses, of what use are a kingdom, happiness, or even life itself when all those for whom we desire such things – our teachers, fathers, sons, grandfathers, maternal uncles, fathers-in-law, grandsons, brothers-in-law and other relatives – are standing here, prepared to die on this battlefield?

1.34-35

mātulāḥ śvaśurāḥ pautrāḥ - śyālāḥ sambandhinas tathā
etān na hantum icchāmi - ghnato 'pi madhusūdana

api trailokya-rājyasya - hetoḥ kiṁ nu mahī-kṛte
nihatya dhārtarāṣṭrān naḥ - kā prītiḥ syāj janārdana

O Madhusūdana, slayer of the illusion of material happiness, I have no desire to kill them, even though they are intent on killing me. O Janārdana, source of inspiration, I am not prepared to fight with them even for the sake of attaining dominion over the entire universe to say nothing of an earthly kingdom. What joy can we take in killing the sons of Dhṛtarāṣṭra?

1.36

pāpam evāśrayed asmān - hatvaitān ātatāyinaḥ
tasmān nārhā vayaṁ hantuṁ - dhārtarāṣṭrān sa-bāndhavān
sva-janaṁ hi kathaṁ hatvā - sukhinaḥ syāma mādhava

Though they are aggressors, killing the sons of Dhṛtarāṣṭra would still be sinful. Therefore, we should desist from killing them or causing the deaths of our friends. What should we gain, O Mādhava, source of all good fortune, and how could we ever be happy after killing our own family?

1.37-38

yady apy ete na paśyanti - lobhopahata-cetasaḥ
kula-kṣaya-kṛtaṁ doṣaṁ - mitra-drohe ca pātakam

kathaṁ na jñeyam asmābhiḥ - pāpād asmān nivartitum
kula-kṣaya-kṛtaṁ doṣaṁ - prapaśyadbhir janārdana

O Janārdana, although these men, overwhelmed by greed, do not see the criminality of killing family members or deceiving friends, why should we, who know better, engage in such sinful acts?

1.39

kula-kṣaye praṇaśyanti - kula-dharmāḥ sanātanāḥ
dharme naṣṭe kulaṁ kṛtsnam - adharmo 'bhibhavaty uta

Our family will be devastated by the downfall of our dynasty. With the very nature of our family destabilized, remaining family members will fall away from the path of righteousness.

1.40

adharmābhibhavāt kṛṣṇa - praduṣyanti kula-striyaḥ
strīṣu duṣṭāsu vārṣṇeya - jāyate varṇa-saṅkaraḥ

O Kṛṣṇa, if righteousness recedes then women will be exploited. O descendant of Vṛṣṇi, when unscrupulous men exploit women then unwanted children are brought into the world.

1.41

saṅkaro narakāyaiva - kula-ghnānāṁ kulasya ca
patanti pitaro hy eṣāṁ - lupta-piṇḍodaka-kriyāḥ

The rise of an unstable population results in a hellish life for both families and for those who destroy the continuity of family traditions. Even the ancestors of such degraded families will fall down when traditional offerings of food and water cease.

1.42

doṣair etaiḥ kula-ghnānāṁ - varṇa-saṅkara-kārakaiḥ
utsādyante jāti-dharmāḥ - kula-dharmāś ca śāśvatāḥ

The foul deeds of those who destabilize family life bring about social unrest, ruined communities, and undermine arrangements that are intended for family welfare.

1.43

utsanna-kula-dharmāṇāṁ - manuṣyāṇāṁ janārdana
narake niyataṁ vāso - bhavatīty anuśuśruma

O Janārdana, I have heard from authoritative sources that those whose family traditions have been lost dwell perpetually in hell.

1.44

aho bata mahat pāpaṁ - kartuṁ vyavasitā vayam
yad rājya-sukha-lobhena - hantuṁ sva-janam udyatāḥ

Alas, how strange it is: we are so driven by the desire for royal happiness that we are prepared to commit such profoundly evil deeds as killing our own kinsmen.

1.45

yadi mām apratīkāram - aśastraṁ śastra-pāṇayaḥ
dhārtarāṣṭrā raṇe hanyus - tan me kṣema-taraṁ bhavet

I would find greater peace if the sons of Dhṛtarāṣṭra, their weapons in hand, were to kill me while I stand on the battlefield unarmed and unresisting.

1.46

sañjaya uvāca
evam uktvārjunaḥ saṅkhye - rathopastha upāviśat
visṛjya sa-śaraṁ cāpaṁ - śoka-saṁvigna-mānasaḥ

Sañjaya said: Having thus spoken on the battlefield, Arjuna dropped back onto the seat of his chariot and cast his bow and arrows aside, his mind overwhelmed by grief.

CHAPTER 2

sāṅkhya-yoga THE YOGA OF ANALYSIS

Prelude

Chapter 1 introduced us to the setting, the situation, the principal combatants, and Arjuna's mindset as he considers the consequences of letting the battle proceed. As the chapter ended, Arjuna did the unthinkable for a dutiful warrior of his matchless caliber: he dropped his weapons. Nothing could have been more out of character.

As we begin Chapter 2, Arjuna argues that causing the deaths of his teachers, family members, and friends is sinful. And yet, he isn't convinced that leaving the battlefield would be the right course of action, either. Bewildered by what appear to be conflicting ethical imperatives, Arjuna turns to Kṛṣṇa for guidance. Kṛṣṇa, in turn, transitions from acting as Arjuna's friend to acting as Arjuna's teacher.

Chapter 2 provides us with a broad overview of Kṛṣṇa's complete teachings and the foundation for Kṛṣṇa's argument that fighting will actually be in Arjuna's best interest. Kṛṣṇa begins his teachings by challenging the most basic underlying assumption of Arjuna's arguments. When examined closely, we'll find that Kṛṣṇa's challenge to Arjuna's unspoken assumption is a profoundly radical departure from an assumption that's shared by both traditional Western monotheism and modern secular humanism: that we come into being at a point in time.

Things to look for:

- Throughout this chapter, the words "soul," "self," and "person" are used synonymously as references to the eternal individual being that inhabits any given temporary material body.
- Verse 12 provides us with the first and most fundamental element of knowledge in the Gītā's spiritual philosophy.
- Verse 26 is of particular interest because Kṛṣṇa juxtaposes the underlying assumption of his argument against a very modern assumption.
- In verse 40, "the greatest danger" is understood to mean the danger of taking birth in a species of life lower than that of a human being. All life forms have their own special kinds of intelligence and capabilities suitable for their bodies, their environments, and their desires. However, in the Gītā's worldview, life forms are regarded as hierarchical based on their capacity for spiritual inquiry. Other life forms have specialized intelligence that allows them to thrive within the precincts of their own realm but the ability to inquire into how and why we exist and if what we appear to be is who we truly are is understood to be a special opportunity for those who have taken birth as a human being. Therefore, a human birth would be considered higher than that of a dog or a fish or a bird, etc.

- In verse 52, "all that has been heard and all that is to be heard" refers to the portions of the Vedas that describe how to act in such a way as to bring about desirable reactions such as material prosperity and enjoyment (good *karma*).
- In verse 54, "how would such a person sit still" refers to the way in which a person who is practicing yoga stills the movements of the mind. Arjuna's question could be re-stated as, "How can I recognize someone who has stilled the fluctuations of the mind?"
- Verse 61 is the first verse in which Kṛṣṇa indicates that he, Kṛṣṇa, is the object of meditation that a yoga practitioner should focus on to achieve the greatest benefit from their practice. Kṛṣṇa will progressively amplify this recommendation throughout the rest of the Gītā.
- Verse 69 may be taken both literally and figuratively, as a difference in lifestyle and as a difference of interests respectively.

2.1

sañjaya uvāca
taṁ tathā kṛpayāviṣṭam - aśru-pūrṇākulekṣaṇam
viṣīdantam idaṁ vākyam - uvāca madhusūdanaḥ

Sañjaya said: Seeing Arjuna overwhelmed by compassion, his tear-filled eyes cast down in despair, Madhusūdana [Kṛṣṇa] spoke to him.

2.2

śrī-bhagavān uvāca
kutas tvā kaśmalam idaṁ - viṣame samupasthitam
anārya-juṣṭam asvargyam - akīrti-karam arjuna

The Blessed Lord said: My dear Arjuna, how has this weakness come upon you at such a critical moment? It is unbefitting a man of your noble character and will lead you not to heavenly glory but to disgrace.

2.3

klaibyaṁ mā sma gamaḥ pārtha - naitat tvayy upapadyate
kṣudraṁ hṛdaya-daurbalyaṁ - tyaktvottiṣṭha paran-tapa

O son of Pṛthā, do not succumb to this unbecoming impotence. Banish this petty weakness from your heart. Rise and breathe fire on your foes!

2.4

arjuna uvāca
kathaṁ bhīṣmam ahaṁ saṅkhye - droṇaṁ ca madhusūdana
iṣubhiḥ pratiyotsyāmi - pūjārhāv ari-sūdana

Arjuna said: O Madhusūdana, Bhīṣma and Droṇa are worthy of my worship! How can I counter-attack such men with arrows in battle, O slayer of enemies?

2.5

gurūn ahatvā hi mahānubhāvān
śreyo bhoktuṁ bhaikṣyam apīha loke
hatvārtha-kāmāṁs tu gurūn ihaiva
bhuñjīya bhogān rudhira-pradigdhān

Even though they are motivated by selfish desires, they are still my noble teachers. I would be better off living as a beggar in this world than to live having slain these great souls who are my mentors, for whatever pleasure I might enjoy thereafter would be tainted with their blood.

2.6

na caitad vidmaḥ kataran no garīyo
yad vā jayema yadi vā no jayeyuḥ
yān eva hatvā na jijīviṣāmas
te 'vasthitāḥ pramukhe dhārtarāṣṭrāḥ

Nor do we know which would be better: conquering them or being conquered by them. If we kill the sons of Dhṛtarāṣṭra, who stand here before us on the battlefield, then we would surely not wish to live.

2.7

kārpaṇya-doṣopahata-svabhāvaḥ
pṛcchāmi tvāṁ dharma-sammūḍha-cetāḥ
yac chreyaḥ syān niścitaṁ brūhi tan me
śiṣyas te 'haṁ śādhi māṁ tvāṁ prapannam

My heart is afflicted by a wretched weakness. My thoughts are in disarray as I try to ascertain which path is virtuous. Therefore, I am asking you to tell me with certainty what course of action would serve the greatest good. Please tell me, for I am now your disciple; a soul surrendered to you.

2.8

na hi prapaśyāmi mamāpanudyād
yac chokam ucchoṣaṇam indriyāṇām
avāpya bhūmāv asapatnam ṛddhaṁ
rājyaṁ surāṇām api cādhipatyam

I cannot envision how the grief that is drying up my senses might be dispelled, for it will remain even if I win an earthly kingdom of unrivaled affluence and reign with sovereignty on par with the celestial beings.

2.9

sañjaya uvāca
evam uktvā hṛṣīkeśaṁ - guḍākeśaḥ paran-tapaḥ
na yotsya iti govindam - uktvā tūṣṇīṁ babhūva ha

Sañjaya said: Having thus spoken to the Lord of the senses, the conqueror of sleep, who burns his foes said to Govinda, "I shall not fight," and fell silent.

2.10

tam uvāca hṛṣīkeśaḥ - prahasann iva bhārata
senayor ubhayor madhye - viṣīdantam idaṁ vacaḥ

O descendant of Bhārata, the Lord of the senses gently smiled as if about to laugh and then, in the midst of both armies, spoke to the despondent Arjuna as follows.

2.11

śrī-bhagavān uvāca
aśocyān anvaśocas tvaṁ - prajñā-vādāṁś ca bhāṣase
gatāsūn agatāsūṁś ca - nānuśocanti paṇḍitāḥ

The Blessed Lord said: Though your words have the sound of wisdom, you grieve for what is unworthy of grief. The wise lament neither for those who have passed away nor for those who have yet to pass.

2.12

na tv evāhaṁ jātu nāsaṁ - na tvaṁ neme janādhipāḥ
na caiva na bhaviṣyāmaḥ - sarve vayam ataḥ param

There has never been a time when I did not exist, nor a time when you did not exist, nor a time when all these kings did not exist; nor is there any possibility that in the future any of us shall ever cease to be.

2.13

dehino 'smin yathā dehe - kaumāraṁ yauvanaṁ jarā
tathā dehāntara-prāptir - dhīras tatra na muhyati

Just as an embodied soul experiences the transformations of their body, from childhood to youth to old age, that same person will pass into another body at the time of death. Those who are wise do not find this bewildering.

2.14

mātrā-sparśās tu kaunteya - śītoṣṇa-sukha-duḥkha-dāḥ
āgamāpāyino 'nityās - tāṁs titikṣasva bhārata

O son of Kuntī, happiness and distress come and go like winter and summer seasons. O descendent of Bhārata, they are transient products of sense perception that one must learn to tolerate without being disturbed.

2.15

yaṁ hi na vyathayanty ete - puruṣaṁ puruṣarṣabha
sama-duḥkha-sukhaṁ dhīraṁ - so 'mṛtatvāya kalpate

Indeed, one who is not troubled by such dualities, who patiently tolerates happiness and distress from a position of equanimity, is eligible for immortality, O best among men.

2.16

nāsato vidyate bhāvo - nābhāvo vidyate sataḥ
ubhayor api dṛṣṭo 'ntas - tv anayos tattva-darśibhiḥ

That which does not endure does not truly exist, whereas that which exists eternally never undergoes change. Seers of the truth have reached this conclusion by studying the nature of both.

2.17

avināśi tu tad viddhi - yena sarvam idaṁ tatam
vināśam avyayasyāsya - na kaścit kartum arhati

That which is present throughout the entire body you should know to be imperishable. No one can bring destruction to that which cannot be destroyed.

2.18

antavanta ime dehā - nityasyoktāḥ śarīriṇaḥ
anāśino 'prameyasya - tasmād yudhyasva bhārata

It is said that the material body, inhabited by the eternal, indestructible, and immeasurable soul, will surely perish. Therefore, fight, O descendent of Bhārata!

2.19

ya enaṁ vetti hantāraṁ - yaś cainaṁ manyate hatam
ubhau tau na vijānīto - nāyaṁ hanti na hanyate

Neither one who thinks of the self as a slayer nor one who thinks that the self can be slain understands that the self can neither slay nor be slain.

2.20

na jāyate mriyate vā kadācin
nāyaṁ bhūtvā bhavitā vā na bhūyaḥ
ajo nityaḥ śāśvato 'yaṁ purāṇo
na hanyate hanyamāne śarīre

The self is never born and never dies, has never come into being and shall never cease to be. Unborn, eternal, everlasting, and primeval, the self is not slain when the body is slain.

2.21

vedāvināśinaṁ nityaṁ - ya enam ajam avyayam
kathaṁ sa puruṣaḥ pārtha - kaṁ ghātayati hanti kam

O son of Pṛthā, how can someone cause the death of another when they know that the self is indestructible, eternal, unborn, and everlasting? Whom does such a person slay?

2.22

vāsāṁsi jīrṇāni yathā vihāya
navāni gṛhṇāti naro 'parāṇi
tathā śarīrāṇi vihāya jīrṇāny
anyāni saṁyāti navāni dehī

As a person relinquishes old and worn-out garments in favor of new ones, the embodied soul similarly acquires a new material body after abandoning the old and inoperative one.

2.23

nainaṁ chindanti śastrāṇi - nainaṁ dahati pāvakaḥ
na cainaṁ kledayanty āpo - na śoṣayati mārutaḥ

The soul cannot be dismembered by weapons, burned by fire, moistened by water, or withered by the wind.

2.24

acchedyo 'yam adāhyo 'yam - akledyo 'śoṣya eva ca
nityaḥ sarva-gataḥ sthāṇur - acalo 'yaṁ sanātanaḥ

Indivisible, inflammable, insoluble, and unwitherable, know for sure that souls are eternal, changeless, motionless, and present everywhere.

2.25

avyakto 'yam acintyo 'yam - avikāryo 'yam ucyate
tasmād evaṁ viditvainaṁ - nānuśocitum arhasi

It is said that the self is invisible, inconceivable, and unchangeable. Understanding the nature of the self, you should not lament for the body.

2.26

atha cainaṁ nitya-jātaṁ - nityaṁ vā manyase mṛtam
tathāpi tvaṁ mahā-bāho - nainaṁ śocitum arhasi

If, on the other hand, you believe that manifestations of consciousness are ever being born and, at the time of death, forever cease to be, you still have no cause for lamentation, O mighty-armed one.

2.27

jātasya hi dhruvo mṛtyur - dhruvaṁ janma mṛtasya ca
tasmād aparihārye 'rthe - na tvaṁ śocitum arhasi

Death is certain for all who are born and all who die will certainly take birth again. Therefore, you should not lament for that which is inevitable.

2.28

avyaktādīni bhūtāni - vyakta-madhyāni bhārata
avyakta-nidhanāny eva - tatra kā paridevanā

O Bhārata, all created beings are unmanifest at the beginning, become manifest during their middle stage, and in the end return to being unmanifest. So, what cause is there for lamentation?

2.29

āścarya-vat paśyati kaścid enam
āścarya-vad vadati tathaiva cānyaḥ
āścarya-vac cainam anyaḥ śṛṇoti
śrutvāpy enaṁ veda na caiva kaścit

Some see this self as astonishing, some describe this self as astonishing, and some hear about this self as astonishing. For others, even after hearing about this, the self remains incomprehensible.

2.30

dehī nityam avadhyo 'yaṁ - dehe sarvasya bhārata
tasmāt sarvāṇi bhūtāni - na tvaṁ śocitum arhasi

The embodied soul can never be killed, O Bharata, Therefore you need not grieve for any living being.

2.31

sva-dharmam api cāvekṣya - na vikampitum arhasi
dharmyād dhi yuddhāc chreyo 'nyat - kṣatriyasya na vidyate

Consider as well that there is nothing better for a warrior than righteous battle. Therefore, do not hesitate in the performance of your duty.

2.32

yadṛcchayā copapannaṁ - svarga-dvāram apāvṛtam
sukhinaḥ kṣatriyāḥ pārtha - labhante yuddham īdṛśam

O son of Pṛthā, such unsought battles thrust the gates of heaven wide open. Warriors are happy to obtain such a fight.

2.33

atha cet tvam imaṁ dharmyaṁ - saṅgrāmaṁ na kariṣyasi
tataḥ sva-dharmaṁ kīrtiṁ ca - hitvā pāpam avāpsyasi

If you do not fight then you will lose your reputation as a warrior. It would be sinful for you to renounce your duty by refusing to fight this righteous battle.

2.34

akīrtiṁ cāpi bhūtāni - kathayiṣyanti te 'vyayām
sambhāvitasya cākīrtir - maraṇād atiricyate

People will forever speak of your infamy; for one so highly esteemed, dishonor is worse than death.

2.35

bhayād raṇād uparataṁ - maṁsyante tvāṁ mahā-rathāḥ
yeṣāṁ ca tvaṁ bahu-mato - bhūtvā yāsyasi lāghavam

The great chariot warriors, thinking that you have left the battlefield out of fear alone, will belittle you. Thus, those who once admired you will consider you insignificant.

2.36

avācya-vādāṁś ca bahūn - vadiṣyanti tavāhitāḥ
nindantas tava sāmarthyaṁ - tato duḥkha-taraṁ nu kim

Your enemies will ridicule you with unkind words. What could be a greater misery than this?

2.37

hato vā prāpsyasi svargaṁ - jitvā vā bhokṣyase mahīm
tasmād uttiṣṭha kaunteya - yuddhāya kṛta-niścayaḥ

O son of Kuntī, either you will meet death in battle and enter the heavenly world or you will be victorious and enjoy an earthly kingdom. Therefore, you should rise with determination and fight.

2.38

sukha-duḥkhe same kṛtvā - lābhālābhau jayājayau
tato yuddhāya yujyasva - naivaṁ pāpam avāpsyasi

Being equipoised in happiness or distress, loss or gain, victory or defeat, fight simply for the sake of fighting, for by so doing you will not invite misfortune.

2.39

eṣā te 'bhihitā sāṅkhye - buddhir yoge tv imāṁ śṛṇu
buddhyā yukto yayā pārtha - karma-bandhaṁ prahāsyasi

Thus far I have described how to see with discernment. Now, hear me as I explain how this same kind of intelligence can be applied to the yoga of action. O son of Pṛthā, by acting on the basis of such intelligence, you will be free from the bondage of reactions.

2.40

nehābhikrama-nāśo 'sti - pratyavāyo na vidyate
sv-alpam apy asya dharmasya - trāyate mahato bhayāt

For those who strive along the path of righteousness, progress is never lost nor minimized, and just a little advancement can save one from the greatest danger.

2.41

vyavasāyātmikā buddhir - ekeha kuru-nandana
bahu-śākhā hy anantāś ca - buddhayo 'vyavasāyinām

O beloved son of the Kurus, those who take to this path pursue a singular goal with resolute determination, whereas the intelligence of those who are irresolute is drawn in countless directions.

2.42-43

yām imāṁ puṣpitāṁ vācaṁ - pravadanty avipaścitaḥ
veda-vāda-ratāḥ pārtha - nānyad astīti vādinaḥ

kāmātmānaḥ svarga-parā - janma-karma-phala-pradām
kriyā-viśeṣa-bahulāṁ - bhogaiśvarya-gatiṁ prati

Those who are delighted by the flowery language of the Vedas, which promise heavenly rewards and a fortuitous future in exchange for extravagantly ritualized offerings, absorb themselves in the pursuit of sensual pleasure and opulence. Bereft of wisdom, they insist that there is nothing more to life than this.

2.44

bhogaiśvarya-prasaktānāṁ - tayāpahṛta-cetasām
vyavasāyātmikā buddhiḥ - samādhau na vidhīyate

Resolute determination to achieve the perfection of meditation never arises in the minds of those who are bewildered by an obsession with affluence, power, and worldly pleasures.

2.45

trai-guṇya-viṣayā vedā - nistrai-guṇyo bhavārjuna
nirdvandvo nitya-sattva-stho - niryoga-kṣema ātmavān

The Vedas are primarily concerned with the three qualities of material nature. Transcend these three qualities, Arjuna. Establish yourself in a state of eternal truth and, thus abiding in your true self, attain freedom from anxieties arising from dualistic conceptions of loss and gain.

2.46

yāvān artha uda-pāne - sarvataḥ samplutodake
tāvān sarveṣu vedeṣu - brāhmaṇasya vijānataḥ

For one who has complete knowledge of the highest truth, the value of the Vedas is equal to that of a small well that's been placed next to a vast reservoir of water.

2.47

karmaṇy evādhikāras te - mā phaleṣu kadācana
mā karma-phala-hetur bhūr - mā te saṅgo 'stv akarmaṇi

You are entitled to act but you are not entitled to the fruits of your actions. You should never let results be your motivation for action nor should you adhere to inaction.

2.48

yoga-sthaḥ kuru karmāṇi - saṅgaṁ tyaktvā dhanañ-jaya
siddhy-asiddhyoḥ samo bhūtvā - samatvaṁ yoga ucyate

Bring your mind and senses under control and act without attachment to success or failure. Such equanimity is called yoga.

2.49

dūreṇa hy avaraṁ karma - buddhi-yogād dhanañ-jaya
buddhau śaranam anviccha - kṛpaṇāḥ phala-hetavaḥ

O winner of wealth, take shelter of discernment and, in that state of consciousness, distance yourself from lesser actions. Those who seek only the fruits of their actions are misers.

2.50

buddhi-yukto jahātīha - ubhe sukṛta-duṣkṛte
tasmād yogāya yujyasva - yogaḥ karmasu kauśalam

Those who are linked to reason shed both good and bad reactions to their actions even in this life. Therefore, absorb yourself in yoga, for yoga is virtuosity in action.

2.51

karma-jaṁ buddhi-yuktā hi - phalaṁ tyaktvā manīṣiṇaḥ
janma-bandha-vinirmuktāḥ - padaṁ gacchanty anāmayam

The great sages, endowed with wisdom, free themselves from reactions to their actions by renouncing the fruits of their actions. Thus liberated from the obligation of future births, they attain a state that is beyond the reach of material miseries.

2.52

yadā te moha-kalilaṁ - buddhir vyatitariṣyati
tadā gantāsi nirvedaṁ - śrotavyasya śrutasya ca

When your intelligence has passed through the dense forest of illusion you will find that you are indifferent to all that has been heard and all that is to be heard.

2.53

śruti-vipratipannā te - yadā sthāsyati niścalā
samādhāv acalā buddhis - tadā yogam avāpsyasi

When you are no longer perplexed by the flowery language of scriptural solicitations and remain fixed in a trance of transcendental awareness, you will have attained the perfect state of union.

2.54

arjuna uvāca
sthita-prajñasya kā bhāṣā - samādhi-sthasya keśava
sthita-dhīḥ kiṁ prabhāṣeta - kim āsīta vrajeta kim

Arjuna said: O Keśava, what are the characteristics of a person who is transcendentally situated in perfect meditation? What is the language of one whose intelligence is sound? How would such a person sit still and how would they move through the world?

2.55

śrī-bhagavān uvāca
prajahāti yadā kāmān - sarvān pārtha mano-gatān
ātmany evātmanā tuṣṭaḥ - sthita-prajñas tadocyate

The Blessed Lord said: O son of Pṛthā, when someone is free from all varieties of material desires that arise from the mind and, with a purified mind, finds satisfaction in the self alone, such a person is understood to be situated in a state of transcendental consciousness.

2.56

duḥkheṣv anudvigna-manāḥ - sukheṣu vigata-spṛhaḥ
vīta-rāga-bhaya-krodhaḥ - sthita-dhīr munir ucyate

One whose mind is free from attachment, fear, and anger, who is undisturbed by the arrival of sources of misery nor euphoric at the arrival of causes for happiness, is called a sage of steady mind.

2.57

yaḥ sarvatrānabhisnehas - tat tat prāpya śubhāśubham
nābhinandati na dveṣṭi - tasya prajñā pratiṣṭhitā

One who remains unfazed in all circumstances by whatever fortune or misfortune they obtain, neither celebrating it nor scorning it, is firmly fixed in perfect knowledge.

2.58

yadā saṁharate cāyaṁ - kūrmo 'ṅgānīva sarvaśaḥ
indriyāṇīndriyārthebhyas - tasya prajñā pratiṣṭhitā

One who can withdraw their senses from the objects of the senses, as a tortoise withdraws its limbs into its shell, is firmly fixed in perfect consciousness.

2.59

viṣayā vinivartante - nirāhārasya dehinaḥ
rasa-varjaṁ raso 'py asya - paraṁ dṛṣṭvā nivartate

Though the objects of the senses recede for the embodied soul who abstains from them, the taste for such objects remains. By acquiring a higher taste for that which is far superior, the taste for sense objects fades as well.

2.60

yatato hy api kaunteya - puruṣasya vipaścitaḥ
indriyāṇi pramāthīni - haranti prasabhaṁ manaḥ

O son of Kuntī, the senses are so powerful and impulsive that they may forcibly carry away even the mind of one who is capable of discernment.

2.61

tāni sarvāṇi saṁyamya - yukta āsīta mat-paraḥ
vaśe hi yasyendriyāṇi - tasya prajñā pratiṣṭhitā

One who retains complete control of the senses through self-discipline and whose consciousness remains linked to me is known to be one whose wisdom is firmly established.

2.62

dhyāyato viṣayān puṁsaḥ - saṅgas teṣūpajāyate
saṅgāt sañjāyate kāmaḥ - kāmāt krodho 'bhijāyate

When one's thoughts dwell on objects that attract the senses, attachment to those objects develops. From attachment to those sense objects, the desire to satisfy the senses is born. And from the desire to satisfy the senses, anger arises.

2.63

krodhād bhavati sammohaḥ - sammohāt smṛti-vibhramaḥ
smṛti-bhraṁśād buddhi-nāśo - buddhi-nāśāt praṇaśyati

Anger gives rise to bewilderment and with bewilderment comes loss of memory. When one's memory is lost, the power of discernment is lost with it. As the power of discernment recedes, the self vanishes from view.

2.64

rāga-dveṣa-vimuktais tu - viṣayān indriyaiś caran
ātma-vaśyair vidheyātmā - prasādam adhigacchati

But those who remain free from attractions and aversions, exercising self-control even as the senses engage with their objects, attain the grace of the Lord.

2.65

prasāde sarva-duḥkhānāṁ - hānir asyopajāyate
prasanna-cetaso hy āśu - buddhiḥ paryavatiṣṭhate

The miseries of material existence cease for a recipient of such grace and, with a clear mind, their power of discernment is firmly established.

2.66

nāsti buddhir ayuktasya - na cāyuktasya bhāvanā
na cābhāvayataḥ śāntir - aśāntasya kutaḥ sukham

Such transcendental intelligence is unattainable without the discipline of yoga, for without the discipline of yoga one cannot attain a state of meditation. Inner peace is only achieved through meditation; how can anyone be happy without inner peace?

2.67

indriyāṇāṁ hi caratāṁ - yan mano 'nuvidhīyate
tad asya harati prajñāṁ - vāyur nāvam ivāmbhasi

A person's intelligence will be carried away, just as a strong gust of wind carries a boat across the water, if the mind yields to even one of the senses that roams toward its objects.

2.68

tasmād yasya mahā-bāho - nigṛhītāni sarvaśaḥ
indriyāṇīndriyārthebhyas - tasya prajñā pratiṣṭhitā

Therefore, O mighty-armed, wisdom is firmly established in those who withdraw their senses from the objects of the senses.

2.69

yā niśā sarva-bhūtānāṁ - tasyāṁ jāgarti saṁyamī
yasyāṁ jāgrati bhūtāni - sā niśā paśyato muneḥ

That which is night for all beings is the time of awakening for those who are self-controlled; the time of awakening for all beings is night for the introspective sage.

2.70

āpūryamāṇam acala-pratiṣṭhaṁ
samudram āpaḥ praviśanti yadvat
tadvat kāmā yaṁ praviśanti sarve
sa śāntim āpnoti na kāma-kāmī

Just as the ocean remains unmoved by the incessant flow of rivers that continually fill it, those who remain unmoved by the incessant flow of desires attain peace; those who pursue such desires do not.

2.71

vihāya kāmān yaḥ sarvān - pumāṁś carati niḥspṛhaḥ
nirmamo nirahaṅkāraḥ - sa śāntim adhigacchati

Those who relinquish all selfish desires move through life in a state of freedom from worldly aspirations. Renouncing all sense of proprietorship and discarding all sense of identification with the material body, they attain peace.

2.72

eṣā brāhmī sthitiḥ pārtha - naināṁ prāpya vimuhyati
sthitvāsyām anta-kāle 'pi - brahma-nirvāṇam ṛcchati

O son of Pṛthā, upon attaining this state of spiritual consciousness, one remains free from bewilderment. Being firmly established in such consciousness, even if only at the moment of death, one extinguishes the forest fire of material existence and attains the spiritual realm.

CHAPTER 3

karma-yoga
THE YOGA OF ACTION

Prelude

In Chapter 2, Kṛṣṇa spoke about spiritual knowledge in general terms, including:

- an overview of the science of discernment (*sāṅkhya*) that reveals the distinction between spirit and matter,
- the art of applying spiritual intelligence to action,
- the process of controlling the senses in order to control the mind, and
- the shift in consciousness that's required for us to be able to act without attachment to the results of our actions.

Not surprisingly, Arjuna sees spiritual knowledge as incompatible with fighting. Therefore, Kṛṣṇa's insistence that Arjuna should fight doesn't make sense to him. Chapter 3 begins with Arjuna's expression of confusion over what specific course of action Kṛṣṇa is advising him to take.

In response to Arjuna's request for clarification, Kṛṣṇa explains why it's impossible to completely abstain from acting, why the renunciation of action alone is insufficient, and that action informed by spiritual knowledge and performed without attachment is called *karma-yoga*.

Things to look for:

- In verse 9, Kṛṣṇa speaks about making every action an offering to Viṣṇu as the essential element of *karma-yoga*. He specifically uses the word *yajñārthāt*, meaning "done only as a sacrifice" or "done only to satisfy Viṣṇu." "Viṣṇu" means "the all-pervading sustainer of existence." The word *yajña* can be translated as "sacrifice" and Viṣṇu is known as the *yajña-puruṣa*, the personification of sacrifice or the person for whom all sacrifices are ultimately intended. Hence, in the Gītā's frame of reference, it's understood that Viṣṇu, the omnipresent maintainer of the entire cosmic manifestation, is synonymous with *yajña*: sacrifice.
- In verse 10, the phrase "the Lord of all creatures," which translates the word *prajāpatiḥ*, has a double meaning: it indicates both the primary creator, Viṣṇu, who propels all souls who have forgotten their true spiritual nature into the illusory material world, and the secondary creator, Brahmā, who is empowered by Viṣṇu to populate the universe by supplying material bodies for all embodied souls.
- Verses 10 through 14 describe a relationship between earthbound human beings and celestial beings who are in charge of the proper administration of cosmic order. Verse 14 in particular includes the curious proposition that "rain is a product of sacrifice." The underlying assumption of the existence of celestial beings who are empowered to administer cosmic affairs, along with the proposition that a ceremony or ritual can influence the weather, may sound like a primitive understanding of how nature works. From

a modern perspective, we assume that nature is impersonal and that the laws of nature are autonomic. From the Gītā's perspective, however, the laws of nature are established by a person, Viṣṇu, and enacted by people who are authorized and empowered to do so: celestial beings, often referred to as "demigods," whose bodies are woven directly into the subtle fabric of the universe.

- In verse 20, Kṛṣṇa refers to King Janaka as a great leader who attained perfection by the same methods that Kṛṣṇa is advising Arjuna to follow. King Janaka is famous in Vedic history as the father of Princess Jānakī, also known as Sītā, the wife of Lord Rāma, who is glorified in the epic story Rāmāyaṇa. The events of the Rāmāyaṇa are understood to have taken place long before the Bhagavad-gītā was spoken.
- Verse 27 is especially significant: the concept that Kṛṣṇa speaks about here will appear again later as an important part of Kṛṣṇa's closing argument in Chapter 18.
- Verse 35 is also particularly significant, so much so that it, too, will be reiterated in Chapter 18.

3.1

arjuna uvāca
jyāyasī cet karmaṇas te - matā buddhir janārdana
tat kiṁ karmaṇi ghore māṁ - niyojayasi keśava

Arjuna said: If discernment and reason are higher than work that's performed for the sake of its result, O Janārdana, then why do you want me to engage in this horrific warfare, O Keśava?

3.2

vyāmiśreṇeva vākyena - buddhiṁ mohayasīva me
tad ekaṁ vada niścitya - yena śreyo 'ham āpnuyām

I'm confused by your bewildering instructions. Therefore, please tell me definitively what singular course of action I should take in order to achieve the greater good.

3.3

śrī-bhagavān uvāca
loke 'smin dvi-vidhā niṣṭhā - purā proktā mayānagha
jñāna-yogena sāṅkhyānāṁ - karma-yogena yoginām

The Blessed Lord said: O sinless one, I have described the steady path through this world as two-fold: for contemplatives it is the yoga of knowledge and for those who are active it is the yoga of action.

3.4

na karmaṇām anārambhān - naiṣkarmyaṁ puruṣo 'śnute
na ca sannyasanād eva - siddhiṁ samadhigacchati

A person cannot gain freedom from reactions to their actions merely by abstaining from action, nor can one attain perfection by renunciation alone.

3.5

na hi kaścit kṣaṇam api - jātu tiṣṭhaty akarma-kṛt
kāryate hy avaśaḥ karma - sarvaḥ prakṛti-jair guṇaiḥ

In fact, no one remains inactive for even a moment; everyone is forced to act according to their natural tendencies by the qualities of material nature that hold sway over them.

3.6

karmendriyāṇi saṁyamya - ya āste manasā smaran
indriyārthān vimūḍhātmā - mithyācāraḥ sa ucyate

One who restrains the senses of action but allows the mind to continuously dwell on the objects of sense attraction deludes oneself and is called a charlatan.

3.7

yas tv indriyāṇi manasā - niyamyārabhate 'rjuna
karmendriyaiḥ karma-yogam - asaktaḥ sa viśiṣyate

On the other hand, one who controls the senses by way of the mind and, relinquishing material attachments, engages the active senses in the yoga of action, is superior by far.

3.8

niyataṁ kuru karma tvaṁ - karma jyāyo hy akarmaṇaḥ
śarīra-yātrāpi ca te - na prasidhyed akarmaṇaḥ

Action in accordance with your prescribed duty is better than inaction. You cannot even maintain your physical body without action.

3.9

yajñārthāt karmaṇo 'nyatra - loko 'yaṁ karma-bandhanaḥ
tad-arthaṁ karma kaunteya - mukta-saṅgaḥ samācara

Act only for the sake of offering your actions to Viṣṇu, free from attachment, O son of Kuntī, for by such perfect action you will be liberated from all reactions associated with your deeds. Otherwise, your actions will bind you to this material world.

3.10

saha-yajñāḥ prajāḥ sṛṣṭvā - purovāca prajāpatiḥ
anena prasaviṣyadhvam - eṣa vo 'stv iṣṭa-kāma-dhuk

At the dawn of creation, the Lord of all beings, having sent forth generations of humans and demigods, along with sacrifices, declared, "By this [sacrifice] may you flourish; let this be the source of your desire's fulfillment."

3.11

devān bhāvayatānena - te devā bhāvayantu vaḥ
parasparaṁ bhāvayantaḥ - śreyaḥ param avāpsyatha

The demigods, satisfied by your offerings, will satisfy you in return. By thus pleasing one another, you shall attain the highest good.

3.12

iṣṭān bhogān hi vo deva - dāsyante yajña-bhāvitāḥ
tair dattān apradāyaibhyo - yo bhuṅkte stena eva saḥ

Satisfied by sacrifice, the demigods will surely fulfill your desires. However, one who enjoys such gifts without offering them back to the giver is surely a thief.

3.13

yajña-śiṣṭāśinaḥ santo - mucyante sarva-kilbiṣaiḥ
bhuñjate te tv aghaṁ papa - ye pacanty ātma-kāraṇāt

The virtuous, whose food consists of sacrificial offerings, are released from complicity in evil, whereas the wicked, who prepare food exclusively for their personal enjoyment, consume only suffering.

3.14

annād bhavanti bhūtāni - parjanyād anna-sambhavaḥ
yajñād bhavati parjanyo - yajñaḥ karma-samudbhavaḥ

All beings subsist on food, food is a product of rain, rain is a product of sacrifice, and sacrifice is a product of the performance of prescribed duties.

3.15

karma brahmodbhavaṁ viddhi - brahmākṣara-samudbhavam
tasmāt sarva-gataṁ brahma - nityaṁ yajñe pratiṣṭhitam

Prescribed duties are set forth in the sacred literature [the Vedas] and sacred literature originates in the imperishable Absolute. Therefore, the all-pervading Absolute Truth is eternally situated in acts of sacrifice.

3.16

evaṁ pravartitaṁ cakraṁ - nānuvartayatīha yaḥ
aghāyur indriyārāmo - moghaṁ pārtha sa jīvati

Thus the cycle of sacrifice is set into motion, my dear son of Pṛthā. One who does not keep this cycle turning, who lives an irresponsible life in pursuit of sense pleasure, lives in vain.

3.17

yas tv ātma-ratir eva syād - ātma-tṛptaś ca mānavaḥ
ātmany eva ca santuṣṭas - tasya kāryaṁ na vidyate

However, for one who takes pleasure in the true self, whose satisfaction and contentment are found exclusively in the true self, for that person there is no duty that needs to be fulfilled.

3.18

naiva tasya kṛtenārtho - nākṛteneha kaścana
na cāsya sarva-bhūteṣu - kaścid artha-vyapāśrayaḥ

Such a person has nothing to gain by acting, no reason to refrain from acting, and no sense of dependence on anyone for any purpose.

3.19

tasmād asaktaḥ satataṁ - kāryaṁ karma samācara
asakto hy ācaran karma - param āpnoti pūruṣaḥ

Therefore, act as a matter of duty, without attachment to the results of your actions, for by acting without attachment one surely attains the highest perfection.

3.20

karmaṇaiva hi saṁsiddhim - āsthitā janakādayaḥ
loka-saṅgraham evāpi - sampaśyan kartum arhasi

Indeed, by proper action alone, kings like Janaka attained perfection. If for no other reason, you are morally obligated to act for the welfare of the world.

3.21

yad yad ācarati śreṣṭhas - tat tad evetaro janaḥ
sa yat pramāṇaṁ kurute - lokas tad anuvartate

The actions of a great leader will surely be emulated by others. And the standards set by such a leader serve as the example for all the world to follow.

3.22

na me pārthāsti kartavyaṁ - triṣu lokeṣu kiñcana
nānavāptam avāptavyaṁ - varta eva ca karmaṇi

O son of Pṛthā, I am not obliged to perform any duties within these three worlds nor is there anything I aspire to obtain. Nevertheless, I myself engage in prescribed duties.

3.23

yadi hy ahaṁ na varteyaṁ - jātu karmaṇy atandritaḥ
mama vartmānuvartante - manuṣyāḥ pārtha sarvaśaḥ

For should I ever cease to engage in carefully performing such prescribed duties, O son of Pṛthā, people would surely follow my example in all respects.

3.24

utsīdeyur ime lokā - na kuryāṁ karma ced aham
saṅkarasya ca kartā syām - upahanyām imāḥ prajāḥ

All these worlds would fall to ruin if I did not act properly. I would be the cause of chaos in society and would thereby bring harm to all beings.

3.25

saktāḥ karmaṇy avidvāṁso - yathā kurvanti bhārata
kuryād vidvāṁs tathāsaktaś - cikīrṣur loka-saṅgraham

O descendent of Bhārata, as those who lack vision act with attachment to the results of their actions, the wise may also act, but without such attachment, for the sake of the world's welfare.

3.26

na buddhi-bhedaṁ janayed - ajñānāṁ karma-saṅginām
joṣayet sarva-karmāṇi - vidvān yuktaḥ samācaran

A learned person should not disturb the minds of those who, due to a poor fund of knowledge, act with attachment to the fruits of their actions. Instead, the wise inspire delight in prescribed duties by performing them in a spirit of devotion.

3.27

prakṛteḥ kriyamāṇāni - guṇaiḥ karmāṇi sarvaśaḥ
ahaṅkāra-vimūḍhātmā - kartāham iti manyate

One who is bewildered by the influence of false ego thinks, "I am the doer of activities." The truth is that all activities are carried out by the qualities of material nature.

3.28

tattva-vit tu mahā-bāho - guṇa-karma-vibhāgayoḥ
guṇā guṇeṣu vartanta - iti matvā na sajjate

But one who knows the truth about how material nature generates action remains detached, O mighty-armed, knowing well that it is only the qualities of material nature that are interacting with one another.

3.29

prakṛter guṇa-sammūḍhāḥ - sajjante guṇa-karmasu
tān akṛtsna-vido mandān - kṛtsna-vin na vicālayet

Those who are bewildered by the influence of material nature become attached to material activities. The wise should not disturb those who are fooled into identifying with material nature due to a lack of knowledge.

3.30

mayi sarvāṇi karmāṇi - sannyasyādhyātma-cetasā
nirāśīr nirmamo bhūtvā - yudhyasva vigata-jvaraḥ

Therefore, cast aside your fever of inertia; offer your actions to me in complete knowledge of the Supreme Self within and fight without yearning for ownership or profit.

3.31

ye me matam idaṁ nityam - anutiṣṭhanti mānavāḥ
śraddhāvanto 'nasūyanto - mucyante te 'pi karmabhiḥ

Those who faithfully act without envy in accordance with my teaching attain freedom from action's reactions.

3.32

ye tv etad abhyasūyanto - nānutiṣṭhanti me matam
sarva-jñāna-vimūḍhāṁs tān - viddhi naṣṭān acetasaḥ

Those who disregard my teachings due to resentment, however, are confused by this knowledge. Know that such people, whose minds are thus confused, are lost.

3.33

sadṛśaṁ ceṣṭate svasyāḥ - prakṛter jñānavān api
prakṛtiṁ yānti bhūtāni - nigrahaḥ kiṁ kariṣyati

Even those who possess knowledge act according to their own nature, for everyone acts according to the tendencies they have acquired due to contact with the qualities of material nature. What will repression accomplish?

3.34

indriyasyendriyasyārthe - rāga-dveṣau vyavasthitau
tayor na vaśam āgacchet - tau hy asya paripanthinau

Attachment and aversion, which reside in each sense object and are rooted in the senses, are stumbling blocks on the path of self-realization. Therefore, you should observe principles to regulate the senses and their objects so as not to come under their control.

3.35

śreyān sva-dharmo viguṇaḥ - para-dharmāt sv-anuṣṭhitāt
sva-dharme nidhanaṁ śreyaḥ - para-dharmo bhayāvahaḥ

Acting in accordance with your own nature, even when such actions appear riddled with fault, is far better than perfectly executing duties prescribed for others. It is better to die in the course of performing your own duty than to risk the peril of following the path of another.

3.36

arjuna uvāca
atha kena prayukto 'yaṁ - pāpaṁ carati pūruṣaḥ
anicchann api vārṣṇeya - balād iva niyojitaḥ

Arjuna said: O descendant of Vṛṣṇi, what impels a person to improper action, as if driven by force against one's will?

3.37

śrī-bhagavān uvāca
kāma eṣa krodha eṣa - rajo-guṇa-samudbhavaḥ
mahāśano mahā-pāpmā - viddhy enam iha vairiṇam

The Blessed Lord said: It is insatiable desire, lust, which transforms into anger as it advances from the mode of passion. Know that this all-consuming force of ruination is one's enemy in this world.

3.38

dhūmenāvriyate vahnir - yathādarśo malena ca
yatholbenāvṛto garbhas - tathā tenedam āvṛtam

Just as fire is covered by smoke, a mirror by dust, and an embryo by the womb, the world is covered by varying degrees of insatiable desire.

3.39

āvṛtaṁ jñānam etena - jñānino nitya-vairiṇā
kāma-rūpeṇa kaunteya - duṣpūreṇānalena ca

With an appetite like fire that is never satisfied, this persistent enemy, in the form of ravenous desire, thus conceals the natural perception of conscious beings.

3.40

indriyāṇi mano buddhir - asyādhiṣṭhānam ucyate
etair vimohayaty eṣa - jñānam āvṛtya dehinam

It is said that the senses, the mind, and the intelligence, are the places wherein this enemy resides. Through them, it covers true knowledge as it bewilders the embodied soul.

3.41

tasmāt tvam indriyāṇy ādau - niyamya bharatarṣabha
pāpmānaṁ prajahi hy enaṁ - jñāna-vijñāna-nāśanam

Therefore, O best of the descendants of Bhārata, control your senses from the outset and thus slay this evil enemy of knowledge and self-realization.

3.42

indriyāṇi parāṇy āhur - indriyebhyaḥ paraṁ manaḥ
manasas tu parā buddhir - yo buddheḥ paratas tu saḥ

It is said that the senses are higher than material sense objects, that the mind is higher than the senses, that the intellect is higher than the mind, and that the self is beyond the intellect.

3.43

evaṁ buddheḥ paraṁ buddhvā - saṁstabhyātmānam ātmanā
jahi śatruṁ mahā-bāho - kāma-rūpaṁ durāsadam

Therefore, O mighty-armed, engage reason to go beyond reason. With knowledge of your transcendental nature, steady your mind by means of spiritual intelligence and slay this formidable enemy known as insatiable desire.

CHAPTER 4

jñāna-yoga
THE YOGA OF KNOWLEDGE

Prelude

At the end of Chapter 3, Kṛṣṇa exposed the true identity of the soul's foremost enemy and advised Arjuna to apply spiritual intelligence to his confrontation with this "evil enemy of knowledge and self-realization."

Now, in Chapter 4, Kṛṣṇa tells Arjuna how transcendental knowledge is transmitted and why Arjuna is especially qualified to receive it. In the process, Kṛṣṇa reveals the truth about his own transcendental position, the reasons for his appearance in the world, and why understanding the transcendental nature of his appearance and activities matters.

This chapter includes advice on the best way to acquire transcendental knowledge, a glorification of the value of transcendental knowledge, and encouragement to think of transcendental knowledge as a weapon we can arm ourselves with to remain transcendentally situated amidst the chaos of war.

Things to look for:

- In verse 1, Kṛṣṇa drops some names that might be unfamiliar to Western readers: Vivasvān, also known as Sūrya, is the name of the celestial being or demigod who currently presides over the Sun. Vivasvān is also the father of Vaivsvata, a demigod who occupies the post of Manu. "Manu" is a title given to the first progenitor of mankind within specific cycles of time according to Vedic calculations. Vaivsvata Manu is the father of Ikṣvāku, the first king of the Earth in a cycle of time that, by Vedic calculation, began about 2,005,000 years ago.
- In verse 13, Kṛṣṇa asserts that he is the origin of a natural division of human society into four general categories. It is very important to note that this four-fold division is based on people's natural aptitudes and inclinations, not on the circumstances of someone's birth. This differentiates Kṛṣṇa's system from the caste system, which is a corrupted deviation from the original system.
- In verse 26, the Sanskrit word "*indriya*," meaning "senses," appears here in two contexts. The first context applies to people who choose the path of celibacy and solitude; monastics who "sacrifice" the "cognitive" senses – the senses associated with hearing, feeling, seeing, tasting, and smelling – by accepting sensory impressions that advance the cause of their spiritual advancement to the exclusion of any and all materialistic distractions. The second context applies to people who choose the path of family life and engagement with the world; householders who "sacrifice" the "active" senses – the senses associated with speaking, touching, looking, tasting, and smelling – by regulating their contact with objects of sense enjoyment or, on a higher level, making every engagement of the active senses an offering to Viṣṇu, as described in Chapter 3, verse 9. The sensations of taste and smell can be either receptive or

active experiences. We therefore see these sensations appearing in both monastic and householder contexts.

- In verse 29, Kṛṣṇa refers to an advanced form of *prāṇāyāma*, the process of liberating the life force by the practice of controlling the breath. This reference foreshadows a deeper discussion about the process of mystic yoga in chapters 5 through 8.
- In verse 41, "the composure of self-reflection" refers to the peace that comes from seeing the true nature of the self reflected in the still mind. This indicates that the perfection of meditation can be achieved by the practice of *karma-yoga*. Kṛṣṇa will begin to speak about how self-realization can also be achieved by the practice of meditation, *dhyāna-yoga*, in the next chapter.

4.1

śrī-bhagavān uvāca
imaṁ vivasvate yogaṁ - proktavān aham avyayam
vivasvān manave prāha - manur ikṣvākave 'bravīt

The Blessed Lord said: I taught this imperishable science of yoga to Vivasvān, Vivasvān taught it to Manu, and Manu in turn taught it to Ikṣvāku.

4.2

evaṁ paramparā-prāptam - imaṁ rājarṣayo viduḥ
sa kāleneha mahatā - yogo naṣṭaḥ paran-tapa

Thus, the visionary kings received and understood this great science through a chain of disciplic succession. Over the course of time this succession was broken and therefore the science of yoga has been lost, O subduer of enemies.

4.3

sa evāyaṁ mayā te 'dya - yogaḥ proktaḥ purātanaḥ
bhakto 'si me sakhā ceti - rahasyaṁ hy etad uttamam

Today, I am teaching you this same ancient science of yoga. Because you are my devotee as well as my friend, I am revealing this transcendental mystery to you.

4.4

arjuna uvāca
aparaṁ bhavato janma - paraṁ janma vivasvataḥ
katham etad vijānīyāṁ - tvam ādau proktavān iti

Arjuna said: Vivasvān's birth preceded yours. How am I to understand that, in the beginning, you instructed this science to him?

4.5

śrī-bhagavān uvāca
bahūni me vyatītāni - janmāni tava cārjuna
tāny ahaṁ veda sarvāṇi - na tvaṁ vettha paran-tapa

The Blessed Lord said: you and I have passed through many births. I remember all of them; you, O subduer of the enemy, do not.

4.6

ajo 'pi sann avyayātmā - bhūtānām īśvaro 'pi san
prakṛtiṁ svām adhiṣṭhāya - sambhavāmy ātma-māyayā

Although I am, by my very nature, unborn, imperishable, and the Lord of all living beings, I appear in every millennium by my own inner power, standing within and yet presiding over my material energy.

4.7

yadā yadā hi dharmasya - glānir bhavati bhārata
abhyutthānam adharmasya - tadātmānaṁ sṛjāmy aham

O descendant of Bhārata, whenever and wherever righteousness declines and unrighteousness ascends – at that time I personally appear.

4.8

paritrāṇāya sādhūnāṁ - vināśāya ca duṣkṛtām
dharma-saṁsthāpanārthāya - sambhavāmi yuge yuge

For the sake of protecting the saintly and destroying the wicked, as well as to re-establish the principles of religion, I appear millennium after millennium.

4.9

janma karma ca me divyam - evaṁ yo vetti tattvataḥ
tyaktvā dehaṁ punar janma - naiti mām eti so 'rjuna

O Arjuna, one who knows the truth about the transcendental nature of my appearance and activities does not, upon leaving their body, take birth again in this material world, but comes to me instead.

4.10

vīta-rāga-bhaya-krodhā - man-mayā mām upāśritāḥ
bahavo jñāna-tapasā - pūtā mad-bhāvam āgatāḥ

Free from attachment, fear, and anger, their minds fully absorbed in me, and fully situated within me as their shelter, many have become purified by the fire of this knowledge and have thus attained my mood of transcendental love.

4.11

ye yathā māṁ prapadyante - tāṁs tathaiva bhajāmy aham
mama vartmānuvartante - manuṣyāḥ pārtha sarvaśaḥ

However one approaches me, I respond accordingly. Everyone, in all circumstances, follows my path, O son of Pṛthā.

4.12

kāṅkṣantaḥ karmaṇāṁ siddhiṁ - yajanta iha devatāḥ
kṣipraṁ hi mānuṣe loke - siddhir bhavati karma-jā

In pursuit of the perfection of their worldly desires, people worship their deities through acts of sacrifice. In the human realm, such fruitive work is quickly met with success.

4.13

cātur-varṇyaṁ mayā sṛṣṭaṁ - guṇa-karma-vibhāgaśa
tasya kartāram api māṁ - viddhy akartāram avyayam

I created the four social orders, which divide human society according to the qualities people acquire and the actions they perform. You should know that, although I am the creator of this system, I have no position within it, for I am eternally transcendental to such qualities and actions.

4.14

na māṁ karmāṇi limpanti - na me karma-phale spṛhā
iti māṁ yo 'bhijānāti - karmabhir na sa badhyate

No action adheres to me nor do I aspire for the fruits of action. One who understands this truth about me is freed from the entanglement of reactions to fruitive work.

4.15

evaṁ jñātvā kṛtaṁ karma - pūrvair api mumukṣubhiḥ
kuru karmaiva tasmāt tvaṁ - pūrvaiḥ pūrva-taraṁ kṛtam

Indeed, the sages of ancient times attained liberation by acting with this understanding. Therefore you should act as the ancients did, following in their footsteps.

4.16

kiṁ karma kim akarmeti - kavayo 'py atra mohitāḥ
tat te karma pravakṣyāmi - yaj jñātvā mokṣyase 'śubhāt

Even greatly learned sages are perplexed by questions about what action and inaction are. Now I shall explain to you what action is, knowing which you will be freed from all misfortune.

4.17

karmaṇo hy api boddhavyaṁ - boddhavyaṁ ca vikarmaṇaḥ
akarmaṇaś ca boddhavyaṁ - gahanā karmaṇo gatiḥ

The path of action is complex. Therefore, one should know how to make distinctions between moral actions, immoral actions, and liberating actions.

4.18

karmaṇy akarma yaḥ paśyed - akarmaṇi ca karma yaḥ
sa buddhimān manuṣyeṣu - sa yuktaḥ kṛtsna-karma-kṛt

In human society, one who sees inaction in action and action in inaction is endowed with the power of discernment. Such a yogī remains transcendentally situated even while engaged in all manner of activities.

4.19

yasya sarve samārambhāḥ - kāma-saṅkalpa-varjitāḥ
jñānāgni-dagdha-karmāṇaṁ - tam āhuḥ paṇḍitaṁ budhāḥ

Those who are wise say that one whose every endeavor is free from the motivation to enjoy the fruits of their endeavors is understood to be a sage whose reactions to their actions have been burned up by the fire of perfect knowledge.

4.20

tyaktvā karma-phalāsaṅgaṁ - nitya-tṛpto nirāśrayaḥ
karmaṇy abhipravṛtto 'pi - naiva kiñcit karoti saḥ

One who is ever satisfied and independent, having given up all attachment to such fruits, does not "do" anything at all despite being engaged in all manner of activities.

4.21

nirāśīr yata-cittātmā - tyakta-sarva-parigrahaḥ
śārīraṁ kevalaṁ karma - kurvan nāpnoti kilbiṣam

Free from the desire to enjoy the fruits of actions, with mind and senses controlled by spiritual intelligence, having relinquished all sense of proprietorship over one's possessions, and doing only what's needed for the basic maintenance of one's body, one remains free from unrighteous reactions.

4.22

yadṛcchā-lābha-santuṣṭo - dvandvātīto vimatsaraḥ
samaḥ siddhāv asiddhau ca - kṛtvāpi na nibadhyate

Content with gain that comes of its own accord, unperturbed by duality or envy, accepting both success and failure with a steady mind - such a person is never entangled by reactions to their actions.

4.23

gata-saṅgasya muktasya - jñānāvasthita-cetasaḥ
yajñāyācarataḥ karma - samagraṁ pravilīyate

For a liberated soul who is thus situated in transcendental knowledge, free from attachment, and whose every action is an act of sacrifice, all reactions to their actions are systematically vanquished.

4.24

brahmārpaṇaṁ brahma havir - brahmāgnau brahmaṇā hutam
brahmaiva tena gantavyaṁ - brahma-karma-samādhinā

In such acts of sacrifice, the instrument by which the offering is made, the act of offering, the offering itself, the person who makes the offering, and the fire that consumes the offering are all of the same spiritual nature. Thus, one who is completely absorbed in meditation on such spiritual actions attains perfect spiritual consciousness.

4.25

daivam evāpare yajñaṁ - yoginaḥ paryupāsate
brahmāgnāv apare yajñaṁ - yajñenaivopajuhvati

Some *yogīs* worship demigods through sacrificial offerings. Others offer themselves in the fire of sacrifice to the Absolute Truth.

4.26

śrotrādīnīndriyāṇy anye - saṁyamāgniṣu juhvati
śabdādīn viṣayān anya - indriyāgniṣu juhvati

Some [monastics] offer their [cognitive] senses into the fire of complete self-discipline. Others [householders] offer the objects of sense enjoyment into the fire of the [active] senses.

4.27

sarvāṇīndriya-karmāṇi - prāṇa-karmāṇi cāpare
ātma-saṁyama-yogāgnau - juhvati jñāna-dīpite

Still others, being motivated by the desire for self-realization, offer the functions of all of their organs, along with the actions of the breath of life, into the fire of yoga, which is kindled by perfect mental discipline.

4.28

dravya-yajñās tapo-yajñā - yoga-yajñās tathāpare
svādhyāya-jñāna-yajñāś ca - yatayaḥ saṁśita-vratāḥ

Some sacrifice their worldly possessions through acts of charity and some sacrifice material comforts through acts of austerity. Some perform sacrifices of the eight-fold path of mystic yoga and some perform sacrifices by accepting severe vows of asceticism, acquiring self-knowledge by engaging in scriptural study.

4.29

apāne juhvati prāṇaṁ - prāṇe 'pānaṁ tathāpare
prāṇāpāna-gatī ruddhvā - prāṇāyāma-parāyaṇāḥ
apare niyatāhārāḥ - prāṇān prāṇeṣu juhvati

Still others practice control of the breath, offering their incoming breath into their outgoing breath and their outgoing breath into their incoming breath. Others sacrifice the act of eating and suspend their breath altogether, thus sacrificing their own vital force.

4.30

sarve 'py ete yajña-vido - yajña-kṣapita-kalmaṣāḥ
yajña-śiṣṭāmṛta-bhujo - yānti brahma sanātanam

Though engaged in different methods, all these performers understand the purpose of sacrifice and become purified by such performances. Having tasted the nectar of sacrificial remnants, they advance toward the supreme and eternal Truth.

4.31

nāyaṁ loko 'sty ayajñasya - kuto 'nyaḥ kuru-sattama

O best of the Kuru dynasty, without engaging in sacrifice one cannot live happily in this world, what to speak of the next.

4.32

evaṁ bahu-vidhā yajñā - vitatā brahmaṇo mukhe
karma-jān viddhi tān sarvān - evaṁ jñātvā vimokṣyase

Thus various kinds of sacrifices emanate from the mouth of sacred texts. They are all born of action. Knowing them in this way, you shall be liberated.

4.33

śreyān dravya-mayād yajñāj - jñāna-yajñaḥ paran-tapa
sarvaṁ karmākhilaṁ pārtha - jñāne parisamāpyate

O scorcher of foes, a sacrifice based on knowledge [for the sake of knowledge] is greater than a sacrifice of worldly possessions, for all acts of sacrifice culminate in knowledge.

4.34

tad viddhi praṇipātena - paripraśnena sevayā
upadekṣyanti te jñānaṁ - jñāninas tattva-darśina

You can learn the truth about these sacrifices by approaching a spiritual master with humility, offering service, and making relevant inquiries. The wise can impart this knowledge unto you, for they are seers of the truth.

4.35

yaj jñātvā na punar moham - evaṁ yāsyasi pāṇḍava
yena bhūtāny aśeṣāṇi - drakṣyasy ātmany atho mayi

O son of Pāṇḍu, having acquired this knowledge, you will never again fall under the influence of illusion, for by this knowledge you will see the shared spiritual essence of all living beings and how they all abide within me.

4.36

api ced asi pāpebhyaḥ - sarvebhyaḥ pāpa-kṛt-tamaḥ
sarvaṁ jñāna-plavenaiva - vṛjinaṁ santariṣyasi

Even if you are the most sinful of all sinners, you will be able to cross over the ocean of afflictions by the boat of transcendental knowledge.

4.37

yathaidhāṁsi samiddho 'gnir - bhasma-sāt kurute 'rjuna
jñānāgniḥ sarva-karmāṇi - bhasma-sāt kurute tathā

O Arjuna, as a blazing fire turns kindling into ashes, the fire of transcendental knowledge burns all reactions to material activities into ashes.

4.38

na hi jñānena sadṛśaṁ - pavitram iha vidyate
tat svayaṁ yoga-saṁsiddhaḥ - kālenātmani vindati

Nothing in this world is as sublimely purifying as transcendental knowledge. One who has achieved the perfection of yoga realizes this knowledge within one's self in due course of time.

4.39

śraddhāvāḻ labhate jñānaṁ - tat-paraḥ saṁyatendriyaḥ
jñānaṁ labdhvā parāṁ śāntim - acireṇādhigacchati

Those who are endowed with faith, who dedicate themselves to the pursuit of transcendental knowledge, and who subdue their senses for the sake of such knowledge, are eligible to attain it. Upon acquiring such knowledge, one quickly attains supreme peace.

4.40

ajñaś cāśraddadhānaś ca - saṁśayātmā vinaśyati
nāyaṁ loko 'sti na paro - na sukhaṁ saṁśayātmanaḥ

Those who remain ignorant and faithless, who distrust such revelations of transcendental knowledge, meet only with failure. The doubtful do not find happiness in this world nor in the next.

4.41

yoga-sannyasta-karmāṇaṁ - jñāna-sañchinna-saṁśayam
ātmavantaṁ na karmāṇi - nibadhnanti dhanañ-jaya

O conqueror of riches, one who renounces the fruits of action in accordance with the principles of sacrifice, whose doubts have been severed by transcendental knowledge, and who has thus regained the composure of self-reflection, is not bound by reactions to their actions.

4.42

tasmād ajñāna-sambhūtaṁ - hṛt-sthaṁ jñānāsinātmanaḥ
chittvainaṁ saṁśayaṁ yogam - ātiṣṭhottiṣṭha bhārata

Therefore, O Bhārata, you should slash with the sword of knowledge the doubts that have arisen in your heart due to ignorance. Armed with yoga, stand and fight.

CHAPTER 5

karma-sannyāsa-yoga
THE YOGA OF RENUNCIATION OF ACTION

Prelude

At this point, Arjuna still thinks that practicing renunciation means disengagement from the world in favor of reclusive study and meditation. Thus, Chapter 5 begins with Arjuna asking once again for a clarification of the true meaning of renunciation.

Kṛṣṇa responds to Arjuna's desire to resolve the apparent paradox of simultaneous engagement and renunciation by explaining how action without attachment (*karma-yoga*) and analytical knowledge (*jñāna-yoga*) go hand-in-hand. We also hear how action informed by analytical knowledge is better than the pursuit of analytical knowledge by itself.

Things to look for:

- In verse 13, the "city of nine gates" refers to the material body, with nine entrances and exits consisting of the two ears, two eyes, two nostrils, one mouth, one genital, and one anus.

- Verse 21 marks the beginning of Kṛṣṇa's segue from the outward-facing yoga of action to the inward-facing yoga of meditative mysticism, the basic mechanics of which are described in verses 27 and 28.
- In verse 25, Kṛṣṇa notes that dedicating one's life to the welfare of others is an attribute of a person who is on the path toward "supreme liberation." Beyond addressing people's material needs, living for "the welfare of all living beings" is also understood to mean dedicating one's life to sharing the science of transcendental knowledge that Kṛṣṇa is presenting in the Bhagavad-gītā. This understanding will be confirmed in subsequent chapters wherein Kṛṣṇa will repeatedly affirm the efficacy of his teachings and express his feelings toward those who share them.

5.1

arjuna uvāca
sannyāsaṁ karmaṇāṁ kṛṣṇa - punar yogaṁ ca śaṁsasi
yac chreya etayor ekaṁ - tan me brūhi su-niścitam

Arjuna said: O Kṛṣṇa, you are praising both the renunciation of action and spiritual action. Please tell me definitively which one of these two is more beneficial.

5.2

śrī-bhagavān uvāca
sannyāsaḥ karma-yogaś ca - niḥśreyasa-karāv ubhau
tayos tu karma-sannyāsāt - karma-yogo viśiṣyate

The Blessed Lord replied: Both renunciation of action and spiritual action lead to the path of liberation. Of the two, however, spiritual action is better than the renunciation of action.

5.3

jñeyaḥ sa nitya-sannyāsī - yo na dveṣṭi na kāṅkṣati
nirdvandvo hi mahā-bāho - sukhaṁ bandhāt pramucyate

One who neither hates nor hankers for the fruits of action is known as a renunciant. O mighty-armed Arjuna, such a person moves beyond duality, easily overcomes material bondage, and thus attains the joy of liberation.

5.4

sāṅkhya-yogau pṛthag bālāḥ - pravadanti na paṇḍitāḥ
ekam apy āsthitaḥ samyag - ubhayor vindate phalam

Those possessed of a child's intelligence say that spiritual action is different from contemplative study. Those possessing mature intelligence say that by perfect practice along either path, one can attain the results of both.

5.5

yat sāṅkhyaiḥ prāpyate sthānaṁ - tad yogair api gamyate
ekaṁ sāṅkhyaṁ ca yogaṁ ca - yaḥ paśyati sa paśyati

The destination attained by means of contemplative study can also be attained by means of spiritual action. Therefore, one who sees the unity of contemplative study and spiritual action sees things as they are.

5.6

sannyāsas tu mahā-bāho - duḥkham āptum ayogataḥ
yoga-yukto munir brahma - na cireṇādhigacchati

However, renunciation is difficult to attain if it is uncoupled from spiritual action, whereas the sage who is absorbed in spiritual action quickly attains the supreme destination.

5.7

yoga-yukto viśuddhātmā - vijitātmā jitendriyaḥ
sarva-bhūtātma-bhūtātmā - kurvann api na lipyate

Having conquered the mind and senses, a purified soul who, by means of spiritual action, remains linked to the Supreme Self within all beings, is never entangled by the actions they perform.

5.8-9

naiva kiñcit karomīti - yukto manyeta tattva-vit
paśyañ śṛṇvan spṛśañ jighrann - aśnan gacchan svapañ śvasan

pralapan visṛjan gṛhṇann - unmiṣan nimiṣann api
indriyāṇīndriyārtheṣu - vartanta iti dhārayan

Those who are acquainted with reality by virtue of a steady yoga practice think, "I am not doing anything; while seeing, hearing, touching, smelling, eating, walking, sleeping, breathing, talking, eliminating, accepting – even when blinking my eyes, it is only the senses that act in relationship to the objects of the senses."

5.10

brahmaṇy ādhāya karmāṇi - saṅgaṁ tyaktvā karoti yaḥ
lipyate na sa pāpena - padma-patram ivāmbhasā

Just as water does not cling to a lotus leaf, misfortune does not cling to those who let go of attachments and offer their actions to the Supreme Absolute Truth.

5.11

kāyena manasā buddhyā - kevalair indriyair api
yoginaḥ karma kurvanti - saṅgaṁ tyaktvātma-śuddhaye

Abandoning attachment, the *karma-yogī* acts with body, mind, intelligence, and even the senses, solely for the sake of purification.

5.12

yuktaḥ karma-phalaṁ tyaktvā - śāntim āpnoti naiṣṭhikīm
ayuktaḥ kāma-kāreṇa - phale sakto nibadhyate

Those who are linked in *karma-yoga*, having renounced the fruits of their actions, attain lasting peace. Those who are unlinked, forsaking this practice, seek enjoyment from the fruits of their work and thus become entangled by selfish desires.

5.13

sarva-karmāṇi manasā - sannyasyāste sukhaṁ vaśī
nava-dvāre pure dehī - naiva kurvan na kārayan

Mentally renouncing all actions, an embodied master of the senses lives happily within the city of nine gates, neither acting nor causing actions to occur.

5.14

na kartṛtvaṁ na karmāṇi - lokasya sṛjati prabhuḥ
na karma-phala-saṁyogaṁ - svabhāvas tu pravartate

The master of this city does not create activities, does not induce people to act, and does not connect actions to their results. All of this is set into motion by the qualities of material nature.

5.15

nādatte kasyacit pāpaṁ - na caiva sukṛtaṁ vibhuḥ
ajñānenāvṛtaṁ jñānaṁ - tena muhyanti jantavaḥ

Nor does the Supreme Lord accept responsibility for anyone's virtuous or evil deeds. All living beings are bewildered by the ignorance that covers their knowledge.

5.16

jñānena tu tad ajñānaṁ - yeṣāṁ nāśitam ātmanaḥ
teṣām āditya-vaj jñānaṁ - prakāśayati tat param

But those whose nescience has been destroyed by knowledge experience enlightenment. Just as the shining sun reveals everything in the daytime, this same knowledge illuminates the Highest Truth.

5.17

tad-buddhayas tad-ātmānas - tan-niṣṭhās tat-parāyaṇāḥ
gacchanty apunar-āvṛttiṁ - jñāna-nirdhūta-kalmaṣāḥ

Those whose intelligence is focused on the Supreme, whose mind is absorbed in the Supreme, whose faith is fully vested in the Supreme, and who have accepted the Supreme as their only shelter, are cleansed of impieties by virtue of complete knowledge. They go to that place from which one need not return.

5.18

vidyā-vinaya-sampanne - brāhmaṇe gavi hastini
śuni caiva śva-pāke ca - paṇḍitāḥ sama-darśinaḥ

Those who are wise see an elevated soul who is endowed with higher learning and a gentle disposition, a cow, an elephant, a dog, and one who eats dogs, with equal vision.

5.19

ihaiva tair jitaḥ sargo - yeṣāṁ sāmye sthitaṁ manaḥ
nirdoṣaṁ hi samaṁ brahma - tasmād brahmaṇi te sthitāḥ

Even here, in this world, those whose minds are fixed in impartiality, seeing all as equal, conquer birth and death. As the Absolute Truth is flawless and forever the same, they, too, are established in the Absolute Truth.

5.20

na prahṛṣyet priyaṁ prāpya - nodvijet prāpya cāpriyam
sthira-buddhir asammūḍho - brahma-vid brahmaṇi sthitaḥ

A person with perfect knowledge of the Absolute Truth neither rejoices upon obtaining that which is pleasant nor laments upon receiving that which is unpleasant. Those with steady intelligence, who remain free of bewilderment, are firmly situated in transcendence.

5.21

bāhya-sparśeṣv asaktātmā - vindaty ātmani yat sukham
sa brahma-yoga-yuktātmā - sukham akṣayam aśnute

One who is not attracted to external sense pleasure and who, looking inward, finds joy in the self, who is linked through yoga to the Absolute Truth, enjoys unlimited happiness.

5.22

ye hi saṁsparśa-jā bhogā - duḥkha-yonaya eva te
ādy-antavantaḥ kaunteya - na teṣu ramate budhaḥ

Pleasures that arise from contact between the material senses and the objects of sense enjoyment are actually sources of misery, O son of Kuntī, for such pleasures have a beginning and an end. The wise do not take delight in them.

5.23

śaknotīhaiva yaḥ soḍhuṁ - prāk śarīra-vimokṣaṇāt
kāma-krodhodbhavaṁ vegaṁ - sa yuktaḥ sa sukhī naraḥ

Happiness comes to one who, absorbed in yoga, tolerates urges born of desire and anger for the duration of their life prior to being liberated from their present body.

5.24

yo 'ntaḥ-sukho 'ntar-ārāmas - tathāntar-jyotir eva yaḥ
sa yogī brahma-nirvāṇaṁ - brahma-bhūto 'dhigacchati

One who finds happiness within, relishes delight from within, and whose light shines from within, is a perfect mystic who is liberated from the forest fire of material existence, having attained the supreme state of being.

5.25

labhante brahma-nirvāṇam - ṛṣayaḥ kṣīṇa-kalmaṣāḥ
chinna-dvaidhā yatātmānaḥ - sarva-bhūta-hite ratāḥ

This supreme liberation is attained by those for whom impiety has been destroyed, for whom dualities arising from doubts have been severed, whose minds are engaged in self-realization, and who live for the welfare of all living beings.

5.26

kāma-krodha-vimuktānāṁ - yatīnāṁ yata-cetasām
abhito brahma-nirvāṇaṁ - vartate viditātmanām

For those wise renunciates who are free from lust and anger, who are constantly endeavoring for perfection with controlled minds, and who know the true nature of the self, freedom from the forest fire of material existence and entry into the abode of Absolute Reality is close at hand.

5.27-28

sparśān kṛtvā bahir bāhyāṁś - cakṣuś caivāntare bhruvoḥ
prāṇāpānau samau kṛtvā - nāsābhyantara-cāriṇau

yatendriya-mano-buddhir - munir mokṣa-parāyaṇaḥ
vigatecchā-bhaya-krodho - yaḥ sadā mukta eva saḥ

Shutting out all external sense objects, with eyes directed toward a point between the eyebrows, equalizing the inward and outward breaths that move through the nose, and thus controlling the mind, senses and intelligence, the transcendentalist who aspires for liberation becomes free from desire, fear and anger. One who maintains this state of being is surely liberated.

5.29

bhoktāraṁ yajña-tapasāṁ - sarva-loka-maheśvaram
suhṛdaṁ sarva-bhūtānāṁ - jñātvā māṁ śāntim ṛcchati

Peace is attained by knowing me to be the beneficiary of all sacrifices and austerities, the Supreme Lord of all worlds, and the most benevolent friend within the heart of all beings.

CHAPTER 6

dhyāna-yoga
THE YOGA OF MEDITATION

Prelude

Up to this point, Kṛṣṇa has spoken about:

- the ability to distinguish between spirit and matter (*sāṅkhya-yoga*),
- action without attachment performed as an offering to the Supreme Being (*karma-yoga*), and
- the infusion of action with transcendental knowledge (*jñāna-yoga*).

Together, these three elements of Kṛṣṇa's argument have established a comprehensive theory of practically applied spiritual intelligence (*buddhi-yoga*).

In Chapter 3, we heard Kṛṣṇa advise Arjuna to act "only for the sake of offering your actions to Viṣṇu." Kṛṣṇa ended Chapter 4 by urging Arjuna to stand and fight. And he ended Chapter 5 by telling Arjuna that "peace is attained by knowing me to be the beneficiary of all sacrifices," alluding to the idea that Viṣṇu and Kṛṣṇa are different versions of the same person.

Kṛṣṇa's focus in Chapter 6 is the yoga of meditation (*dhyāna-yoga*), wherein we hear about the renunciation of material desires as a mandatory prerequisite for a successful meditation practice, the importance of controlling the mind, the results of controlling the mind, the process for controlling the mind, and *samādhi*; the perfectional stage of spontaneous absorption in an object of meditation.

Things to look for:

- In verse 6, we find a curious characterization of the uncontrolled mind as being motivated by "enmity." The Sanskrit word *śatrutve*, meaning "because of enmity," suggests that the mind has a mind of its own, which is certainly how it seems to almost anyone who's attempted to still the mind through the practice of meditation.
- In verse 11, the *āsana* or seat of the *yogī* who goes to the forest to meditate is described as consisting of *kuśa* grass. *Kuśa* grass is a very tough and sharp variety of grass, similar to straw, that's said to have purifying properties. It's also symbolic in that its sharpness likens it to a sword with which the *yogī* can pierce the veil of ignorance.
- Also in verse 11, it's understood that the deerskin that the *yogī* is advised to place on top of the *kuśa* grass should be obtained from the body of a deer that has already died. A *yogī* does not hunt and kill a deer for the sake of acquiring such a deerskin.
- Beginning in verse 14 and continuing throughout this chapter, Kṛṣṇa alternates between referring to himself in the first person as "me" and in the third person as the "Supreme Self" or "transcendent Self." In so doing, he allows the context of his instructions to make it clear that he and the Supreme Self to whom he's referring are identical. Again, Kṛṣṇa's references to himself as the Supreme

Self shouldn't be confused with the individual self who is seeking self-realization; Kṛṣṇa, by definition, is always fully "Self-realized" and therefore has no need to practice meditation for the sake of attaining self-realization.

6.1

śrī-bhagavān uvāca
anāśritaḥ karma-phalaṁ - kāryaṁ karma karoti yaḥ
sa sannyāsī ca yogī ca - na niragnir na cākriyaḥ

The Blessed Lord said: One who performs their duty without attachment to the fruits of their actions is both a renunciate and a *yogī*, not one who lights no sacred fire nor performs any act of sacrifice.

6.2

yaṁ sannyāsam iti prāhur - yogaṁ taṁ viddhi pāṇḍava
na hy asannyasta-saṅkalpo - yogī bhavati kaścana

O son of Pāṇḍu, that which is said to be renunciation should be known as yoga, for no one becomes a *yogī* without renouncing the desire to gratify their material senses.

6.3

ārurukṣor muner yogaṁ - karma kāraṇam ucyate
yogārūḍhasya tasyaiva - śamaḥ kāraṇam ucyate

For the sage who aspires to perfection on the path of yoga, action is said to be the means. For one who has attained perfection on the path of yoga, cessation of activity is said to be the means.

6.4

yadā hi nendriyārtheṣu - na karmasv anuṣajjate
sarva-saṅkalpa-sannyāsī - yogārūḍhas tadocyate

One is said to have ascended to union with the Supreme when they have renounced all material desires and clings neither to the objects of the senses nor to action in pursuit of such objects.

6.5

uddhared ātmanātmānaṁ - nātmānam avasādayet
ātmaiva hy ātmano bandhur - ātmaiva ripur ātmanaḥ

One should elevate oneself with the help of the mind, and not degrade oneself. Indeed, the mind may surely be the friend of the self or, just as certainly, the self's enemy.

6.6

bandhur ātmātmanas tasya - yenātmaivātmanā jitaḥ
anātmanas tu śatrutve - vartetātmaiva śatru-vat

The mind is the best of friends to one who has conquered the mind. For one who has failed to do so, the mind will, out of enmity, remain a tenacious enemy.

6.7

jitātmanaḥ praśāntasya - paramātmā samāhitaḥ
śītoṣṇa-sukha-duḥkheṣu - tathā mānāpamānayoḥ

One who has conquered the mind reaches the Supreme Self within the heart and attains tranquility. For one so situated, heat and cold, pleasure and displeasure, and honor and dishonor are all the same.

6.8

jñāna-vijñāna-tṛptātmā - kūṭa-stho vijitendriyaḥ
yukta ity ucyate yogi - sama-loṣṭrāśma-kāñcanaḥ

One who is spiritually situated by virtue of both acquired knowledge and realized knowledge, who has conquered the senses, and who sees a clump of earth, a common stone, or gold as all being of equal value, is said to be fixed in yoga.

6.9

suhṛn-mitrāry-udāsīna- - madhyastha-dveṣya-bandhuṣu
sādhuṣv api ca pāpeṣu - sama-buddhir viśiṣyate

Those who are even more advanced see well-wishing friends, kind-hearted benefactors, enemies, those who are disinterested, neutral mediators, the saintly and the sinful, all through a lens of steady intelligence.

6.10

yogī yuñjīta satatam - ātmānaṁ rahasi sthitaḥ
ekākī yata-cittātmā - nirāśīr aparigrahaḥ

Living alone in a secluded place, free from material desires and possessiveness, with mind and body vigilantly controlled, a transcendentalist should direct their full and complete attention exclusively toward the self in relationship with the Supreme.

6.11

śucau deśe pratiṣṭhāpya - sthiram āsanam ātmanaḥ
nāty-ucchritaṁ nāti-nīcaṁ - cailājina-kuśottaram

To practice yoga, one should go to a holy place and prepare a stable sitting place that is neither too high nor too low by laying *kuśa* grass on the ground and covering it with a deerskin and a soft cloth.

6.12

tatraikāgraṁ manaḥ kṛtvā - yata-cittendriya-kriyaḥ
upaviśyāsane yuñjyād - yogam ātma-viśuddhaye

Then the *yogī* should sit firmly on this seat and, for the sake of self-purification, practice yoga by keeping thoughts and sense activity restrained and the mind actively focused on a singular point.

6.13-14

samaṁ kāya-śiro-grīvaṁ - dhārayann acalaṁ sthiraḥ
samprekṣya nāsikāgraṁ svaṁ - diśaś cānavalokayan
praśāntātmā vigata-bhīr - brahmacāri-vrate sthitaḥ
manaḥ saṁyamya mac-citto - yukta āsīta mat-paraḥ

With body, neck, and head aligned, steady, without movement, with vision focused on the tip of the nose and nowhere else, a *yogī* thus brings their mind to me, the ultimate goal. With tranquility of mind, free from fear, and firmly established in a vow of celibacy, such a *yogī* remains linked to me.

6.15

yuñjann evaṁ sadātmānaṁ - yogī niyata-mānasaḥ
śāntiṁ nirvāṇa-paramāṁ - mat-saṁsthām adhigacchati

The mystic whose subdued mind is always absorbed in union with the Supreme transcends the forest fire of material existence. Residing in my spiritual abode, such a transcendentalist thus attains the highest peace.

6.16

nāty-aśnatas tu yogo 'sti - na caikāntam anaśnataḥ
na cāti-svapna-śīlasya - jāgrato naiva cārjuna

The state of yoga is never attained by one who either eats too much or abstains from eating, nor by one who either sleeps too much or remains ever awake.

6.17

yuktāhāra-vihārasya - yukta-ceṣṭasya karmasu
yukta-svapnāvabodhasya - yogo bhavati duḥkha-hā

But for one who appropriately balances their eating, action, recreation, sleeping, and wakefulness, linking all such activities to the practice of yoga, all miseries are vanquished.

6.18

yadā viniyataṁ cittam - ātmany evāvatiṣṭhate
nispṛhaḥ sarva-kāmebhyo - yukta ity ucyate tadā

One is said to be firmly ensconced in harmonic union when, by virtue of having disciplined the fluctuations of the mind to the point where the desire for the gratification of the material senses has vanished, they are transcendentally situated in the state of self-realization.

6.19

yathā dīpo nivāta-stho - neṅgate sopamā smṛtā
yogino yata-cittasya - yuñjato yogam ātmanaḥ

Just as the flame of a lamp in a windless place does not flicker, the controlled mind of a *yogī* remains steadily absorbed in meditation on the transcendent Self.

6.20-22

yatroparamate cittaṁ - niruddhaṁ yoga-sevayā
yatra caivātmanātmānaṁ - paśyann ātmani tuṣyati

sukham ātyantikaṁ yat tad - buddhi-grāhyam atīndriyam
vetti yatra na caivāyaṁ - sthitaś calati tattvataḥ

yaṁ labdhvā cāparaṁ lābhaṁ - manyate nādhikaṁ tataḥ
yasmin sthito na duḥkhena - guruṇāpi vicālyate

The perfection of yoga is that state of meditative absorption in which the mind is held still by the practice of yoga; in which one finds contentment by seeing the Supreme Self within oneself through the clear lens of the pure mind; by which one experiences boundless joy through the agency of spiritual intelligence that transcends the material senses; from which, having seen the truth, one remains firmly situated and never departs; and, upon attaining it, one knows that there is nothing further to be attained. Being so situated, one is never perturbed, even in the most challenging of circumstances.

6.23

taṁ vidyād duḥkha-saṁyoga- - viyogaṁ yoga-saṁjñitam
sa niścayena yoktavyo - yogo 'nirviṇṇa-cetasā

One should understand that this complete state of meditative absorption called yoga, which is attained through steady practice with deep conviction and complete confidence, severs one's connection to all the miseries that arise due to contact with material nature.

6.24-25

saṅkalpa-prabhavān kāmāṁs - tyaktvā sarvān aśeṣataḥ
manasaivendriya-grāmaṁ - viniyamya samantataḥ

śanaiḥ śanair uparamed - buddhyā dhṛti-gṛhītayā
ātma-saṁsthaṁ manaḥ kṛtvā - na kiñcid api cintayet

Completely relinquishing all aspirations born of material desires and bringing the collective senses under the exclusive control of the mind, one should gradually, step by step, give up material engagements and, by means of spiritual intelligence sustained by resolute conviction, fix one's mind on the transcendent Self, thinking of nothing else.

6.26

yato yato niścalati - manaś cañcalam asthiram
tatas tato niyamyaitad - ātmany eva vaśaṁ nayet

Indeed, one must retrieve the agitated mind from wherever it wanders due to its flickering and unsteady nature and place the mind under the control of the Self.

6.27

praśānta-manasaṁ hy enaṁ - yoginaṁ sukham uttamam
upaiti śānta-rajasaṁ - brahma-bhūtam akalmaṣam

A *yogī* whose mind is peaceful will surely achieve liberation by union with the Supreme and will thus attain the highest perfection of transcendental happiness. Situated beyond the influence of passion, one is thus freed from all reactions to past deeds.

6.28

yuñjann evaṁ sadātmānaṁ - yogī vigata-kalmaṣaḥ
sukhena brahma-saṁsparśam - atyantaṁ sukham aśnute

By constant engagement in the practice of yoga, the self remains connected to the Supreme Self, becomes free from all material impurities, and easily attains infinite joy.

6.29

sarva-bhūta-stham ātmānaṁ - sarva-bhūtāni cātmani
īkṣate yoga-yuktātmā - sarvatra sama-darśanaḥ

An adept *yogī* sees the Supreme Self within all beings and sees all beings within the Supreme Self. Indeed, one who is truly linked to the Supreme by the process of yoga sees the same Supreme Self everywhere.

6.30

yo māṁ paśyati sarvatra - sarvaṁ ca mayi paśyati
tasyāhaṁ na praṇaśyāmi - sa ca me na praṇaśyati

For one who sees me everywhere and sees everything in me, I am never lost, nor are they ever lost to me.

6.31

sarva-bhūta-sthitaṁ yo māṁ - bhajaty ekatvam āsthitaḥ
sarvathā vartamāno 'pi - sa yogī mayi vartate

The *yogī* who is immersed in this experience of unity offers their love to me as the One who abides in all beings. Such a transcendentalist always lives within me, irrespective of any external circumstances.

6.32

ātmaupamyena sarvatra - samaṁ paśyati yo 'rjuna
sukhaṁ vā yadi vā duḥkhaṁ - sa yogī paramo mataḥ

O Arjuna, a perfect *yogī* who sees the true equality of all beings, sees the happiness or distress of all beings as if it were their own.

6.33

arjuna uvāca
yo 'yaṁ yogas tvayā proktaḥ - sāmyena madhusūdana
etasyāhaṁ na paśyāmi - cañcalatvāt sthitiṁ sthirām

Arjuna said: O slayer of the illusion of material happiness, the system of mystic equanimity that you have described seems unsustainable for me, for the mind is restless and unsteady.

6.34

cañcalaṁ hi manaḥ kṛṣṇa - pramāthi balavad dṛḍham
tasyāhaṁ nigrahaṁ manye - vāyor iva su-duṣkaram

The mind is so fickle, turbulent, obstinate, and powerful, O Kṛṣṇa, that to subdue the mind would be more difficult than to control the wind.

6.35

śrī-bhagavān uvāca
asaṁśayaṁ mahā-bāho - mano durnigrahaṁ calam
abhyāsena tu kaunteya - vairāgyeṇa ca gṛhyate

The Blessed Lord said: O mighty-armed, the restless mind is undoubtedly difficult to control. However, O son of Kuntī, such control can be achieved by suitable practice and detachment.

6.36

asaṁyatātmanā yogo - duṣprāpa iti me matiḥ
vaśyātmanā tu yatatā - śakyo 'vāptum upāyataḥ

In my opinion, self-realization is indeed difficult for one whose mind is unrestrained. But anyone who controls the mind and endeavors by appropriate means is assured of success.

6.37

arjuna uvāca
ayatiḥ śraddhayopeto - yogāc calita-mānasaḥ
aprāpya yoga-saṁsiddhiṁ - kāṁ gatiṁ kṛṣṇa gacchati

Arjuna said: O Kṛṣṇa, what is the destiny of an unsuccessful transcendentalist who takes to the process of self-realization with faith but who later falls away from their practice due to worldly-mindedness and thus does not attain the perfection of yogic mysticism?

6.38

kaccin nobhaya-vibhraṣṭaś - chinnābhram iva naśyati
apratiṣṭho mahā-bāho - vimūḍho brahmaṇaḥ pathi

O mighty-armed Kṛṣṇa, do those who stray from the path of transcendence, achieving neither spiritual nor material success, perish like a dissipated cloud, without any position in either world?

6.39

etan me saṁśayaṁ kṛṣṇa - chettum arhasy aśeṣataḥ
tvad-anyaḥ saṁśayasyāsya - chettā na hy upapadyate

This is my doubt, O Kṛṣṇa, and I ask you to dispel it completely. Other than you, there is no one to be found who can remove this doubt.

6.40

śrī-bhagavān uvāca
pārtha naiveha nāmutra - vināśas tasya vidyate
na hi kalyāṇa-kṛt kaścid - durgatiṁ tāta gacchati

The Blessed Lord said: O Son of Pṛthā, a transcendentalist does not meet with destruction either in this world or in the next. My dear friend, anyone who sincerely engages in such auspicious activities is never overcome by misfortune.

6.41

prāpya puṇya-kṛtāṁ lokān - uṣitvā śāśvatīḥ samāḥ
śucīnāṁ śrīmatāṁ gehe - yoga-bhraṣṭo 'bhijāyate

One who falls from the path of yoga takes a celestial birth and, after many years of enjoyment, is born into a righteous or aristocratic family.

6.42

atha vā yoginām eva - kule bhavati dhīmatām
etad dhi durlabha-taraṁ - loke janma yad īdṛśam

Otherwise, one who is unsuccessful after practicing yoga for a long time takes birth in a family of learned transcendentalists who are endowed with great wisdom. Indeed, such a birth is very rare in this world.

6.43

tatra taṁ buddhi-saṁyogaṁ - labhate paurva-dehikam
yatate ca tato bhūyaḥ - saṁsiddhau kuru-nandana

Upon taking such a birth, they reconnect to the spiritual intelligence that they cultivated in their previous life and once again strive for complete perfection, O beloved son of the Kuru dynasty.

6.44

pūrvābhyāsena tenaiva - hriyate hy avaśo 'pi saḥ
jijñāsur api yogasya - śabda-brahmātivartate

By virtue of the practice that has carried over from their previous life, they are spontaneously attracted to yogic principles. Such a transcendentalist, who merely inquires about yoga, transcends the ritualistic recitations of worldly mantras.

6.45

prayatnād yatamānas tu - yogī saṁśuddha-kilbiṣaḥ
aneka-janma-saṁsiddhas - tato yāti parāṁ gatim

By sincere endeavor and perseverance, one becomes cleansed of all impurities and, after many births of such practice, they ultimately attain the supreme goal.

6.46

tapasvibhyo 'dhiko yogi - jñānibhyo 'pi mato 'dhikaḥ
karmibhyaś cādhiko yogi - tasmād yogī bhavārjuna

A *yogī* is superior to the ascetic, superior to the empiricist, and superior to the ritualist worker. Therefore, Arjuna, become a *yogī*.

6.47

yoginām api sarveṣāṁ - mad-gatenāntar-ātmanā
śraddhāvān bhajate yo māṁ - sa me yukta-tamo mataḥ

And of all types of *yogīs*, one whose inner self is absorbed in me, who is always thinking of me within oneself, and who, with complete faith, engages in devotional service to me, is the one whom I consider to have attained the highest connection of yoga.

CHAPTER 7

jñāna-vijñāna-yoga
THE YOGA OF KNOWLEDGE AND REALIZATION

Prelude

In the first six chapters of the Bhagavad-gītā, the yoga of action, *karma-yoga*, was the primary topic. The infusion of action with transcendental knowledge, *jñāna-yoga*, and linking with the Supreme through meditation, *dhyāna-yoga*, were secondary topics. In the next six chapters, the yoga of devotional service, *bhakti-yoga*, will be the primary topic.

Kṛṣṇa begins Chapter 7 by explaining why he, Kṛṣṇa, is the ultimate object of meditation and how reality, in its entirety, is comprised of just two components: Kṛṣṇa and Kṛṣṇa's energies. After describing his energies, Kṛṣṇa suggests ways in which he can be seen as the superlative feature of various aspects of the world of our experience, explains why so many people are either unable to see him or are unwilling to engage in a relationship with him, and describes what kinds of people are most likely to approach him.

Returning to the topic of demigod worship, Kṛṣṇa speaks about how and why most people's faith is likely to be misplaced, how he facilitates this willful misplacement of faith, and the position of those who have freed themselves from material consciousness.

Things to look for:

- In verse 12, the phrase "be they illuminative, passionate, or opaque" refers to the three qualities of material nature.
- In verse 19, the name *Vāsudeva* has a dual meaning. When translated as "all-pervading," it's one of the many names of Viṣnu. When translated as a patronymic, it's a name of Kṛṣṇa: the long first *ā* in Vāsudeva indicates the son of a father whose name is Vasudeva, with a short *a*. Kṛṣṇa's appearance as the son of Vasudeva and his wife Devakī is described in the Bhāgavata Purāṇa, also known as the Śrīmad-Bhāgavatam. The context and composition of this verse clearly indicate that Kṛṣṇa is identifying himself as Vāsudeva.
- In verse 27, the phrase "dualities that arise from desire and hostility" is particularly interesting because it can be understood in two ways. The first way is to think of "desire and hostility" as being synonymous with "attachment and aversion," two of the five "afflictions" specified in the Yoga-sūtra as obstacles to the experience of yoga (or, more specifically, the experience of *samādhi*; the perfection of yoga). The second way is a little more nuanced and a lot more revelatory: traditional commentators describe the word "desire," which translates the Sanskrit word *icchā*, as indicating the desire to be the enjoyer and controller of the world, i.e. to occupy the position of God. They describe the word "hostility," which translates the Sanskrit word *dveṣa*, as indicating anger: a particularly inimical mood of envy that's directed at the person who holds the position they covet.

  The implication of this understanding is that the material world exists for the sake of facilitating the desire of those living beings who, somehow or other, have developed the attitude that it would be better to rule in Hell than to serve in Heaven.

The infinitesimal self, as opposed to the Supreme Self, is said to be "marginal," meaning that we can be influenced by God's interior spiritual energy or God's exterior material energy. The inexplicable development of this combination of desire and resentment within the heart of a marginal spirit soul triggers the influence of God's external material energy on that soul as a way to provide them with an opportunity to entertain the illusion that they can make the universe revolve around them.

Unlike the biblical idea of "original sin," enviousness of God is considered to be a reversible affliction, like catching a cold, rather than an inherent state of being for which there is no cure.

7.1

śrī-bhagavān uvāca
mayy āsakta-manāḥ pārtha - yogaṁ yuñjan mad-āśrayaḥ
asaṁśayaṁ samagraṁ māṁ - yathā jñāsyasi tac chṛṇu

The Blessed Lord said: Now hear, O son of Pṛthā, how, by practicing yoga with your mind joined to me, with me as your shelter, you can know me completely, beyond any doubt.

7.2

jñānaṁ te 'haṁ sa-vijñānam - idaṁ vakṣyāmy aśeṣataḥ
yaj jñātvā neha bhūyo 'nyaj - jñātavyam avaśiṣyate

I shall explain this knowledge and wisdom to you in its entirety. Knowing this, nothing further of this world shall be left for you to know.

7.3

manuṣyāṇāṁ sahasreṣu - kaścid yatati siddhaye
yatatām api siddhānāṁ - kaścin māṁ vetti tattvataḥ

Of many thousands among mankind, one may strive for perfection, and amongst those who attain perfection, hardly one may know me in truth.

7.4

bhūmir āpo 'nalo vāyuḥ - khaṁ mano buddhir eva ca
ahaṅkāra itīyaṁ me - bhinnā prakṛtir aṣṭadhā

Earth, water, fire, air, ether, the mind, the intellect, and the false ego constitute the eight-fold division of my separated material energy.

7.5

apareyam itas tv anyāṁ - prakṛtiṁ viddhi me parām
jīva-bhūtāṁ mahā-bāho - yayedaṁ dhāryate jagat

Besides this inferior energy, O mighty-armed, know that I have another, superior energy, of which the living beings who animate this world are comprised.

7.6

etad-yonīni bhūtāni - sarvāṇīty upadhāraya
ahaṁ kṛtsnasya jagataḥ - prabhavaḥ pralayas tathā

Thus, you should understand that these two energies are the source of all beings and that I am both the origin and the dissolution of the entire cosmos.

7.7

mattaḥ parataraṁ nānyat - kiñcid asti dhanañ-jaya
mayi sarvam idaṁ protaṁ - sūtre maṇi-gaṇā iva

There is nothing beyond me, O winner of wealth. Everything rests upon me like pearls strung on a thread.

7.8

raso 'ham apsu kaunteya - prabhāsmi śaśi-sūryayoḥ
praṇavaḥ sarva-vedeṣu - śabdaḥ khe pauruṣaṁ nṛṣu

I am the taste of water, O son of Kuntī, the radiance of the moon and the sun, the sacred vibration *oṁ* in the Vedas, the sound in space and valor in men.

7.9

puṇyo gandhaḥ pṛthivyāṁ ca - tejaś cāsmi vibhāvasau
jīvanaṁ sarva-bhūteṣu - tapaś cāsmi tapasviṣu

I am also the pure fragrance of the earth and the brilliance in fire. I am the life of all who live and I am the austerity of all ascetics.

7.10

bījaṁ māṁ sarva-bhūtānāṁ - viddhi pārtha sanātanam
buddhir buddhimatām asmi - tejas tejasvinām aham

O son of Pṛthā, try to understand me as the original seed of all living beings, as the intelligence of the intelligent, and the prowess of the powerful.

7.11

balaṁ balavatāṁ cāhaṁ - kāma-rāga-vivarjitam
dharmāviruddho bhūteṣu - kāmo 'smi bharatarṣabha

O best of the Bhāratas, among the strong I am strength that is free from passion and attachment. Within all beings, I am the expression of erotic desire that does not conflict with the principles of religion.

7.12

ye caiva sāttvikā bhāvā - rājasās tāmasāś ca ye
matta eveti tān viddhi - na tv ahaṁ teṣu te mayi

Indeed, you should know that all states of being – be they illuminative, passionate, or opaque – arise from me alone. Yet I am not influenced by these modes of being, for they are all within me.

7.13

tribhir guṇa-mayair bhāvair - ebhiḥ sarvam idaṁ jagat
mohitaṁ nābhijānāti - mām ebhyaḥ param avyayam

Bewildered by these three states of being, the whole world does not know me; I am beyond these states of being, infinite, and everlasting.

7.14

daivī hy eṣā guṇa-mayī - mama māyā duratyayā
mām eva ye prapadyante - māyām etāṁ taranti te

My divine power of illusion, composed of the qualities of material nature, is nearly impossible to overcome. But those who offer themselves to me can easily cross beyond this bewildering power.

7.15

na māṁ duṣkṛtino mūḍhāḥ - prapadyante narādhamāḥ
māyayāpahṛta-jñānā - āsuraṁ bhāvam āśritāḥ

Those who are foolish, who are the lowest of mankind, whose knowledge has been stolen by illusion, and who have acquiesced to an ungodly nature; these miscreants do not offer themselves to me.

7.16

catur-vidhā bhajante māṁ - janāḥ su-kṛtino 'rjuna
ārto jijñāsur arthārthī - jñānī ca bharatarṣabha

O Arjuna, best of the Bhāratas, there are four kinds of people who are inclined to offer their devotion to me: those who are distressed, those who seek knowledge, those who seek wealth, and those who have obtained knowledge.

7.17

teṣāṁ jñānī nitya-yukta - eka-bhaktir viśiṣyate
priyo hi jñānino 'tyartham - ahaṁ sa ca mama priyaḥ

Of these, the one who has complete knowledge and thus remains ever united with me through singular devotion is the best. I am very dear to one in possession of such knowledge, and they are dearly loved by me.

7.18

udārāḥ sarva evaite - jñānī tv ātmaiva me matam
āsthitaḥ sa hi yuktātmā - mām evānuttamāṁ gatim

All of them are undoubtedly exalted. Still, I consider one who is in possession of knowledge to be just like my own Self, for a soul who is linked to me alone surely abides in me, the ultimate goal.

7.19

bahūnāṁ janmanām ante - jñānavān māṁ prapadyate
vāsudevaḥ sarvam iti - sa mahātmā su-durlabhaḥ

After many births, those in possession of knowledge approach me with the realization that "Vāsudeva is the source and substance of all that is." Such a great soul is rarely seen.

7.20

kāmais tais tair hṛta-jñānāḥ - prapadyante 'nya-devatāḥ
taṁ taṁ niyamam āsthāya - prakṛtyā niyatāḥ svayā

Those whose knowledge has been stolen by material desires approach other deities. Following various prescriptions for ritualistic observances, they are ruled by their own worldly nature.

7.21

yo yo yāṁ yāṁ tanuṁ bhaktaḥ - śraddhayārcitum icchati
tasya tasyācalāṁ śraddhāṁ - tām eva vidadhāmy aham

To whoever wishes to be thus devoted, I provide the conviction required for faithful worship of whatever conception of divinity they choose.

7.22

sa tayā śraddhayā yuktas - tasyārādhanam īhate
labhate ca tataḥ kāmān - mayaiva vihitān hi tān

Endowed with such faith, they worship a particular deity and obtain their desires, though the fulfillment of their desires is actually bestowed by me alone.

7.23

antavat tu phalaṁ teṣāṁ - tad bhavaty alpa-medhasām
devān deva-yajo yānti - mad-bhaktā yānti mām api

The fruits of worship obtained by those of lesser acumen are fleeting. The worshippers of the demigods go to the demigods, but my devotees surely come to me.

7.24

avyaktaṁ vyaktim āpannaṁ - manyante mām abuddhayaḥ
paraṁ bhāvam ajānanto - mamāvyayam anuttamam

Unaware of my higher nature, which is eternal and supreme, those who are bereft of spiritual intelligence think of me as a formless existence that has assumed a visible personality.

7.25

nāhaṁ prakāśaḥ sarvasya - yoga-māyā-samāvṛtaḥ
mūḍho 'yaṁ nābhijānāti - loko mām ajam avyayam

I do not reveal myself to everyone. Being hidden by my divine power of illusion, this bewildered world does not understand that I am unborn and infallible.

7.26

vedāhaṁ samatītāni - vartamānāni cārjuna
bhaviṣyāṇi ca bhūtāni - māṁ tu veda na kaścana

O Arjuna, I know the past, present, and future of all beings; none of them know me.

7.27

icchā-dveṣa-samutthena - dvandva-mohena bhārata
sarva-bhūtāni sammohaṁ - sarge yānti paran-tapa

O descendant of Bhārata, scorcher of foes, all beings enter this world in a state of delusion, bewildered by dualities that arise from desire and hostility.

7.28

yeṣāṁ tv anta-gataṁ pāpaṁ - janānāṁ puṇya-karmaṇām
te dvandva-moha-nirmuktā - bhajante māṁ dṛḍha-vratāḥ

Those whose misdeeds have come to an end, whose actions have been virtuous, and who are free from the bewilderment of dualities, express their love for me with firm vows.

7.29

jarā-maraṇa-mokṣāya - mām āśritya yatanti ye
te brahma tad viduḥ kṛtsnam - adhyātmaṁ karma cākhilam

Striving for liberation from old age and death, those who take refuge in me are situated in transcendence, for they have obtained a complete understanding of the principle of the self and the intricacies of action.

7.30

sādhibhūtādhidaivaṁ māṁ - sādhiyajñaṁ ca ye viduḥ
prayāṇa-kāle 'pi ca māṁ - te vidur yukta-cetasaḥ

Those whose minds are absorbed in thoughts of me, who know me to be the highest principle of divinity as well as the governing principle of the material manifestation, of all the demigods, and of all methods of sacrifice, can know me even at the time of death.

CHAPTER 8

tāraka-brahma-yoga
THE YOGA OF ATTAINING THE ABSOLUTE TRUTH

Prelude

In the last two verses of Chapter 7, Kṛṣṇa made references to transcendence (*brahma*), the principle of the self (*adhyātmaṁ*), action (*karma*), the governing principle of the material manifestation (*adhibhūta*), the governing principle of the demigods (*adhidaivam*), and the governing principle of sacrifices (*adhiyajñam*). As we begin Chapter 8, Arjuna asks Kṛṣṇa to elaborate on each of these six topics as well as two more: how the governing principle of sacrifices (Viṣṇu) resides within everyone's body and how those who practice self-control can know Kṛṣṇa at the time of death.

As the chapter proceeds, Kṛṣṇa describes methods for meditating on him (*dhyāna-yoga*), how devotion can be mixed with techniques of mystic yoga, and the characteristics of pure devotion (*bhakti-yoga*). Kṛṣṇa will go on to explain how and why the material world is inherently a place of unhappiness, juxtapose the nature of the material world (his external energy) with that of the spiritual world (his internal energy), and how anyone who engages exclusively in the process of *bhakti-yoga* obtains all of the benefits, both material and spiritual, that might otherwise be sought through other means.

Things to look for:

- In verses 16 and 17, Kṛṣṇa refers to the world of Brahmā and the duration of Brahmā's life. In Vedic cosmology, Brahmā is understood to be the first created being and his realm is said to be situated in the highest dimension of the universe, where time operates very differently from the way we experience it. Brahmā's "day" of "a thousand ages" refers to a day that lasts for a thousand cycles of four "seasons" of time. Each set of four "seasons" lasts for 4,320,000 years. When multiplied by a thousand, we get the duration of Brahmā's "day"—4,320,000,000 years. Brahmā's "night" is just as long as his "day" and Brahmā lives for one hundred years made up of such "days" and "nights" (you do the math). In addition to the Bhagavad-gītā, other Vedic texts, such as the Bhāgavata Purāṇa and the Sūrya Siddhānta, describe measurements of time, from microseconds to trillions of years, in terms of multi-dimensional cosmic cycles.
- The Sanskrit word *avyakta*, meaning "unmanifest," appears in verses 18 and 20. However, the implications of the word "unmanifest" are significantly different in each verse. In verse 18, "unmanifest" indicates a formless state of undifferentiated potential into which all of creation beneath the plateau of Brahmā dissolves at regular intervals. In verse 20, "unmanifest" indicates invisibility; a region of reality that can't be seen from the vantage point of material consciousness.

- In verse 25, the phrase "attains the light of the moon" indicates that the *yogī* who leaves their body under the circumstances being described transmigrates to a celestial body suitable for a life of extraordinary sensual pleasure over a lifespan of 10,000 lunar years, wherein one lunar day is the equivalent of one solar month, resulting in a lifespan of approximately 120,000 solar years.

8.1

arjuna uvāca
kiṁ tad brahma kim adhyātmaṁ - kiṁ karma puruṣottama
adhibhūtaṁ ca kiṁ proktam - adhidaivaṁ kim ucyate

Arjuna said: What is the nature of Brahman, what is the nature of the self, and what is the nature of action, O Ultimate Person? What is the governing principle of this material manifestation and what is the governing principle of the demigods called?

8.2

adhiyajñaḥ kathaṁ ko 'tra - dehe 'smin madhusūdana
prayāṇa-kāle ca kathaṁ - jñeyo 'si niyatātmabhiḥ

O Madhusūdana, what is the governing principle of sacrifice, how does it reside here, within the body, and how can you be known by those who are self-controlled at the time of death?

8.3

śrī-bhagavān uvāca
akṣaraṁ brahma paramaṁ - svabhāvo 'dhyātmam ucyate
bhūta-bhāvodbhava-karo - visargaḥ karma-saṁjñitaḥ

The Blessed Lord said: Brahman is the imperishable transcendence, which is the eternal nature of the self. Karma is action that creates the succession of future material bodies for a living being.

8.4

adhibhūtaṁ kṣaro bhāvaḥ - puruṣaś cādhidaivatam
adhiyajño 'ham evātra - dehe deha-bhṛtāṁ vara

O best of embodied beings, the governing principle of this material manifestation is to be subject to perpetual change. The principle by which the demigods are governed is called the "Universal Form" of the Lord. And I alone, situated within the body, am the governing principle of sacrifice.

8.5

anta-kāle ca mām eva - smaran muktvā kalevaram
yaḥ prayāti sa mad-bhāvaṁ - yāti nāsty atra saṁśayaḥ

And whoever, at the end of their life, remembers me alone as they leave their body, goes to my state of being; of this there is no doubt.

8.6

yaṁ yaṁ vāpi smaran bhāvaṁ - tyajaty ante kalevaram
taṁ tam evaiti kaunteya - sadā tad-bhāva-bhāvitaḥ

O son of Kuntī, whatever state of being one remembers at the end of one's life is the state of being they will carry into their next life, for one is certain to attain whatever state of being one's mind is absorbed in.

8.7

tasmāt sarveṣu kāleṣu - mām anusmara yudhya ca
mayy arpita-mano-buddhir - mām evaiṣyasy asaṁśayaḥ

Therefore, you should think of me at all times and fight. With your mind and intelligence offered to me, you will, beyond any doubt, surely come to me.

8.8

abhyāsa-yoga-yuktena - cetasā nānya-gāminā
paramaṁ puruṣaṁ divyaṁ - yāti pārthānucintayan

One approaches the Supreme Divine Person by practicing yoga without deviation, keeping one's thoughts continuously focused on him.

8.9

kaviṁ purāṇam anuśāsitāram
aṇor aṇīyāṁsam anusmared yaḥ
sarvasya dhātāram acintya-rūpam
āditya-varṇaṁ tamasaḥ parastāt

One should continuously meditate upon the Supreme Person as the one who is the most wise, the most ancient, and the perpetual ruler of all; who is smaller than the smallest and the maintainer of everything; whose form is inconceivable; who is luminous like the sun and transcendental to the darkness of material nature.

8.10

prayāṇa-kāle manasācalena
bhaktyā yukto yoga-balena caiva
bhruvor madhye prāṇam āveśya samyak
sa taṁ paraṁ puruṣam upaiti divyam

One who is filled with pure devotion and propelled by the power of yoga at the time of passing away, whose mind is undisturbed, and whose life air is held firmly between the eyebrows, will surely attain the transcendental abode of the Supreme Personality of Godhead.

8.11

yad akṣaraṁ veda-vido vadanti
viśanti yad yatayo vīta-rāgāḥ
yad icchanto brahma-caryaṁ caranti
tat te padaṁ saṅgraheṇa pravakṣye

I shall now briefly describe to you that which those who are conversant in the Vedas know as the imperishable, which great sages seek to enter by means of renunciation and chastity.

8.12

sarva-dvārāṇi saṁyamya - mano hṛdi nirudhya ca
mūrdhny ādhāyātmanaḥ prāṇam - āsthito yoga-dhāraṇām

Closing the gates of the senses, controlling the mind from within the heart, and placing the life air at the top of the head, they remain situated in the state of yogic concentration.

8.13

oṁ ity ekākṣaraṁ brahma - vyāharan mām anusmaran
yaḥ prayāti tyajan dehaṁ - sa yāti paramāṁ gatim

Anyone who leaves their body while vibrating the single-syllable sound of transcendence, *oṁ*, and who continually remembers me, will certainly reach the supreme destination.

8.14

ananya-cetāḥ satataṁ - yo māṁ smarati nityaśaḥ
tasyāhaṁ su-labhaḥ pārtha - nitya-yuktasya yoginaḥ

O son of Pṛthā, for one whose mind is continually immersed in remembrance of me, who is united with me through their constant absorption in me, I am easy to obtain.

8.15

mām upetya punar janma - duḥkhālayam aśāśvatam
nāpnuvanti mahātmānaḥ - saṁsiddhiṁ paramāṁ gatāḥ

Upon reaching me, these great souls never take birth again in this transient place of sorrows, for they have attained the highest perfection.

8.16

ā-brahma-bhuvanāl lokāḥ - punar āvartino 'rjuna
mām upetya tu kaunteya - punar janma na vidyate

O Arjuna, all realms of this material world, from the highest – the abode of Brahmā – down to this earth, are places of repeated birth and death. But one who reaches me, O son of Kuntī, never takes birth again.

8.17

sahasra-yuga-paryantam - ahar yad brahmaṇo viduḥ
ātriṁ yuga-sahasrāntāṁ - te 'ho-rātra-vido janāḥ

Those who understand the truth about day and night know that Brahmā's day lasts for a thousand ages and that his night ends after the passage of yet another thousand ages.

8.18

avyaktād vyaktayaḥ sarvāḥ - prabhavanty ahar-āgame
rātry-āgame pralīyante - tatraivāvyakta-saṁjñake

At the dawn of Brahmā's day, all beings emerge from the unmanifest state; with the arrival of Brahmā's nightfall, they are absorbed once again into the unmanifest.

8.19

bhūta-grāmaḥ sa evāyaṁ - bhūtvā bhūtvā pralīyate
rātry-āgame 'vaśaḥ pārtha - prabhavaty ahar-āgame

Over and over, all are helplessly annihilated with the arrival of Brahmā's night only to come into being once again upon the commencement of Brahmā's day.

8.20

paras tasmāt tu bhāvo 'nyo - 'vyakto 'vyaktāt sanātanaḥ
yaḥ sa sarveṣu bhūteṣu - naśyatsu na vinaśyati

Beyond this, there is yet another unmanifest state of being that is eternal and transcendental. When all who are in this world vanish, that part remains as it is.

8.21

avyakto 'kṣara ity uktas - tam āhuḥ paramāṁ gatim
yaṁ prāpya na nivartante - tad dhāma paramaṁ mama

That unmanifest realm is said to be infallible and is known as the ultimate destination; that place from which one never returns after having attained it is my supreme abode.

8.22

puruṣaḥ sa paraḥ pārtha - bhaktyā labhyas tv ananyayā
yasyāntaḥ-sthāni bhūtāni - yena sarvam idaṁ tatam

O Pārtha, the Supreme Person, the greatest of all, who enters into everything and within whom all the worlds reside, is attainable by unalloyed devotion.

8.23

yatra kāle tv anāvṛttim - āvṛttiṁ caiva yoginaḥ
prayātā yānti taṁ kālaṁ - vakṣyāmi bharatarṣabha

O best of the Bhāratas, I shall now describe the times at which different kinds of mystics depart from this world, either to return once again or never to return.

8.24

agnir jyotir ahaḥ śuklaḥ - ṣaṇ-māsā uttarāyaṇam
tatra prayātā gacchanti - brahma brahma-vido janāḥ

Those who know Absolute Reality attain that Supreme Absolute by leaving this world under the influence of fire and light: within the six months when the sun follows a northern path, during the bright fortnight of the waxing moon, and at an auspicious time of day.

8.25

dhūmo rātris tathā kṛṣṇaḥ - ṣaṇ-māsā dakṣiṇāyanam
tatra cāndramasaṁ jyotir - yogī prāpya nivartate

The mystic who leaves this world under the influence of smoke and darkness, within the six months when the sun follows a southern path, during the waning lunar fortnight, attains the light of the moon but returns once again.

8.26

śukla-kṛṣṇe gatī hy ete - jagataḥ śāśvate mate
ekayā yāty anāvṛttim - anyayāvartate punaḥ

These two ways of passage from this world - one in light and one in darkness - are known to be primeval. Those who pass in light do not come back; by the other passage, one returns.

8.27

naite sṛtī pārtha jānan - yogī muhyati kaścana
tasmāt sarveṣu kāleṣu - yoga-yukto bhavārjuna

These two paths do not bewilder a mystic who knows them. Therefore, O Arjuna, remain firmly situated in union with the Supreme.

8.28

vedeṣu yajñeṣu tapaḥsu caiva
dāneṣu yat puṇya-phalaṁ pradiṣṭam
atyeti tat sarvam idaṁ viditvā
yogī paraṁ sthānam upaiti cādyam

With such a complete understanding, a mystic transcends the fruits to be obtained by the study of the Vedas, the performance of sacrifice, the observance of austerities, and the giving of charitable gifts. Thus they reach the supreme, original abode.

CHAPTER 9

rāja-guhya-yoga
THE YOGA OF THE KING OF SECRETS

Prelude

In Chapter 8, Kṛṣṇa spoke of the ultimate goal of mystic yoga. In Chapter, 9 Kṛṣṇa will present himself as the ultimate mystic *yogī* by whose divine power the entire cosmic creation comes into being and goes out of being.

Several of the verses in this chapter expand on elements of Chapter 7: Kṛṣṇa reiterates his sense of urgency about Arjuna hearing what he has to say, elaborates on his relationship with material nature, and speaks further about the difference between worshiping demigods and worshipping him.

This chapter is also distinct from previous chapters in that Kṛṣṇa begins to speak more directly about his identity as the Supreme Person and reveal confidential details about his relationship with those who devote themselves to him.

Things to look for:

- In verse 1, Kṛṣṇa expands on Arjuna's qualification for receiving and understanding the "confidential secret" that he is about to reveal.

- In verse 15, Kṛṣṇa describes three different features of his divine nature. The phrase "undifferentiated Oneness" indicates his feature as *Brahman*, the phrase "as diverse within many" indicates his feature as the *Paramātmā*, and the phrase "the all-pervading Lord of the universe whose face is turned everywhere" indicates the *viśva-rūpa* or Universal Form, which Kṛṣṇa will reveal to Arjuna in Chapter 11.

- In verse 20, the "nectar of the gods," known as *soma* in Sanskrit, is said to be a beverage, available only in higher or "heavenly" planetary systems, that increases one's mental, sensual, and physical strength.

- Also in verse 20, Kṛṣṇa uses the Sanskrit phrase *surendra-lokam* to indicate "the world of Indra." Indra is the name of a particularly significant demigod who reigns over the most heavenly of all the planets in the higher planetary systems. Hence, Indra is known as the "Lord of Heaven."

- At the beginning of Chapter 4, Kṛṣṇa indicated that the scientific knowledge of yoga that he's revealing to Arjuna is meant for leaders of society. In verse 32 of this chapter, Kṛṣṇa clearly indicates that everyone, irrespective of their gender, social position, or family situation, can access this knowledge and attain the highest perfection of yoga.

- Verse 34, the conclusive verse of Chapter 9, is located at the literary center of the Bhagavad-gītā, which gives us an indication of its significance. In fact, this verse is so important that Kṛṣṇa will repeat it almost verbatim near the end of Chapter 18.

9.1

śrī-bhagavān uvāca
idaṁ tu te guhya-tamaṁ - pravakṣyāmy anasūyave
jñānaṁ vijñāna-sahitaṁ - yaj jñātvā mokṣyase 'śubhāt

The Blessed Lord said: Now, because you are free from envy, I will reveal the most confidential secret to you. It is theoretical knowledge realized as experiential wisdom; knowing this, you shall be freed from all misfortune.

9.2

rāja-vidyā rāja-guhyaṁ - pavitram idam uttamam
pratyakṣāvagamaṁ dharmyaṁ - su-sukhaṁ kartum avyayam

This knowledge is the king of all knowledge, the most secret of all secrets, and the ultimate purifier. Understood by direct experience, it is the everlasting and supremely joyful perfection of religious principles.

9.3

aśraddadhānāḥ puruṣā - dharmasyāsya paran-tapa
aprāpya māṁ nivartante - mṛtyu-saṁsāra-vartmani

Those who do not have faith in this process of ultimate harmony cannot attain me, O conqueror of enemies. They therefore return to the path of recurring death.

9.4

mayā tatam idaṁ sarvaṁ - jagad avyakta-mūrtinā
mat-sthāni sarva-bhūtāni - na cāhaṁ teṣv avasthitaḥ

I pervade the entirety of creation with my invisible form. All beings are situated in me, but I am not in them.

9.5

na ca mat-sthāni bhūtāni - paśya me yogam aiśvaram
bhūta-bhṛn na ca bhūta-stho - mamātmā bhūta-bhāvanaḥ

And yet, all that is created does not rest in me. Behold my magnificent mystic power! Although I am situated everywhere as the maintainer of all beings, I am not a part of this world, for my very Self is the cause of all that is created.

9.6

yathākāśa-sthito nityaṁ - vāyuḥ sarvatra-go mahān
tathā sarvāṇi bhūtāni - mat-sthānīty upadhāraya

Try to understand that just as the wind, which blows everywhere, always resides in the sky, all created beings reside in me.

9.7

sarva-bhūtāni kaunteya - prakṛtiṁ yānti māmikām
kalpa-kṣaye punas tāni - kalpādau visṛjāmy aham

O son of Kuntī, at the end of a cycle of eons all beings enter into my primordial nature. At the beginning of another cycle, I release them again.

9.8

prakṛtiṁ svām avaṣṭabhya - visṛjāmi punaḥ punaḥ
bhūta-grāmam imaṁ kṛtsnam - avaśaṁ prakṛter vaśāt

By my will, all beings, who are powerless against the force of material nature, are released again and again into the cosmic manifestation.

9.9

na ca māṁ tāni karmāṇi - nibadhnanti dhanañ-jaya
udāsīna-vad āsīnam - asaktaṁ teṣu karmasu

O conqueror of riches, I am never bound by these activities. I remain detached from all such activities, as if seated at a distance.

9.10

mayādhyakṣeṇa prakṛtiḥ - sūyate sa-carācaram
hetunānena kaunteya - jagad viparivartate

Under my direction, O son of Kuntī, all moving and nonmoving beings are brought forth by the power of this material nature. Hence, this cosmic manifestation revolves in cycles.

9.11

avajānanti māṁ mūḍhā - mānuṣīṁ tanum āśritam
paraṁ bhāvam ajānanto - mama bhūta-maheśvaram

Fools dismiss me when I appear in a diminutive human form. They do not comprehend my transcendental position as the Supreme Lord of all that be.

9.12

moghāśā mogha-karmāṇo - mogha-jñānā vicetasaḥ
rākṣasīm āsurīṁ caiva - prakṛtiṁ mohinīṁ śritāḥ

Acting in vain, pursuing knowledge in vain, and baffled in their various aspirations, they take shelter of the bewildering material energy and thus embrace a demonic and godless disposition.

9.13

mahātmānas tu māṁ pārtha - daivīṁ prakṛtim āśritāḥ
bhajanty ananya-manaso - jñātvā bhūtādim avyayam

But, O son of Pṛthā, those great souls who take refuge in my divine nature, whose minds are focused exclusively on me; they offer their love to me because they know me to be the imperishable origin of all beings.

9.14

satataṁ kīrtayanto māṁ - yatantaś ca dṛḍha-vratāḥ
namasyantaś ca māṁ bhaktyā - nitya-yuktā upāsate

Always glorifying me, endeavoring with great determination, and honoring me by their devotion, they worship me in a state of perpetual union.

9.15

jñāna-yajñena cāpy anye - yajanto mām upāsate
ekatvena pṛthaktvena - bahudhā viśvato-mukham

There are also others: those whose sacrificial offerings consist of the cultivation of knowledge as well as those who worship me as undifferentiated Oneness, as diverse within many, and as the all-pervading Lord of the universe whose face is turned everywhere.

9.16

ahaṁ kratur ahaṁ yajñaḥ - svadhāham aham auṣadham
mantro 'ham aham evājyam - aham agnir ahaṁ hutam

I am the ritual, I am the sacrifice, and I am the offering to the ancestors. I am the healing herb and the transcendental chant. Indeed, it is I alone who am the clarified butter, I who am the fire, and I who am the offering.

9.17

pitāham asya jagato - mātā dhātā pitāmahaḥ
vedyaṁ pavitram oṁ-kāra - ṛk sāma yajur eva ca

I am the father of this universe, the mother, the creator, and the grandfather. I am what is to be known, that which purifies, and the vibration *oṁ*. Know me to be the Ṛg Veda, the Sāma Veda, and the Yajur Veda as well.

9.18

gatir bhartā prabhuḥ sākṣī - nivāsaḥ śaraṇaṁ suhṛt
prabhavaḥ pralayaḥ sthānaṁ - nidhānaṁ bījam avyayam

I am the goal, the sustainer, the master, and the witness. I am the abode, the shelter, and the most intimate friend. I am the origin and the dissolution, the foundation of existence, the resting place, and the imperishable seed.

9.19

tapāmy aham ahaṁ varṣaṁ - nigṛhṇāmy utsṛjāmi ca
amṛtaṁ caiva mṛtyuś ca - sad asac cāham arjuna

O Arjuna, I radiate heat and I both withhold and send forth rain. I am both immortality and certain death, both being and non-being.

9.20

trai-vidyā māṁ soma-pāḥ pūta-pāpā
yajñair iṣṭvā svar-gatiṁ prārthayante
te puṇyam āsādya surendra-lokam
aśnanti divyān divi deva-bhogān

Praying for passage to the realms of heaven, those who know the three Vedas drink the nectar of the gods. Purified of sin, their worship is enacted through sacrificial offerings. Thus they attain the pious world of Indra, the Lord of Heaven, where they enjoy godly delights.

9.21

te taṁ bhuktvā svarga-lokaṁ viśālaṁ
kṣīṇe puṇye martya-lokaṁ viśanti
evaṁ trayī-dharmam anuprapannā
gatāgataṁ kāma-kāmā labhante

Having enjoyed the pleasures of the vast heavenly realm, with their pious credits exhausted, they return once again to the world of mortals. Thus following the religious principles of the three Vedas in pursuit of material sense pleasure, they attain only such repeated comings and goings.

9.22

ananyāś cintayanto māṁ - ye janāḥ paryupāsate
teṣāṁ nityābhiyuktānāṁ - yoga-kṣemaṁ vahāmy aham

But for those who have no object of meditation other than me, who worship me with complete devotion, I bring support and protection.

9.23

ye 'py anya-devatā-bhaktā - yajante śraddhayānvitāḥ
te 'pi mām eva kaunteya - yajanty avidhi-pūrvakam

Even those who faithfully worship other gods to whom they are devoted are actually worshipping me alone, O son of Kuntī, but they do so improperly.

9.24

ahaṁ hi sarva-yajñānāṁ - bhoktā ca prabhur eva ca
na tu mām abhijānanti - tattvenātaś cyavanti te

I am the only enjoyer and the master of all sacrifices. But, because they do not know the truth about me, they fall down.

9.25

yānti deva-vratā devān - pitṝn yānti pitṛ-vratāḥ
bhūtāni yānti bhūtejyā - yānti mad-yājino 'pi mām

Those who make a covenant with the demigods go to the demigods, those who make solemn vows to ancestors go to such ancestors, and worshipers of ghosts and spirits go to those ghosts and spirits. My devotees, however, come to me.

9.26

patraṁ puṣpaṁ phalaṁ toyaṁ - yo me bhaktyā prayacchati
tad ahaṁ bhakty-upahṛtam - aśnāmi prayatātmanaḥ

If one who is pure in heart presents a leaf, a flower, fruit, or water to me as an offering of love, I will accept such a devotional offering.

9.27

yat karoṣi yad aśnāsi - yaj juhoṣi dadāsi yat
yat tapasyasi kaunteya - tat kuruṣva mad-arpaṇam

Whatever you do, whatever you eat, whatever you sacrifice, whatever gifts you give, whatever austerities you perform – do it as an offering to me.

9.28

śubhāśubha-phalair evaṁ - mokṣyase karma-bandhanaiḥ
sannyāsa-yoga-yuktātmā - vimukto mām upaiṣyasi

By doing so you will be freed from the bondage of reactions to your actions, both good and bad. By linking yourself to me through this principle of renunciation, you shall attain liberation and come to me.

9.29

samo 'haṁ sarva-bhūteṣu - na me dveṣyo 'sti na priyaḥ
ye bhajanti tu māṁ bhaktyā - mayi te teṣu cāpy aham

I am equally disposed toward all living beings. I hate no one nor do I favor anyone. Even so, I hold those who honor me with offerings of love within me. Indeed, I am within them as well.

9.30

api cet su-durācāro - bhajate mām ananya-bhāk
sādhur eva sa mantavyaḥ - samyag vyavasito hi saḥ

If one offers their love to me without deviation then, even if they have engaged in dreadful behavior, they are to be considered saintly, for they are perfectly situated in their determination.

9.31

kṣipraṁ bhavati dharmātmā - śaśvac-chāntiṁ nigacchati
kaunteya pratijānīhi - na me bhaktaḥ praṇaśyati

Such a person quickly becomes righteous and attains lasting peace. Let it be known, O son of Kuntī, that one who offers their love to me is never lost.

9.32

māṁ hi pārtha vyapāśritya - ye 'pi syuḥ pāpa-yonayaḥ
striyo vaiśyās tathā śūdrās - te 'pi yānti parāṁ gatim

O son of Pṛthā, those who take shelter of me, whether they are women, merchants, laborers, or are born of a troubled family, will also attain the supreme goal of life.

9.33

kiṁ punar brāhmaṇāḥ puṇyā - bhaktā rājarṣayas tathā
anityam asukhaṁ lokam - imaṁ prāpya bhajasva mām

How much more so, then, for the saintly caretakers of religious principles and the wise monarchs who are devoted to me. Therefore, having come to this temporary and unhappy world, now offer your love to me.

9.34

man-manā bhava mad-bhakto - mad-yājī māṁ namaskuru
mām evaiṣyasi yuktvaivam - ātmānaṁ mat-parāyaṇaḥ

Direct your mind toward me, become my devotee, offer your sacrifices to me and act in reverence for me. Thus, you will surely come to me, having completely absorbed yourself in me alone.

CHAPTER 10

vibhūti-yoga

THE YOGA OF DIVINE MANIFESTATIONS

Prelude

In Chapter 9, Kṛṣṇa glorified those who devote themselves to him, described how he reciprocates with his devotees, and, in the last verse, explained the mental, emotional, and practical elements that guarantee success on the path of devotional yoga. In Chapter 10, Kṛṣṇa will expand on his revelation of "the most secret of all secrets" by giving Arjuna examples of the limitless grandeur of his supreme personality.

It is particularly noteworthy that Kṛṣṇa begins this chapter by revealing his motivation for sharing such personal information about himself and that he regards this personal information as his "supreme message."

Things to look for:

- In verse 6, the "seven great sages of antiquity" refers to the seven sages mentioned in the Upaniṣads as the patriarchs of Vedic religion. The "four prior to them" refers to the sages known as the four Kumaras: Sanaka, Sananda,

Sanātana and Sanat-kumāra. The "progenitors from whom all living beings in this world descend" refers to the 14 Manus who are responsible for populating the universe during each day of Brahmā.

- Verses 8 through 11 are known as the *catuḥ-ślokī*: the four essential verses around which the entirety of the Bhagavad-gītā revolves. It is said that understanding these four verses is the key to understanding the rest of the Gītā.

- From verse 12 onward, Arjuna's questions shift from doubt-based questions that arose from his confusion to faith-based questions that arise from his desire to gain a deeper understanding.

- In verse 13, Arjuna references four sages: Nārada, Asita, Devala and Vyāsa. Nārada is the foremost sage among the demigods and the guru of Vyāsa. Vyāsa is the sage who is credited with compiling all of the Vedic literature, including the Bhagavad-gītā. And, as noted earlier, Vyāsa plays an important role in the events leading up to the battle of Kurukṣetra. Asita and Devala are both renowned sages who counseled the ruling classes in Arjuna's time.

- In verses 21 through 37, Kṛṣṇa references various types of people, places, and things and the names of the topmost person, place, or thing within each of these categories. In each case, he likens the topmost person, place, or thing to himself. Kṛṣṇa is using these examples to convey the idea that he, Kṛṣṇa, is the origin of the superlative qualities that distinguish the topmost person, place, or thing from all others in their category. The principle that Kṛṣṇa's universally superlative qualities are represented by the topmost person, place, or thing in any given category is more important than specific knowledge of who or what he's referring to. The examples that Kṛṣṇa uses in these verses would have been familiar to Arjuna but are likely to be foreign to most Western readers. For the sake of placing the principle in a somewhat more contemporary cultural frame of reference, Kṛṣṇa might just as well be saying, "of popular musicians I am the Beatles."

- In verse 35, Gāyatrī refers to the shortest and most sacred of poetic meters in the Vedic literary tradition, not the mantra of the same name.

10.1

śrī-bhagavān uvāca
bhūya eva mahā-bāho - śṛṇu me paramaṁ vacaḥ
yat te 'haṁ prīyamāṇāya - vakṣyāmi hita-kāmyayā

The Blessed Lord said: O mighty armed, just hear my voice once again. Because I think of you as my dear friend, I shall speak my supreme message for the sake of your well-being.

10.2

na me viduḥ sura-gaṇāḥ - prabhavaṁ na maharṣayaḥ
aham ādir hi devānāṁ - maharṣīṇāṁ ca sarvaśaḥ

Neither the gods nor the great sages understand how I have come to be, for I am, in all respects, the source of all the gods and great sages.

10.3

yo māṁ ajam anādiṁ ca - vetti loka-maheśvaram
asammūḍhaḥ sa martyeṣu - sarva-pāpaiḥ pramucyate

Those who understand me as unborn, beginningless, and the Supreme Lord of all the worlds – they alone are undeluded among mortals and are freed from all misfortune.

10.4

buddhir jñānam asammohaḥ - kṣamā satyaṁ damaḥ śamaḥ
sukhaṁ duḥkhaṁ bhavo 'bhāvo - bhayaṁ cābhayam eva ca

Discernment, knowledge, freedom from delusion, forgiveness, truthfulness, control of the mind and senses, serenity, happiness and distress, birth and death, and fear and fearlessness as well; . . .

10.5

ahiṁsā samatā tuṣṭis - tapo dānaṁ yaśo 'yaśaḥ
bhavanti bhāvā bhūtānāṁ - matta eva pṛthag-vidhāḥ

non-violence, impartiality, satisfaction, austerity, charity, fame, and infamy – all these conditions and the various forms in which they appear in living beings arise from me alone.

10.6

maharṣayaḥ sapta pūrve - catvāro manavas tathā
mad-bhāvā mānasā jātā - yeṣāṁ loka imāḥ prajāḥ

The seven great sages of antiquity, as well as the four prior to them and the progenitors from whom all living beings in this world descend, are born from me as emanations from my mind.

10.7

etāṁ vibhūtiṁ yogaṁ ca - mama yo vetti tattvataḥ
so 'vikalpena yogena - yujyate nātra saṁśayaḥ

One who knows the truth about my immeasurable mystic power remains united with me through an unwavering yoga practice. Of this there is no doubt.

10.8

ahaṁ sarvasya prabhavo - mattaḥ sarvaṁ pravartate
iti matvā bhajante māṁ - budhā bhāva-samanvitāḥ

I am the source of everything. Everything emanates from me. Those who are wise, whose knowledge is perfect, serve me with devotion and worship me with all their heart.

10.9

mac-cittā mad-gata-prāṇā - bodhayantaḥ parasparam
kathayantaś ca māṁ nityaṁ - tuṣyanti ca ramanti ca

With their thoughts dwelling in me and every breath of life offered to me, those who are devoted to me experience complete satisfaction and transcendental bliss by continually enlightening one another and speaking about me.

10.10

teṣāṁ satata-yuktānāṁ - bhajatāṁ prīti-pūrvakam
dadāmi buddhi-yogaṁ taṁ - yena mām upayānti te

To those who are constantly associating with me through offerings of devotional affection, I give the spiritual intelligence by which they can come to me.

10.11

teṣām evānukampārtham - aham ajñāna-jaṁ tamaḥ
nāśayāmy ātma-bhāva-stho - jñāna-dīpena bhāsvatā

Feeling especially compassionate for those who are devoted to me, I, dwelling within their hearts, dispel the darkness born of ignorance with the radiant lamp of knowledge.

10.12

arjuna uvāca
paraṁ brahma paraṁ dhāma - pavitraṁ paramaṁ bhavan
puruṣaṁ śāśvataṁ divyam - ādi-devam ajaṁ vibhum

Arjuna said: You are the supreme truth, the supreme abode, the supreme purifier, the eternal divine person and the original divinity, unborn and all-powerful.

10.13

āhus tvām ṛṣayaḥ sarve - devarṣir nāradas tathā
asito devalo vyāsaḥ - svayaṁ caiva bravīṣi me

All the great seers, including the divine sage Nārada, Asita, Devala, and Vyāsa say this about you, and now you are personally affirming this truth to me.

10.14

sarvam etad ṛtaṁ manye - yan māṁ vadasi keśava
na hi te bhagavan vyaktiṁ - vidur devā na dānavāḥ

O Keśava, I accept all that you have told me as the truth. O blessed Lord, neither the demigods nor the demons can comprehend your personality.

10.15

svayam evātmanātmānaṁ - vettha tvaṁ puruṣottama
bhūta-bhāvana bhūteśa - deva-deva jagat-pate

Indeed, you alone know yourself by your own power. O Supreme Person, you are the origin of all, the Lord of all beings, the Lord of all gods, and the Lord of the universe!

10.16

vaktum arhasy aśeṣeṇa - divyā hy ātma-vibhūtayaḥ
yābhir vibhūtibhir lokān - imāṁs tvaṁ vyāpya tiṣṭhasi

Please tell me in detail of your infinite divine powers and the opulence through which you pervade and reside in all these worlds.

10.17

kathaṁ vidyām ahaṁ yogiṁs - tvāṁ sadā paricintayan
keṣu keṣu ca bhāveṣu - cintyo 'si bhagavan mayā

O supreme mystic, how shall I know you and constantly meditate upon you? What various states of being should I remember for the sake of meditating on you, O Lord?

10.18

vistareṇātmano yogaṁ - vibhūtiṁ ca janārdana
bhūyaḥ kathaya tṛptir hi - śṛṇvato nāsti me 'mṛtam

O Janārdana, please describe your magnificent mystic power in detail yet again, for there is no limit to my satisfaction in hearing the nectar of your words.

10.19

śrī-bhagavān uvāca
hanta te kathayiṣyāmi - divyā hy ātma-vibhūtayaḥ
prādhānyataḥ kuru-śreṣṭha - nāsty anto vistarasya me

The Blessed Lord said: Yes, I will indeed tell you about my magnificent personal powers, O best of the Kuru dynasty, but only of those that are most prominent, for the extent of my divine power is limitless.

10.20

aham ātmā guḍākeśa - sarva-bhūtāśaya-sthitaḥ
aham ādiś ca madhyaṁ ca - bhūtānām anta eva ca

I am the innermost soul of all souls, O conqueror of sleep, seated within the hearts of all living beings. I am the beginning, middle, and end of all beings and of all being.

10.21

ādityānām ahaṁ viṣṇur - jyotiṣāṁ ravir aṁśumān
marīcir marutām asmi - nakṣatrāṇām ahaṁ śaśī

Of the Ādityas I am Viṣṇu; of luminaries I am the radiant sun; among the Maruts I am Marīci; and among the stars I am the moon.

10.22

vedānāṁ sāma-vedo 'smi - devānām asmi vāsavaḥ
indriyāṇāṁ manaś cāsmi - bhūtānām asmi cetanā

Of the Vedas I am the Sāma Veda; of the demigods I am Vasava [Indra]; of the senses I am the mind and of living beings I am consciousness.

10.23

udrāṇāṁ śaṅkaraś cāsmi - vitteśo yakṣa-rakṣasām
vasūnāṁ pāvakaś cāsmi - meruḥ śikhariṇām aham

Of the Rudras I am Śaṅkara [Śiva]. Of the Yakṣas and Rākṣasas I am Kuvera, the lord of wealth. Of the Vasus I am fire [Agni], and of towering mountains I am Meru.

10.24

purodhasāṁ ca mukhyaṁ māṁ - viddhi pārtha bṛhaspatim
senānīnām ahaṁ skandaḥ - sarasām asmi sāgaraḥ

Of priests, O son of Pṛthā, know me to be the foremost, Bṛhaspati. Of military leaders I am Kārttikeya, and amongst bodies of water I am the ocean.

10.25

maharṣīṇāṁ bhṛgur ahaṁ - girām asmy ekam akṣaram
yajñānāṁ japa-yajño 'smi - sthāvarāṇāṁ himālayaḥ

Of the great sages I am Bhṛgu, of vibrations I am the singular transcendental syllable [*oṁ*]. Of sacrifices I am the quiet chant, and of all that is immovable I am the Himālayas.

10.26

aśvatthaḥ sarva-vṛkṣāṇāṁ - devarṣīṇāṁ ca nāradaḥ
gandharvāṇāṁ citrarathaḥ - siddhānāṁ kapilo muniḥ

Of all trees I am the banyan tree, of the seers among the celestials I am Nārada. Among the Gandharvas I am Citraratha, and among perfected beings I am the sage Kapila.

10.27

uccaiḥśravasam aśvānāṁ - viddhi mām amṛtodbhavam
airāvataṁ gajendrāṇāṁ - narāṇāṁ ca narādhipam

Of horses I am Uccaiḥśravā, who appeared from the ocean of nectar. Of lordly elephants I am Airāvata, and among human beings I am the ruler.

10.28

āyudhānām ahaṁ vajraṁ - dhenūnām asmi kāma-dhuk
prajanaś cāsmi kandarpaḥ - sarpāṇām asmi vāsukiḥ

Of weapons I am the thunderbolt; among cows I am the giver of unlimited milk. Of procreative impulses I am Kandarpa [Cupid], and of serpents I am Vāsuki.

10.29

anantaś cāsmi nāgānāṁ - varuṇo yādasām aham
pitṝṇām aryamā cāsmi - yamaḥ saṁyamatām aham

Of great serpents I am Ananta, and of the great aquatics I am Varuṇa, the lord of the waters. Of departed ancestors I am Aryamā, and of subduers I am Yama, the lord of death.

10.30

prahlādaś cāsmi daityānāṁ - kālaḥ kalayatām aham
mṛgāṇāṁ ca mṛgendro 'haṁ - vainateyaś ca pakṣiṇām

Among the Daityas I am the devoted Prahlāda, among all that move through time I am time itself. Among animals I am the lion, lord of beasts, and among the winged, I am the son of Vinata [Garuḍa].

10.31

pavanaḥ pavatām asmi - rāmaḥ śastra-bhṛtām aham
jhaṣāṇāṁ makaraś cāsmi - srotasām asmi jāhnavī

Of all that purifies I am the purifying wind, of the wielders of weapons I am Rāma. Of great fish I am the shark, and of flowing rivers I am Jāhnavī [the Ganges].

10.32

sargāṇām ādir antaś ca - madhyaṁ caivāham arjuna
adhyātma-vidyā vidyānāṁ - vādaḥ pravadatām aham

O Arjuna, of creations I am the beginning, the end, and the middle as well. Of sciences I am the science of self-realization, and among logicians I am the conclusive truth.

10.33

akṣarāṇām a-kāro 'smi - dvandvaḥ sāmāsikasya ca
aham evākṣayaḥ kālo - dhātāhaṁ viśvato-mukhaḥ

Of letters I am the letter A and of compound words I am the dual compound. I am eternal time and I am the creator of the world whose faces are turned everywhere.

10.34

mṛtyuḥ sarva-haraś cāham - udbhavaś ca bhaviṣyatām
kīrtiḥ śrīr vāk ca nārīṇāṁ - smṛtir medhā dhṛtiḥ kṣamā

I am all-devouring death and the coming forth of all that is yet to be. Of feminine attributes I am fame, beauty, refined speech, memory, practical intelligence, firmness, and forgiveness.

10.35

bṛhat-sāma tathā sāmnāṁ - gāyatrī chandasām aham
māsānāṁ mārga-śīrṣo 'ham - ṛtūnāṁ kusumākaraḥ

Of hymns I am the "Great Song" and of poetic meters I am Gāyatrī. Of months I am Mārgaśīrṣa [November – December], and of seasons I am the season of abundant flowers [spring].

10.36

dyūtaṁ chalayatām asmi - tejas tejasvinām aham
jayo 'smi vyavasāyo 'smi - sattvaṁ sattvavatām aham

Among cheaters I am gambling and of the splendid I am the splendor. I am victory, I am determination, and I am the courage of the courageous.

10.37

vṛṣṇīnāṁ vāsudevo 'smi - pāṇḍavānāṁ dhanañ-jayaḥ
munīnām apy ahaṁ vyāsaḥ - kavīnām uśanā kaviḥ

Of the descendants of Vṛṣṇi I am the son of Vasudeva; of the Pāṇḍavas I am you, the winner of wealth; of the sages I am Vyāsa and of poets I am the learned Uśanā.

10.38

daṇḍo damayatām asmi - nītir asmi jigīṣatām
maunaṁ caivāsmi guhyānāṁ - jñānaṁ jñānavatām aham

Among tamers I am the rod of chastisement; among those who seek victory I am moral conduct; I am the silence of secrets and the wisdom of the wise.

10.39

yac cāpi sarva-bhūtānāṁ - bījaṁ tad aham arjuna
na tad asti vinā yat syān - mayā bhūtaṁ carācaram

Furthermore, O Arjuna, I am the seed of created beings. No being, moving or nonmoving, can exist without me.

10.40

nānto 'sti mama divyānāṁ - vibhūtīnāṁ paran-tapa
eṣa tūddeśataḥ prokto - vibhūter vistaro mayā

O scorcher of foes, the vast expanse of my divine manifestations has no limit. What I have described to you is merely a sample of my infinite opulence.

10.41

yad yad vibhūtimat sattvaṁ - śrīmad ūrjitam eva vā
tat tad evāvagaccha tvaṁ - mama tejo-'ṁśa-sambhavam

Know with certainty that all creations endowed with power, beauty, and excellence spring from but a spark of my splendor.

10.42

atha vā bahunaitena - kiṁ jñātena tavārjuna
viṣṭabhyāham idaṁ kṛtsnam - ekāṁśena sthito jagat

But what is the need for you to have so much detailed knowledge, O Arjuna? With just a fragment of myself, I continuously support this entire universe.

CHAPTER 11

viśva-rūpa-darśana-yoga
THE YOGA OF SEEING THE UNIVERSAL FORM

Prelude

In Chapter 10, Arjuna heard Kṛṣṇa speak about himself as the one fully independent being upon whom all beings, as well as being itself, depends. We also heard Kṛṣṇa say that he pervades and supports the entire universe with a small fraction of himself. Now, in Chapter 11, Arjuna, asks Kṛṣṇa to let him see the form by which Kṛṣṇa's omniscience, omnipresence, inconceivable power, and supreme majesty can be experienced. This "Universal Form" that Arjuna asks to see is a visual representation of Kṛṣṇa's role as the ultimate source, sustainer, and, most significantly, destroyer of the complete material cosmic manifestation.

Since Arjuna has already accepted that Kṛṣṇa is uniquely qualified to occupy the position of God, his request doesn't imply a lack of faith. According to traditional commentaries, Arjuna's request to see an indisputable visual confirmation of Kṛṣṇa's divinity is based on curiosity and a desire to set the criterion by which anyone else's claim of God-hood may be confirmed or denied. In other words, since only God can display the form that Arjuna is requesting to see, anyone who claims to be God must also be able to display this form to back up their claim.

Things to look for:

- In verse 15, "Brahmā" refers to the first of the demigods, who is said to have appeared from within the whorl of a lotus flower that rises from Viṣṇu's naval, and "Śiva" refers to a transformation of Viṣṇu who enters the material world through the agency of Brahmā. Together, Brahmā, Viṣṇu, and Śiva are known as the *guna-avatar*s; the administrators of the material qualities of passion, luminance, and darkness respectively. The Vedic tradition offers a very wide range of theological interpretations about the nature of these three personalities.
- Verse 32 was made famous by J. Robert Oppenheimer, the "father of the atomic bomb," who quoted a translation of it when he witnessed the first successful test detonation of a nuclear weapon in the New Mexico desert in 1945.
- In verse 43, Arjuna references "the three worlds." The Vedic conception of the structure of the universe describes a vertical arrangement of three planetary systems: upper, middle, and lower. The Earth is understood to be in the middle planetary system.
- In verse 50, the Sanskrit phrase *svakaṁ rūpaṁ* is understood to mean Kṛṣṇa's magnificent four-armed Viṣṇu form and the phrase *saumya-vapur* is understood to indicate Kṛṣṇa's beautiful, human-like two-armed form. The phrase "as before" (*bhūyaḥ*) isn't referring to a previous verse or chapter in the Gītā; it refers to the time of Kṛṣṇa's "birth" when he appeared in his four-armed Viṣṇu form prior to assuming a form resembling that of an ordinary baby.

- In verse 54, the Sanskrit word *bhaktyā* is significant: it indicates that the practice of devotional yoga is the only means by which one can understand the form that Kṛṣṇa has revealed to Arjuna in this chapter.

11.1

arjuna uvāca
mad-anugrahāya paramaṁ - guhyam adhyātma-saṁjñitam
yat tvayoktaṁ vacas tena - moho 'yaṁ vigato mama

Arjuna said: Out of compassion you have revealed your supreme spiritual secret to me. The words that you have so kindly spoken to me have thus dispelled my illusion.

11.2

bhavāpyayau hi bhūtānāṁ - śrutau vistaraśo mayā
tvattaḥ kamala-patrākṣa - māhātmyam api cāvyayam

I have heard a detailed explanation from you, whose eyes are like the petals of a lotus flower, about the appearance and disappearance of living beings, as well as about your own inexhaustible grandeur.

11.3

evam etad yathāttha tvam - ātmānaṁ parameśvara
draṣṭum icchāmi te rūpam - aiśvaraṁ puruṣottama

O Supreme Lord, though you have perfectly described yourself, I wish to see the glorious form of divine majesty by which you enter into this world as the Ultimate Person.

11.4

manyase yadi tac chakyaṁ - mayā draṣṭum iti prabho
yogeśvara tato me tvaṁ - darśayātmānam avyayam

If you think that it is possible for me to see you in this way, O Supreme Lord, master of all mystic power, then kindly reveal this imperishable form of yours to me.

11.5

śrī-bhagavān uvāca
paśya me pārtha rūpāṇi - śataśo 'tha sahasraśaḥ
nānā-vidhāni divyāni - nānā-varṇākṛtīni ca

The Blessed Lord said: O son of Pṛthā, behold my hundreds and thousands of divine forms appearing in a wonderful multitude of categories, colors, and shapes.

11.6

paśyādityān vasūn rudrān - aśvinau marutas tathā
bahūny adṛṣṭa-pūrvāṇi - paśyāścaryāṇi bhārata

Behold the Ādityas, Vasus, Rudras, Aśvinī-kumāras, Maruts, and all the other demigods. O best of the Bhāratas, behold many wonders that no one has seen before.

11.7

ihaika-sthaṁ jagat kṛtsnaṁ - paśyādya sa-carācaram
mama dehe guḍākeśa - yac cānyad draṣṭum icchasi

Now behold the entire universe, with all that moves and all that is still, all in one place. O conqueror of ignorance, whatever else you may wish to see is here, within this form of mine.

11.8

na tu māṁ śakyase draṣṭum - anenaiva sva-cakṣuṣā
divyaṁ dadāmi te cakṣuḥ - paśya me yogam aiśvaram

But you cannot see me in this form with just your own eyes. Therefore I give you divine eyes: behold my mystic power!

11.9

sañjaya uvāca
evam uktvā tato rājan - mahā-yogeśvaro hariḥ
darśayām āsa pārthāya - paramaṁ rūpam aiśvaram

Sañjaya said: Having thus spoken, O King, the greatest of all mystic yogīs, who removes darkness and sorrow from the hearts of his devotees, revealed his form of supreme power and divine majesty to the son of Pāṇḍu.

11.10-11

aneka-vaktra-nayanam - anekādbhuta-darśanam
aneka-divyābharaṇaṁ - divyānekodyatāyudham

divya-mālyāmbara-dharaṁ - divya-gandhānulepanam
sarvāścarya-mayaṁ devam - anantaṁ viśvato-mukham

[Arjuna could see] innumerable mouths, innumerable eyes, and innumerable wondrous visions; a form decorated with countless divine ornaments and carrying countless divine upraised weapons; wearing divine garlands and garments, smeared with divine scents and ointments; consisting of endless divine wonders and facing in all directions.

11.12

divi sūrya-sahasrasya - bhaved yugapad utthitā
yadi bhāḥ sadṛśī sā syād - bhāsas tasya mahātmanaḥ

If a thousand suns were to burst into the sky all at once, their radiance might resemble the brilliance of the Supreme Self.

11.13

tatraika-sthaṁ jagat kṛtsnaṁ - pravibhaktam anekadhā
apaśyad deva-devasya - śarīre pāṇḍavas tadā

Then and there, the son of Pāṇḍu beheld the complete expanse of the universe situated in one place yet infinitely divided within the body of the God of gods.

11.14

tataḥ sa vismayāviṣṭo - hṛṣṭa-romā dhanañ-jayaḥ
praṇamya śirasā devaṁ - kṛtāñjalir abhāṣata

Then, overwhelmed with amazement, with the hairs on his body standing on end, Arjuna, the conqueror of wealth, bowed his head to the divine Lord and, with palms prayerfully joined, began to speak.

11.15

arjuna uvāca
paśyāmi devāṁs tava deva dehe
sarvāṁs tathā bhūta-viśeṣa-saṅghān
brahmāṇam īśaṁ kamalāsana-stham
ṛṣīṁś ca sarvān uragāṁś ca divyān

Arjuna said: O my Lord, I see all the demigods along with all manner of other beings assembled in your body. I see Brahmā sitting on the lotus flower, Śiva, and all the great sages and divine serpents.

11.16

aneka-bāhūdara-vaktra-netraṁ
paśyāmi tvāṁ sarvato 'nanta-rūpam
nāntaṁ na madhyaṁ na punas tavādiṁ
paśyāmi viśveśvara viśva-rūpa

O Lord of the universe in the form of the universe, I see innumerable arms, bellies, mouths and eyes, expanding without limit in every direction. I see no end, no middle, nor any beginning to your unlimited form.

11.17

kirīṭinaṁ gadinaṁ cakriṇaṁ ca
tejo-rāśiṁ sarvato dīptimantam
paśyāmi tvāṁ durnirīkṣyaṁ samantād
dīptānalārka-dyutim aprameyam

I see you everywhere, adorned with various crowns, clubs and discs; a limitless form of shining splendor glowing on all sides like blazing fire, like the immeasurable radiance of the sun, so difficult to behold all at once.

11.18

tvam akṣaraṁ paramaṁ veditavyaṁ
tvam asya viśvasya paraṁ nidhānam
tvam avyayaḥ śāśvata-dharma-goptā
sanātanas tvaṁ puruṣo mato me

You are imperishable, the ultimate object of knowledge, and the supreme resting place of all. You are inexhaustible, the eternal maintainer of eternal religious principles. In my opinion, you are the Supreme Person.

11.19

anādi-madhyāntam ananta-vīryam
ananta-bāhuṁ śaśi-sūrya-netram
paśyāmi tvāṁ dīpta-hutāśa-vaktraṁ
sva-tejasā viśvam idaṁ tapantam

You have no beginning, no middle, nor any end. Your power is limitless, your arms are limitless, and the sun and moon are your eyes. I see you with blazing fire pouring forth from your mouth, burning this entire universe with the heat of your radiance.

11.20

dyāv ā-pṛthivyor idam antaraṁ hi
vyāptaṁ tvayaikena diśaś ca sarvāḥ
dṛṣṭvādbhutaṁ rūpam ugraṁ tavedaṁ
loka-trayaṁ pravyathitaṁ mahātman

O Great Self, you alone fill the space between heaven and earth in all directions; the three worlds tremble at the sight of your fierce and wonderful form.

11.21

amī hi tvāṁ sura-saṅghā viśanti
kecid bhītāḥ prāñjalayo gṛṇanti
svastīty uktvā maharṣi-siddha-saṅghāḥ
stuvanti tvāṁ stutibhiḥ puṣkalābhiḥ

The assembled multitudes of celestial beings are entering into you, some stricken with fear and offering prayers with folded hands. Hosts of great sages and perfected beings are crying out to you by singing hymns of praise and petitions for peace and prosperity.

11.22

rudrādityā vasavo ye ca sādhyā
viśve 'śvinau marutaś coṣmapāś ca
gandharva-yakṣāsura-siddha-saṅghā
vīkṣante tvāṁ vismitāś caiva sarve

All the various manifestations of Śiva, the twelve principal demigods, the Vasus, the Sādhyas, the Viśvedevas, the two Aśvīs, the Maruts, the forefathers, angels, spirits, demons, and the perfected beings are all beholding you with complete amazement.

11.23

rūpaṁ mahat te bahu-vaktra-netraṁ
mahā-bāho bahu-bāhūru-pādam
bahūdaraṁ bahu-daṁṣṭrā-karālaṁ
dṛṣṭvā lokāḥ pravyathitās tathāham

O mighty-armed, seeing your exalted form, with its innumerable faces, eyes, arms, thighs, legs and bellies and your many terrible teeth, the entire universe trembles in fear, as do I.

11.24

nabhaḥ-spṛśaṁ dīptam aneka-varṇaṁ
vyāttānanaṁ dīpta-viśāla-netram
dṛṣṭvā hi tvāṁ pravyathitāntar-ātmā
dhṛtiṁ na vindāmi śamaṁ ca viṣṇo

O all-pervading Viṣṇu, seeing you touching the sky with your endless array of electrifying colors, your gaping mouths and huge glowing eyes, my inner self trembles; my reeling mind can find neither stability nor serenity.

11.25

daṁṣṭrā-karālāni ca te mukhāni
dṛṣṭvaiva kālānala-sannibhāni
diśo na jāne na labhe ca śarma
prasīda deveśa jagan-nivāsa

Seeing your mouths with their terrible teeth and your deathly faces bellowing blazing fires of cosmic devastation, I have lost all sense of direction and can find no place of shelter. O Lord of lords, abode of the universe, please be merciful to me.

11.26-27

mī ca tvāṁ dhṛtarāṣṭrasya putrāḥ
sarve sahaivāvani-pāla-saṅghaiḥ
bhīṣmo droṇaḥ sūta-putras tathāsau
sahāsmadīyair api yodha-mukhyaiḥ

vaktrāṇi te tvaramāṇā viśanti
daṁṣṭrā-karālāni bhayānakāni
kecid vilagnā daśanāntareṣu
sandṛśyante cūrṇitair uttamāṅgaiḥ

All the sons of Dhṛtarāṣṭra, along with multitudes of earthly rulers such as Bhīṣma, Droṇa, and Karṇa, and the best of our warriors as well, are rushing into your mouths, so dreadful with their terrifying teeth. I clearly see some trapped between your teeth with their heads crushed.

11.28

yathā nadīnāṁ bahavo 'mbu-vegāḥ
samudram evābhimukhā dravanti
tathā tavāmī nara-loka-vīrā
viśanti vaktrāṇy abhivijvalanti

As surely as the countless currents of rivers flow only to the sea, so, too, do all these heroes of the mortal world enter into your fiercely blazing mouths.

11.29

yathā pradīptaṁ jvalanaṁ pataṅgā
viśanti nāśāya samṛddha-vegāḥ
tathaiva nāśāya viśanti lokās
tavāpi vaktrāṇi samṛddha-vegāḥ

As moths race madly to their destruction into a blazing fire, I see all the worlds racing furiously to their destruction into your mouths.

11.30

lelihyase grasamānaḥ samantāl
lokān samagrān vadanair jvaladbhiḥ
tejobhir āpūrya jagat samagraṁ
bhāsas tavogrāḥ pratapanti viṣṇo

Devouring them from all sides, I see you licking up all the worlds into your flaming mouths. O all-pervading Lord, the terrible splendor of your scorching radiance fills the entire universe.

11.31

ākhyāhi me ko bhavān ugra-rūpo
namo 'stu te deva-vara prasīda
vijñātum icchāmi bhavantam ādyaṁ
na hi prajānāmi tava pravṛttim

O Lord of lords, so fierce of form, please tell me who you are. I bow down before you. Please be merciful to me. O primal Lord, I want to understand you, for I do not know what your mission is.

11.32

śrī-bhagavān uvāca
kālo 'smi loka-kṣaya-kṛt pravṛddho
lokān samāhartum iha pravṛttaḥ
ṛte 'pi tvāṁ na bhaviṣyanti sarve
ye 'vasthitāḥ praty-anīkeṣu yodhāḥ

The Blessed Lord said: I am time, the great destroyer of worlds, and I come to consume all. Even if you do nothing, all the warriors arrayed in opposition here will be slain.

11.33

tasmāt tvam uttiṣṭha yaśo labhasva
jitvā śatrūn bhuṅkṣva rājyaṁ samṛddham
mayaivaite nihatāḥ pūrvam eva
nimitta-mātraṁ bhava savya-sācin

Therefore you should rise up, attain glory by the conquest of your enemies, and enjoy a flourishing kingdom. All these men have already been slain by me alone. You, O masterful archer, can be but an instrument.

11.34

droṇaṁ ca bhīṣmaṁ ca jayadrathaṁ ca
karṇaṁ tathānyān api yodha-vīrān
mayā hatāṁs tvaṁ jahi mā vyathiṣṭhā
yudhyasva jetāsi raṇe sapatnān

I have already slain Droṇa and Bhīṣma, as well as Jayadratha and Karṇa and the other great warriors. Therefore, do not hesitate; simply fight, and you will surely conquer your enemies in battle.

11.35

sañjaya uvāca
etac chrutvā vacanaṁ keśavasya
kṛtāñjalir vepamānaḥ kirīṭī
namaskṛtvā bhūya evāha kṛṣṇaṁ
sa-gadgadaṁ bhīta-bhītaḥ praṇamya

Sanjaya said: After hearing the words of Kṛṣṇa, the eradicator of false pride, he whose head was adorned with a symbol of sovereignty trembled and, with hands pressed together in a prayerful fold, bowed down as he spoke, stuttering and terrified, to Kṛṣṇa once again.

11.36

arjuna uvāca
sthāne hṛṣīkeśa tava prakīrtyā
jagat prahṛṣyaty anurajyate ca
rakṣāṁsi bhītāni diśo dravanti
sarve namasyanti ca siddha-saṅghāḥ

Arjuna said: O master of the senses, all the world rightly rejoices upon the display of your glories, which they find delightful. Out of fear, the demonic take flight in all directions while the hosts of perfected beings bow down in adoration.

11.37

kasmāc ca te na nameran mahātman
garīyase brahmaṇo 'py ādi-kartre
ananta deveśa jagan-nivāsa
tvam akṣaraṁ sad-asat tat paraṁ yat

And why should they not bow down to you, O Great Self, who is even greater than Brahmā? You are the original creator. O unlimited God of the gods, O refuge of the whole universe, you are invincible; you are being and non-being and that which is beyond both.

11.38

tvam ādi-devaḥ puruṣaḥ purāṇas
tvam asya viśvasya paraṁ nidhānam
vettāsi vedyaṁ ca paraṁ ca dhāma
tvayā tataṁ viśvam ananta-rūpa

You are the original Divinity, the primal Person, and the ultimate resting place of the whole universe. You are the knower, you are all that is knowable, and you are the supreme abode. O Infinite Form, you pervade this entire universe.

11.39

vāyur yamo 'gnir varuṇaḥ śaśāṅkaḥ
prajāpatis tvaṁ prapitāmahaś ca
namo namas te 'stu sahasra-kṛtvaḥ
punaś ca bhūyo 'pi namo namas te

You are the embodiment of the wind and you are the disciplinarian. You are the personification of fire, the ocean, and the moon. You are the first progenitor and the great grandfather of this universe. I bow to you, offering my respects to you again and again and a thousand times and yet again.

11.40

namaḥ purastād atha pṛṣṭhatas te
namo 'stu te sarvata eva sarva
ananta-vīryāmita-vikramas tvaṁ
sarvaṁ samāpnoṣi tato 'si sarvaḥ

Let me offer my respects to you from the front, from behind, and from all sides. You are unlimited power and unlimited prowess. You complete everything and thus, you truly are everything.

11.41

sakheti matvā prasabhaṁ yad uktaṁ
he kṛṣṇa he yādava he sakheti
ajānatā mahimānaṁ tavedaṁ
mayā pramādāt praṇayena vāpi

Thinking of you as my friend, I have spoken presumptuously to you; "O Kṛṣṇa, O Yādava, O my dear friend" – due to foolishness or out of love, without knowing your majesty.

11.42

yac cāvahāsārtham asat-kṛto 'si
vihāra-śayyāsana-bhojaneṣu
eko 'tha vāpy acyuta tat-samakṣaṁ
tat kṣāmaye tvām aham aprameyam

I have dishonored you in jest as we sported together, rested together, reclined or sat or ate together – alone or even in the midst of others; O immeasurable one, please forgive me for all of these offenses.

11.43

pitāsi lokasya carācarasya
tvam asya pūjyaś ca gurur garīyān
na tvat-samo 'sty abhyadhikaḥ kuto 'nyo
loka-traye 'py apratima-prabhāva

You are the father of the entire world, of the moving and the nonmoving. You are also the most glorious and worshipable spiritual master. How is it possible for anyone within the three worlds to be equal to or greater than You, O Lord of immeasurable power?

11.44

tasmāt praṇamya praṇidhāya kāyaṁ
prasādaye tvām aham īśam īḍyam
piteva putrasya sakheva sakhyuḥ
priyaḥ priyāyārhasi deva soḍhum

Therefore, I fall down before you to offer you my prostrated obeisances and beg for your mercy. O Supreme Lord, as a father forgives the impudence of his son, a friend the presumption of a friend, or a husband the familiarity of his wife, please forgive me with the same loving kindness.

11.45

adṛṣṭa-pūrvaṁ hṛṣito 'smi dṛṣṭvā
bhayena ca pravyathitaṁ mano me
tad eva me darśaya deva rūpaṁ
prasīda deveśa jagan-nivāsa

I am thrilled to have seen this form that has never been seen before. Nevertheless, my mind is filled with fear. Therefore, O Lord of lords within whom all the world resides, please bestow your grace upon me and just let me see your own personal form.

11.46

kirīṭinaṁ gadinaṁ cakra-hastam
icchāmi tvāṁ draṣṭum ahaṁ tathaiva
tenaiva rūpeṇa catur-bhujena
sahasra-bāho bhava viśva-mūrte

O Universal Form, O thousand-armed Lord, I wish to see your four-armed form, wearing a crown and carrying a club and a disc in your hands. Please let me see you in just this way.

11.47

śrī-bhagavān uvāca
mayā prasannena tavārjunedaṁ
rūpaṁ paraṁ darśitam ātma-yogāt
tejo-mayaṁ viśvam anantam ādyaṁ
yan me tvad anyena na dṛṣṭa-pūrvam

The Blessed Lord said: My dear Arjuna, bestowing my grace upon you, I have shown you my supreme cosmic form by the power of my inner mystic yoga. No one before you has ever seen this radiant and infinite Universal Form.

11.48

na veda-yajñādhyayanair na dānair
na ca kriyābhir na tapobhir ugraiḥ
evaṁ-rūpaḥ śakya ahaṁ nṛ-loke
draṣṭuṁ tvad anyena kuru-pravīra

This form of mine cannot be seen in the human realm by reciting the hymns of the Vedas, by performing ritualistic sacrifices, by studious research, by giving charitable gifts, or by executing severe austerities. No one before you has ever seen this form, O most valiant of the Kuru warriors.

11.49

mā te vyathā mā ca vimūḍha-bhāvo
dṛṣṭvā rūpaṁ ghoram īdṛṅ mamedam
vyapeta-bhīḥ prīta-manāḥ punas tvaṁ
tad eva me rūpam idaṁ prapaśya

Do not be afraid; do not be bewildered by the sight of this astounding and horrifying form of mine. Be free from fear and, with a peaceful mind, once again see just my personal form.

11.50

sañjaya uvāca
ity arjunaṁ vāsudevas tathoktvā
svakaṁ rūpaṁ darśayām āsa bhūyaḥ
āśvāsayām āsa ca bhītam enaṁ
bhūtvā punaḥ saumya-vapur mahatma

Sañjaya said: The son of Vasudeva, having thus spoken to Arjuna, displayed his own [four-armed] form as before. That great soul then once again assumed his sublime [two-armed] human-like form, thus calming the fearful Arjuna.

11.51

arjuna uvāca
dṛṣṭvedaṁ mānuṣaṁ rūpaṁ - tava saumyaṁ janārdana
idānīm asmi saṁvṛttaḥ - sa-cetāḥ prakṛtiṁ gataḥ

Arjuna said: O Lord who thrills all beings, now that I see this beautiful human-like form of yours, my mind is settled and my consciousness has been restored to its true nature.

11.52

śrī-bhagavān uvāca
su-durdarśam idaṁ rūpaṁ - dṛṣṭavān asi yan mama
devā apy asya rūpasya - nityaṁ darśana-kāṅkṣiṇaḥ

The Blessed Lord said: this form of mine that you now see before you is very difficult to behold. Even the demigods eternally aspire to see this form.

11.53

nāhaṁ vedair na tapasā - na dānena na cejyayā
śakya evaṁ-vidho draṣṭuṁ - dṛṣṭavān asi māṁ yathā

Neither by study of the Vedas, nor by performing austerities, nor by charitable giving, nor by sacrificial worship can I be seen as you see me.

11.54

bhaktyā tv ananyayā śakya - aham evaṁ-vidho 'rjuna
jñātuṁ draṣṭuṁ ca tattvena - praveṣṭuṁ ca paran-tapa

However, O Arjuna, by pure devotional service alone, one can see and understand the truth about this form of mine. Thus, one attains me, O subduer of enemies.

11.55

mat-karma-kṛn mat-paramo - mad-bhaktaḥ saṅga-varjitaḥ
nirvairaḥ sarva-bhūteṣu - yaḥ sa mām eti pāṇḍava

O son of Pāṇḍu, one whose actions are acts on my behalf, who understands me to be the supreme goal of one's life, who devotes themselves to me, who is free from all material association, and who holds no animosity toward any living being, is one who comes to me.

CHAPTER 12

bhakti-yoga
THE YOGA OF DEVOTIONAL SERVICE

Prelude

Having regained his composure from the overwhelming experience of seeing Kṛṣṇa's Universal Form, Arjuna resumes his series of faith-based questions with an inquiry into the relative merits of personal and impersonal conceptions of the Absolute Truth.

Kṛṣṇa's unambiguous response puts to rest any idea that his personal form is a lower, material representation of a higher, formless and impersonal spiritual reality. This chapter, which closes out the middle section of the Gītā, clearly establishes that perpetual meditation on Kṛṣṇa, in his personal feature, is the ultimate culmination of yogic practice rather than a preliminary step toward merging into an undifferentiated Oneness of being.

Things to look for:

- In verse 4, the statement "they, too, will surely attain me" should not be taken as an indication that those whose goal is to merge into the impersonal feature of the Absolute Truth

(*Brahman*) are on the same level of spiritual advancement as those who focus on entering into a personal relationship of love with Kṛṣṇa. As will be made clear in subsequent verses, Kṛṣṇa regards himself as the ultimate goal of yoga and that those who open their hearts directly to him are already close to him. By contrast, those who approach Kṛṣṇa through the gradual cultivation of detachment from material life (*karma-yoga*), meditation on the Supreme Self residing within their heart (*dhyāna-yoga*), or through study and contemplation of the impersonal feature of the Absolute Truth (*jñāna-yoga*), are taking the scenic route to Kṛṣṇa.

- Verses 8 through 12 offer us reassurance that we can begin from wherever we are and feel confident about our ability to make gradual progress along the path of spiritual awakening.

12.1

arjuna uvāca
evaṁ satata-yuktā ye - bhaktās tvāṁ paryupāsate
ye cāpy akṣaram avyaktaṁ - teṣāṁ ke yoga-vittamāḥ

Arjuna inquired: Whom do you consider to have the most perfect knowledge of yoga: the devotees who are always connected with you through worshipful offerings of love or those who worship the imperishable unmanifest?

12.2

śrī-bhagavān uvāca
mayy āveśya mano ye māṁ - nitya-yuktā upāsate
śraddhayā parayopetās - te me yukta-tamā matāḥ

The Blessed Lord said: I consider those endowed with transcendental faith, who worship me and remain united with me by perpetually directing their minds toward me, to have the most perfect knowledge of yoga.

12.3

ye tv akṣaram anirdeśyam - avyaktaṁ paryupāsate
sarvatra-gam acintyaṁ ca - kūṭa-stham acalaṁ dhruvam

But those who worship the imperishable, ineffable, invisible, omnipresent, inconceivable, unchanging, immovable and unceasing; . . .

12.4

sanniyamyendriya-grāmaṁ - sarvatra sama-buddhayaḥ
te prāpnuvanti mām eva - sarva-bhūta-hite ratāḥ

who bring all the various senses under their control, who are equally disposed to all, and whose actions are intended for the welfare of all beings; they, too, will surely attain me.

12.5

kleśo 'dhika-taras teṣām - avyaktāsakta-cetasām
avyaktā hi gatir duḥkhaṁ - dehavadbhir avāpyate

Those whose minds are attached to the unmanifest face more formidable obstacles. Indeed, such embodied souls proceed through a far higher degree of difficulty along the invisible path to the ultimate goal.

12.6-7

ye tu sarvāṇi karmāṇi - mayi sannyasya mat-parāḥ
ananyenaiva yogena - māṁ dhyāyanta upāsate

teṣām ahaṁ samuddhartā - mṛtyu-saṁsāra-sāgarāt
bhavāmi na cirāt pārtha - mayy āveśita-cetasām

But for those who worship me, who completely release all their activities to me, who are unequivocal in their devotion to me, who worship me and meditate on me, by this practice of yoga alone, O son of Pṛthā, I swiftly lift them from the ocean of repeated birth and death, for their consciousness is absorbed in me.

12.8

mayy eva mana ādhatsva - mayi buddhiṁ niveśaya
nivasiṣyasi mayy eva - ata ūrdhvaṁ na saṁśayaḥ

Fix your mind exclusively on me, invest your intelligence in me; thus you will always dwell in me alone – of this there is no doubt.

12.9

atha cittaṁ samādhātuṁ - na śaknoṣi mayi sthiram
abhyāsa-yogena tato - mām icchāptuṁ dhanañ-jaya

O winner of wealth, if you cannot fix your mind on me without deviation, then develop a desire to attain me through a steady practice of yoga.

12.10

abhyāse 'py asamartho 'si - mat-karma-paramo bhava
mad-artham api karmāṇi - kurvan siddhim avāpsyasi

Even if you are unable to engage in such a practice, just try to become devoted to me through action. By offering your actions to me you will surely achieve perfection.

12.11

athaitad apy aśakto 'si - kartuṁ mad-yogam āśritaḥ
sarva-karma-phala-tyāgaṁ - tataḥ kuru yatātmavān

But if even this is not possible for you, then remain self-situated under the shelter of my yoga and try to relinquish the fruits of your actions.

12.12

śreyo hi jñānam abhyāsāj - jñānād dhyānaṁ viśiṣyate
dhyānāt karma-phala-tyāgas - tyāgāc chāntir anantaram

The cultivation of knowledge is better than the practice [of self-restraint], meditation is better than knowledge, and renunciation of the fruits of action is better than meditation, for by such renunciation one can attain peace of mind forevermore.

12.13-14

adveṣṭā sarva-bhūtānāṁ - maitraḥ karuṇa eva ca
nirmamo nirahaṅkāraḥ - sama-duḥkha-sukhaḥ kṣamī

santuṣṭaḥ satataṁ yogi - yatātmā dṛḍha-niścayaḥ
mayy arpita-mano-buddhir - yo mad-bhaktaḥ sa me priyaḥ

One who is free from envy, who is a kind friend to all living beings, who is not controlled by illusory conceptions of "I" and "mine," who is equipoised in both happiness and distress, who is quick to forgive and who always remains satisfied, who offers service to me with determination and devotion, and whose mind and intelligence are fully invested in me – such a devotee is very dear to me.

12.15

yasmān nodvijate loko - lokān nodvijate ca yaḥ
harṣāmarṣa-bhayodvegair - mukto yaḥ sa ca me priyaḥ

One who neither disturbs the world nor is disturbed by the world, who is free from propensities for jubilation, intolerance, fearfulness, and anxiety, is very dear to me.

12.16

anapekṣaḥ śucir dakṣa - udāsīno gata-vyathaḥ
sarvārambha-parityāgī - yo mad-bhaktaḥ sa me priyaḥ

One who is impartial, pure, skillful, free from anxiety and distress, and who has renounced striving for some result – such a devotee of mine is very dear to me.

12.17

yo na hṛṣyati na dveṣṭi - na śocati na kāṅkṣati
śubhāśubha-parityāgī - bhaktimān yaḥ sa me priyaḥ

One who neither rejoices nor grieves, who neither laments nor desires, and who renounces both pleasant and unpleasant things – such a devotee is very dear to me.

12.18

samaḥ śatrau ca mitre ca - tathā mānāpamānayoḥ
śītoṣṇa-sukha-duḥkheṣu - samaḥ saṅga-vivarjitaḥ

One who is equal to friends and enemies; who is equipoised in honor and dishonor, heat and cold, happiness and distress, fame and infamy; who is always free from mundane association; . . .

12.19

tulya-nindā-stutir maunī - santuṣṭo yena kenacit
aniketaḥ sthira-matir - bhaktimān me priyo naraḥ

who is silent and satisfied with whatever comes of its own accord; who is not attached to any particular place of residence, steady in their intelligence, and always engaged in devotional service to me – such a person is very dear to me.

12.20

ye tu dharmāmṛtam idaṁ - yathoktaṁ paryupāsate
śraddadhānā mat-paramā - bhaktās te 'tīva me priyāḥ

Indeed, those who revere this immortal essence of religious principles that I have spoken and who, with full faith, completely engage themselves in making me the supreme goal of their lives, are deeply loved by me.

CHAPTER 13

prakṛiti-puruṣa-viveka-yoga

THE YOGA OF DIFFERENTIATING MATERIAL NATURE FROM THE SPIRITUAL PERSON

Prelude

In Chapter 12, Kṛṣṇa proposed that the best way to understand transcendental knowledge is from within a devotional context. This was both a fitting conclusion to the middle section of the Gītā, where the focus was on devotional yoga, and a natural segue into this section of the Gītā, where the focus will be on the yoga of knowledge.

Chapter 13 marks the beginning of the third and final major section of the Bhagavad-gītā. From this point forward, Arjuna's desire to gain a deeper understanding of everything that Kṛṣṇa has spoken about will drive the conversation.

This chapter primarily consists of an elaboration on Kṛṣṇa's first instructive verses from Chapter 2 about the difference between matter and spirit.

Things to look for:

- In verses 2 and 3, Kṛṣṇa proposes that there are three "selves":
  1. The temporal bodily self, which includes both the physical body made of the five gross material elements (earth, water, fire, air, and ether) and the metaphysical body made of the three subtle material elements (mind, intelligence, and false ego). Kṛṣṇa will refer to the bodily self as the "field of activity."
  2. The eternal spiritual self, the presence of whom is symptomized by consciousness. Kṛṣṇa will refer to the spiritual self as "the knower of the field."
  3. The Supreme Self; the one person who is present within the hearts of all beings and is thus the knower of all fields. Kṛṣṇa will refer to the Supreme Self as the "knower of the field" in *all* bodies.

  A popular assumption in contemporary spirituality is that we have two selves: a lower self, usually identified with the ego, and a higher self, usually identified as the 'true' self. This assumption is often taken a step further to the notion that there's only one 'true' self and that, on the level of the "true" self, we're all One.

  Here, however, Kṛṣṇa is once again making a clear distinction between himself, as the one being who is uniquely capable of universal consciousness, and all other beings, who are only capable of local consciousness. Kṛṣṇa explicitly reiterates this proposition in verse 23.
- In verse 5, "the aphorisms that encapsulate knowledge of Absolute Reality with conclusive logic" refers to the Vedānta-sūtras, which are a systematic philosophical codification of the Upaniṣads.

- In verse 22, Kṛṣṇa concisely integrates five concepts that were spoken about in more general terms at various times throughout the first section of the Gītā: the eternal spiritual person, the interactions of the three qualities of material nature, the law of karma, the transmigration of the soul, and the spiritual equality of all living beings irrespective of the life form any given living being may inhabit.

13.1

arjuna uvāca
prakṛtiṁ puruṣaṁ caiva - kṣetraṁ kṣetra-jñam eva ca
etad veditum icchāmi - jñānaṁ jñeyaṁ ca keśava

Arjuna said: O Keśava, I wish to understand material nature and the spiritual person, the field of activity and the knower of the field, knowledge and the object of knowledge.

13.2

śrī-bhagavān uvāca
idaṁ śarīraṁ kaunteya - kṣetram ity abhidhīyate
etad yo vetti taṁ prāhuḥ - kṣetra-jña iti tad-vidaḥ

The Blessed Lord said: O son of Kuntī, this body is called the field and those with a complete understanding of this call the one who knows the body "the knower of the field."

13.3

kṣetra-jñaṁ cāpi māṁ viddhi - sarva-kṣetreṣu bhārata
kṣetra-kṣetrajñayor jñānaṁ - yat taj jñānaṁ mataṁ mama

O descendent of Bhārata, understand that I am also the "knower of the field" in *all* bodies. In my opinion, knowledge is the understanding of both this body and its knower.

13.4

tat kṣetraṁ yac ca yādṛk ca - yad-vikāri yataś ca yat
sa ca yo yat-prabhāvaś ca - tat samāsena me śṛṇu

Now hear my summary of what the nature of this field of activity is, what its transformations are and how it originates, who the knower of the field of activities is, and what the powers of the knower are.

13.5

ṛṣibhir bahudhā gītaṁ - chandobhir vividhaiḥ pṛthak
brahma-sūtra-padaiś caiva - hetumadbhir viniścitaiḥ

Sages have sung of this in many ways, in various kinds of sacred hymns, especially in the aphorisms that encapsulate knowledge of Absolute Reality with conclusive logic.

13.6

mahā-bhūtāny ahaṅkāro - buddhir avyaktam eva ca
indriyāṇi daśaikaṁ ca - pañca cendriya-gocarāḥ

The five great elements, the false ego, the intelligence, the unmanifested, the ten senses along with the eleventh [the mind], the five sense objects, . . .

13.7

icchā dveṣaḥ sukhaṁ duḥkhaṁ - saṅghātaś cetanā dhṛtiḥ
etat kṣetraṁ samāsena - sa-vikāram udāhṛtam

desire, aversion, happiness, sorrow, the total sum and substance, consciousness, and constancy – all these are considered, in summary, to be the field of activities and its transformations.

13.8

amānitvam adambhitvam - ahiṁsā kṣāntir ārjavam
ācāryopāsanaṁ śaucaṁ - sthairyam ātma-vinigrahaḥ

Humility, honesty, nonviolence, tolerance, simplicity, honoring one's spiritual teacher, cleanliness, steadiness, self-control, . . .

13.9

indriyārtheṣu vairāgyam - anahaṅkāra eva ca
janma-mṛtyu-jarā-vyādhi- - duḥkha-doṣānudarśanam

detachment from the objects of the senses, the absence of egoism along with an awareness of the suffering associated with birth, death, old age and disease, . . .

13.10

asaktir anabhiṣvaṅgaḥ - putra-dāra-gṛhādiṣu
nityaṁ ca sama-cittatvam - iṣṭāniṣṭopapattiṣu

detachment, freedom from the entanglements of children, a spouse, a home, and the rest, equanimity in both desirable and undesirable situations, . . .

13.11

mayi cānanya-yogena - bhaktir avyabhicāriṇī
vivikta-deśa-sevitvam - aratir jana-saṁsadi

constant and exclusive devotion to me, aspiring to live in a secluded place, disinterest in social gatherings, . . .

13.12

adhyātma-jñāna-nityatvaṁ - tattva-jñānārtha-darśanam
etaj jñānam iti proktam - ajñānaṁ yad ato 'nyathā

consistently prioritizing the pursuit of self-realization and seeing the value of the philosophical search for the Truth – this I declare to be knowledge and all that is contrary to this should be understood to be the absence of knowledge.

13.13

jñeyaṁ yat tat pravakṣyāmi - yaj jñātvāmṛtam aśnute
anādi mat-paraṁ brahma - na sat tan nāsad ucyate

Now I will explain the knowable, knowing which one tastes the nectar of immortality. The beginningless spiritual substratum of existence [*Brahman*], which is subordinate to me, is said to be neither existing nor non-existent, for it lies beyond the cause and effect of this material world.

13.14

sarvataḥ pāṇi-pādaṁ tat - sarvato 'kṣi-śiro-mukham
sarvataḥ śrutimal loke - sarvam āvṛtya tiṣṭhati

With hands and legs everywhere, with eyes, heads and faces everywhere, having ears everywhere in the world, all encompassing, it [Universal Consciousness] is constant.

13.15

sarvendriya-guṇābhāsaṁ - sarvendriya-vivarjitam
asaktaṁ sarva-bhṛc caiva - nirguṇaṁ guṇa-bhoktṛ ca

The original source of all senses yet devoid of all senses, unattached and yet the maintainer of all, free of qualities born of material nature and, at the same time, the master of all the qualities of material nature; . . .

13.16

bahir antaś ca bhūtānām - acaraṁ caram eva ca
sūkṣmatvāt tad avijñeyaṁ - dūra-sthaṁ cāntike ca tat

within all living beings as well as without, moving without moving, too subtle to be seen or known, both distant and yet nearby, . . .

13.17

avibhaktam ca bhutesu - vibhaktam iva ca sthitam
bhuta-bhartr ca taj jneyam - grasisnu prabhavisnu ca

appearing to be divided among all beings yet never divided, the maintainer of all living beings is also to be known as the one who absorbs all living beings and the one who sends all beings forth into being.

13.18

jyotisam api taj jyotis - tamasah param ucyate
jnanam jneyam jnana-gamyam - hrdi sarvasya visthitam

He is also known as the illuminator of luminaries, the source of the light beyond darkness. He is knowledge, the object of knowledge, the goal of knowledge, and is situated in the hearts of all beings.

13.19

iti ksetram tatha jnanam - jneyam coktam samasatah
mad-bhakta etad vijnaya - mad-bhavayopapadyate

I have summarily described the field of activities, knowledge, and the knowable. Only my devotees can realize this and thus attain to my nature.

13.20

prakrtim purusam caiva - viddhy anadi ubhav api
vikarams ca gunams caiva - viddhi prakrti-sambhavan

Know for certain that both material nature and the living beings are beginningless. Their transformations, and those of the qualities [luminance, passion, and darkness], are products of material nature.

13.21

karya-karana-kartrtve - hetuh prakrtir ucyate
purusah sukha-duhkhanam - bhoktrtve hetur ucyate

Material nature is said to be the cause of the creation of the instrument of action [the body] and all subsequent causes and effects, whereas the person within the instrument is said to be the cause of the experience of joy and sorrow.

13.22

puruṣaḥ prakṛti-stho hi - bhuṅkte prakṛti-jān guṇān
kāraṇaṁ guṇa-saṅgo 'sya - sad-asad-yoni-janmasu

A person thus situated in material nature experiences a mode of being born of that nature. Clinging to an identity that arises from the qualities of material nature, one meets with good and evil in the course of taking birth among various species.

13.23

upadraṣṭānumantā ca - bhartā bhoktā maheśvaraḥ
paramātmeti cāpy ukto - dehe 'smin puruṣaḥ paraḥ

There is yet another in this body; the witness, sustainer, and giver of consent, the transcendental enjoyer known as the Supreme Self, who is the Highest Person.

13.24

ya evaṁ vetti puruṣaṁ - prakṛtiṁ ca guṇaiḥ saha
sarvathā vartamāno 'pi - na sa bhūyo 'bhijāyate

One who understands the soul, material nature, and the interactions of the qualities of material nature, will not take birth here again, no matter what their present position may be.

13.25

dhyānenātmani paśyanti - kecid ātmānam ātmanā
anye sāṅkhyena yogena - karma-yogena cāpare

Some see the Supreme Self within themselves by means of meditation, others through the yoga of analytical study, and still others through the yoga of action.

13.26

anye tv evam ajānantaḥ - śrutvānyebhya upāsate
te 'pi cātitaranty eva - mṛtyuṁ śruti-parāyaṇāḥ

Still others, without spiritual knowledge, begin to worship the Supreme Person upon hearing about him from others. They, too, surely transcend the path of death by virtue of their attraction to hearing.

13.27

yāvat sañjāyate kiñcit - sattvaṁ sthāvara-jaṅgamam
kṣetra-kṣetrajña-saṁyogāt - tad viddhi bharatarṣabha

O best of the Bhāratas, know that whatever comes into being, be it moving or nonmoving, exists due to the union of the field of activities with the knower of the field.

13.28

samaṁ sarveṣu bhūteṣu - tiṣṭhantaṁ parameśvaram
vinaśyatsv avinaśyantaṁ - yaḥ paśyati sa paśyati

One who sees the same Supreme Lord residing within all living beings, who sees the imperishable within the perishable, actually sees.

13.29

samaṁ paśyan hi sarvatra - samavasthitam īśvaram
na hinasty ātmanātmānaṁ - tato yāti parāṁ gatim

Indeed, one who sees the same Supreme Lord equally present everywhere does not allow the self to become degraded by the mind. Thus, one approaches the supreme destination.

13.30

prakṛtyaiva ca karmāṇi - kriyamāṇāni sarvaśaḥ
yaḥ paśyati tathātmānam - akartāraṁ sa paśyati

One who sees that all activities are enacted exclusively by material nature, and sees that the self is not the source of such action, actually sees.

13.31

yadā bhūta-pṛthag-bhāvam - eka-stham anupaśyati
tata eva ca vistāraṁ - brahma sampadyate tadā

When one perceives the distinctive states of all beings as abiding in a unity from which all such states emanate, one advances to the experience of Absolute Reality.

13.32

anāditvān nirguṇatvāt - paramātmāyam avyayaḥ
śarīra-stho 'pi kaunteya - na karoti na lipyate

Without beginning and untouched by the qualities of material nature, the imperishable Supersoul dwelling within all bodies neither acts nor is affected by action, O son of Kuntī.

13.33

yathā sarva-gataṁ saukṣmyād - ākāśaṁ nopalipyate
sarvatrāvasthito dehe - tathātmā nopalipyate

Just as all-pervading space does not mix with anything due to its subtle nature, the self does not mix with the body, though situated in that body.

13.34

yathā prakāśayaty ekaḥ - kṛtsnaṁ lokam imaṁ raviḥ
kṣetraṁ kṣetrī tathā kṛtsnaṁ - prakāśayati bhārata

O son of Bhārata, just as the sun alone illuminates the whole world, the soul who resides within the field of activities illuminates the entire field.

13.35

kṣetra-kṣetrajñayor evam - antaraṁ jñāna-cakṣuṣā
bhūta-prakṛti-mokṣaṁ ca - ye vidur yānti te param

Those with eyes of knowledge, who can see the difference between the field and the knower of the field, and who can understand the process of liberation from the influence of material nature, attain the Supreme.

CHAPTER 14

guṇa-traya-vibhāga-yoga

THE YOGA OF SEEING THE THREE QUALITIES OF MATERIAL NATURE

Prelude

In Chapter 13, as in Chapter 2, Kṛṣṇa described how the material body (the "field") is different from the person who experiences the various transformations of the material body (the "knower of the field"). However, this time Kṛṣṇa added a significant piece of information: that there is a singular and categorically different conscious entity, the "imperishable Supersoul dwelling within all bodies" who is "the knower of all fields."

This Supersoul (*Paramātmā*) is none other than Kṛṣṇa himself, as we heard Kṛṣṇa say in Chapter 10 (verses 11 and 20). We'll hear Kṛṣṇa confirm his identity as the Supersoul again in Chapter 15.

Unlike all other beings, Kṛṣṇa is never under the influence of the three qualities of material nature, as per his statement to this effect in Chapter 7 and Arjuna's concurring opinion in Chapter 11. In Chapter 13 we heard that, unlike Kṛṣṇa, we, the infinitesimal knowers of our own respective fields, are subject to the influence of the three qualities of material nature to the extent that we may be completely controlled by them. Now, in Chapter 14, Kṛṣṇa speaks about the three qualities of material nature in detail.

Things to look for:

- In verse 2, Kṛṣṇa alludes to a qualitative oneness that the self-realized soul shares with him by using the phrase "one can attain the same nature as my own" *(mama sādharmyam āgatāḥ).* It's worth noting that having the same nature as someone isn't the same thing as *being* that someone. A tiny drop of ocean water has the same qualities as the whole ocean but, quantitatively, the drop and the ocean are not the same: the ocean can effortlessly support hundreds of thousands of boats but a drop of ocean water can't support even the smallest of boats. Similarly, the oneness that Kṛṣṇa refers to in this verse is qualitative oneness, not quantitative Oneness.
- In verse 3, the Sanskrit phrase *mahad brahma,* rendered as "the great *Brahman,*" signifies the infinite extension of the foundation of material existence. The foundation of material existence is understood to be the primal principle of divine cosmic femininity. Kṛṣṇa, in his capacity as the masculine aspect of divinity, places the seed of all possible varieties of life forms into the feminine aspect of divinity. The appearance of the feminine aspect of divinity in the form of the foundation of material existence is understood to be a transformation of the feminine aspect of divinity that forms the foundation of spiritual existence. Hence, we have an element of duality in transcendence: Kṛṣṇa's essentially masculine characteristic as the source of all spiritual and material energies and the essentially feminine characteristic of the energies themselves.

  However, it's also understood that Kṛṣṇa is non-dual, meaning that there's no difference between Kṛṣṇa and

Kṛṣṇa's energies. This presents us with an inconceivable synthesis of duality and non-duality: the simultaneous oneness and difference of Kṛṣṇa and Kṛṣṇa's energies.

- In verse 11, the phrase "the gates of the body" refers to the nine points of entrance or egress on a human body: eyes, ears, etc.
- In verse 25, a "mundane endeavor" is any endeavor, from leading a nation to writing poetry to doing the laundry, that isn't intentionally connected to serving a higher, spiritual purpose.
- Arjuna's questions in verse 21, with the exception of the last question, are a reiteration of the same questions he asked in Chapter 2, verse 54. The difference is that now Arjuna is inquiring from a position of faith rather than from a position of doubt. As such, Kṛṣṇa's replies to Arjuna's questions in this chapter differ somewhat from his replies in Chapter 2. Arjuna's last question, in verse 21, will be answered in verse 26.

14.1

śrī-bhagavān uvāca
paraṁ bhūyaḥ pravakṣyāmi - jñānānāṁ jñānam uttamam
yaj jñātvā munayaḥ sarve - parāṁ siddhim ito gatāḥ

The Blessed Lord said: I shall further explain this ultimate knowledge of all knowledge, knowing which all the sages have ascended from this world to the highest perfection.

14.2

idaṁ jñānam upāśritya - mama sādharmyam āgatāḥ
sarge 'pi nopajāyante - pralaye na vyathanti ca

By taking shelter of this knowledge, one can attain the same nature as my own. One so situated does not take birth at the time of creation nor are they disturbed at the time of destruction.

14.3

mama yonir mahad brahma - tasmin garbhaṁ dadhāmy aham
sambhavaḥ sarva-bhūtānāṁ - tato bhavati bhārata

The infinite substratum of my complete material energy is the womb into which I place the cosmic embryo, thus making it possible for all living beings to come into being, O son of Bhārata.

14.4

sarva-yoniṣu kaunteya - mūrtayaḥ sambhavanti yāḥ
tāsāṁ brahma mahad yonir - ahaṁ bīja-pradaḥ pitā

I am the seed-giving father of all forms of life that come into being, irrespective of the womb from which they appear, O son of Kuntī, for they ultimately appear from the great cosmic womb of this material nature.

14.5

sattvaṁ rajas tama iti - guṇāḥ prakṛti-sambhavāḥ
nibadhnanti mahā-bāho - dehe dehinam avyayam

Material nature is composed of three qualities – luminance, passion, and darkness – that bind the eternal living being to modes of material embodiment, O mighty-armed Arjuna.

14.6

tatra sattvaṁ nirmalatvāt - prakāśakam anāmayam
sukha-saṅgena badhnāti - jñāna-saṅgena cānagha

O sinless one, the quality of luminance, being the purest of qualities, is radiant and untainted by afflictions. Those who associate with this quality become bound by an attachment to happiness and knowledge.

14.7

rajo rāgātmakaṁ viddhi - tṛṣṇā-saṅga-samudbhavam
tan nibadhnāti kaunteya - karma-saṅgena dehinam

Attachment to the pursuit of insatiable desires is the expression of the quality of passion, O son of Kuntī, which binds the embodied soul by attachment to action.

14.8

tamas tv ajñāna-jaṁ viddhi - mohanaṁ sarva-dehinām
pramādālasya-nidrābhis - tan nibadhnāti bhārata

O son of Bhārata, know that the quality of darkness, born of the absence of knowledge, is the delusional condition of all embodied beings. By this quality, one becomes bound by attachment to derangement, lethargy, and sleep.

14.9

sattvaṁ sukhe sañjayati - rajaḥ karmaṇi bhārata
jñānam āvṛtya tu tamaḥ - pramāde sañjayaty uta

O son of Bhārata, the quality of luminance binds one to happiness, passion binds one to action that is driven by desires, and darkness, covering one's knowledge, binds one to foolishness.

14.10

rajas tamaś cābhibhūya - sattvaṁ bhavati bhārata
rajaḥ sattvaṁ tamaś caiva - tamaḥ sattvaṁ rajas tathā

O son of Bhārata, sometimes the quality of luminance prevails, subduing the qualities of passion and darkness. Similarly, passion becomes prominent when it prevails over luminance and darkness becomes prominent when it prevails over luminance and passion.

14.11

sarva-dvāreṣu dehe 'smin - prakāśa upajāyate
jñānaṁ yadā tadā vidyād - vivṛddhaṁ sattvam ity uta

It is said that when the quality of luminance prevails, the clear light of knowledge illuminates all the gates of the body.

14.12

lobhaḥ pravṛttir ārambhaḥ - karmaṇām aśamaḥ spṛhā
rajasy etāni jāyante - vivṛddhe bharatarṣabha

Greed, striving with great effort, ambition, stress, and restlessness arise when the quality of passion is ascendant, O chief of the Bhāratas.

14.13

aprakāśo 'pravṛttiś ca - pramādo moha eva ca
tamasy etāni jāyante - vivṛddhe kuru-nandana

Ignorance, inertia, madness, and bewilderment arise when the quality of darkness prevails, O son of Kuru.

14.14

yadā sattve pravṛddhe tu - pralayaṁ yāti deha-bhṛt
tadottama-vidāṁ lokān - amalān pratipadyate

When one leaves their body while influenced by the quality of luminance, they attain the pure world of the great sages.

14.15

rajasi pralayaṁ gatvā - karma-saṅgiṣu jāyate
tathā pralīnas tamasi - mūḍha-yoniṣu jāyate

When one meets death under the influence of the quality of passion, they take birth among those who cling to action driven by desires. And when one dies under the influence of darkness, they take birth from the wombs of the foolish.

14.16

karmaṇaḥ sukṛtasyāhuḥ - sāttvikaṁ nirmalaṁ phalam
rajasas tu phalaṁ duḥkham - ajñānaṁ tamasaḥ phalam

It is said that the fruit of righteous action is pure, being comprised of the mode of luminance. The fruit of action performed in the mode of passion, however, is misery, and the fruit of action performed in the mode of darkness results in the disappearance of knowledge.

14.17

sattvāt sañjāyate jñānaṁ - rajaso lobha eva ca
pramāda-mohau tamaso - bhavato 'jñānam eva ca

Knowledge arises from luminance, greed arises from passion, and madness, delusion, and the disappearance of knowledge arise from darkness.

14.18

ūrdhvaṁ gacchanti sattva-sthā - madhye tiṣṭhanti rājasāḥ
jaghanya-guṇa-vṛtti-sthā - adho gacchanti tāmasāḥ

Those who are situated in luminance ascend to higher states of being, those who are situated in passion remain in the middle, and those who are situated in the mode of darkness descend to lower states of being.

14.19

nānyaṁ guṇebhyaḥ kartāraṁ - yadā draṣṭānupaśyati
guṇebhyaś ca paraṁ vetti - mad-bhāvaṁ so 'dhigacchati

One who sees no agent of action other than these qualities, and sees that which transcends these qualities, attains my state of being.

14.20

guṇān etān atītya trīn - dehī deha-samudbhavān
janma-mṛtyu-jarā-duḥkhair - vimukto 'mṛtam aśnute

When the embodied soul transcends these three qualities, which are associated with the material body, they become free from birth, death, old age and suffering, for they have attained the nectar of immortality.

14.21

arjuna uvāca
kair liṅgais trīn guṇān etān - atīto bhavati prabho
kim-ācāraḥ kathaṁ caitāṁs - trīn guṇān ativartate

Arjuna said: My dear Lord, what are the characteristics that define those who have transcended these three modes? How do they conduct themselves? And how does one transcend these three modes of nature?

14.22

śrī-bhagavān uvāca
prakāśaṁ ca pravṛttiṁ ca - moham eva ca pāṇḍava
na dveṣṭi sampravṛttāni - na nivṛttāni kāṅkṣati

The Blessed Lord said: O son of Pāṇḍu, one who feels no hatred for illumination, attachment, and delusion when they appear nor longs for them when they disappear; . . .

14.23

udāsīna-vad āsīno - guṇair yo na vicālyate
guṇā vartanta ity evaṁ - yo 'vatiṣṭhati neṅgate

who is situated as if at a distance, undisturbed by these qualities; who knows that it is these qualities alone that are active; who proceeds without wavering and remains unperturbed; . . .

14.24

sama-duḥkha-sukhaḥ sva-sthaḥ - sama-loṣṭāśma-kāñcanaḥ
tulya-priyāpriyo dhīras - tulya-nindātma-saṁstutiḥ

who is equally disposed toward joy and sorrow and, being satisfied by an awareness of their own true self, sees a clump of earth, a stone, and gold as if they were the same; who is equipoised in desirable and undesirable circumstances; who is unmoved by either commendation or denunciation; . . .

14.25

mānāpamānayos tulyas - tulyo mitrāri-pakṣayoḥ
sarvārambha-parityāgī - guṇātītaḥ sa ucyate

who regards honor and dishonor as the same; who treats friend and foe alike; and who renounces all mundane endeavors – such a person is said to have transcended the qualities of material nature.

14.26

māṁ ca yo 'vyabhicāreṇa - bhakti-yogena sevate
sa guṇān samatītyaitān - brahma-bhūyāya kalpate

And one who renders undeviating service to me by means of devotional yoga transcends these modes of material nature and rises to the realization of Ultimate Reality.

14.27

brahmaṇo hi pratiṣṭhāham - amṛtasyāvyayasya ca
śāśvatasya ca dharmasya - sukhasyaikāntikasya ca

Indeed, I am the foundation of Ultimate Reality, of everlasting righteousness, and of happiness that is beyond compare.

CHAPTER 15

puruṣottama-yoga
THE YOGA OF THE SUPREME PERSON

Prelude

In Chapter 15, Kṛṣṇa gives Arjuna further examples of how he can be seen in or associated with elements and experiences in the material world. In so doing, Kṛṣṇa reiterates and expands on the concepts that he spoke about in the previous two chapters as well as those he spoke about in Chapter 10.

Things to look for:

- Verse 1 is a clear example of when a metaphorical rather than a literal understanding is intended. Here, Kṛṣṇa is using an upside-down banyan tree as a metaphor to illustrate how the illusory material world is situated in relationship to the spiritual world and how the Vedas are like a manual for learning the ins and outs of the material world's operating system. The metaphorical tree itself is variously understood as either a banyan tree, a fig tree, or a "Cosmic Tree."

- Also in verse 1, the Sanskrit word *aśvatthaṁ*, rendered as "banyan tree," can also be grammatically deconstructed in such a way as to mean "that which won't exist tomorrow." In other words, while material nature is an eternal feature of reality, as indicated by the Sanskrit word *avyayam*, everything *in* the material world is temporary. Hence, *aśvatthaṁ* can be colloquially understood to mean something that's "here today, gone tomorrow."
- In verse 8, the Sanskrit word *īśvaraḥ*, with a lower case *ī*, is used here to indicate the infinitesimal individual "knower of the field" as opposed to the infinite universal "knower of all fields," and is therefore rendered as "the lord of the material body" with a lower case *l*. This is in juxtaposition to the usual use of the word *Īśvaraḥ* with a capital *Ī*, indicating the Supreme Lord.
- In verse 15, the Sanskrit word *vedānta* means "the end of knowledge" and refers to the ultimate conclusion of the Upaniṣadṣ. The Vedānta-sūtra, also known as the Brahma-sūtra, is a systematic summary of philosophical conclusions found in the Upaniṣads. Vyāsa, the sage traditionally credited with authorship of the Vedānta-sūtra, is considered to be the "literary incarnation" of Viṣṇu or Kṛṣṇa.

15.1

śrī-bhagavān uvāca
ūrdhva-mūlam adhaḥ-śākham - aśvatthaṁ prāhur avyayam
chandāṁsi yasya parṇāni - yas taṁ veda sa veda-vit

The Blessed Lord said: They say that there is an imperishable banyan tree with roots that reach upward and branches reaching down and whose leaves are the Vedic hymns. The knower of this tree is a knower of the Vedas.

15.2

adhaś cordhvaṁ prasṛtās tasya śākhā
guṇa-pravṛddhā viṣaya-pravālāḥ
adhaś ca mūlāny anusantatāni
karmānubandhīni manuṣya-loke

Extending both downward and upward, the branches of this tree are nourished by the three qualities of material nature. Its fresh shoots are the objects of the senses. Its roots, bound to actions, reach downward into the realm of human beings.

15.3

na rūpam asyeha tathopalabhyate
nānto na cādir na ca sampratiṣṭhā
aśvattham enaṁ su-virūḍha-mūlam
asaṅga-śastreṇa dṛḍhena chittvā

The true form of this tree is imperceptible from within this world; no one can understand where it ends, where it begins, or where its foundation is. One must cut down this firmly rooted banyan tree with the mighty weapon of detachment.

15.4

tataḥ padaṁ tat parimārgitavyaṁ
yasmin gatā na nivartanti bhūyaḥ
tam eva cādyaṁ puruṣaṁ prapadye
yataḥ pravṛttiḥ prasṛtā purāṇī

Then one must search for that place from which, having gone, one never returns, and there proclaim, "I surrender myself exclusively to the Original Person from whom the perpetual cycles of coming into being has proceeded since time immemorial."

15.5

nirmāna-mohā jita-saṅga-doṣā
adhyātma-nityā vinivṛtta-kāmāḥ
vandvair vimuktāḥ sukha-duḥkha-saṁjñair
gacchanty amūḍhāḥ padam avyayaṁ tat

Free from vanity, confusion, and the flaw of attraction to degrading association, those who know the eternal spiritual nature of the self, who have turned away from material desires, who are liberated from the dualities of joy and sorrow, they, unbewildered, attain that eternal abode.

15.6

na tad bhāsayate sūryo - na śaśāṅko na pāvakaḥ
yad gatvā na nivartante - tad dhāma paramaṁ mama

Neither the sun, nor the moon, nor electrical radiance illuminates my supreme domain. Those who go there never return.

15.7

mamaivāṁśo jīva-loke - jīva-bhūtaḥ sanātanaḥ
manaḥ-ṣaṣṭhānīndriyāṇi - prakṛti-sthāni karṣati

The living beings in this world of conditioned life are eternal fragments of my very Self. Drawn to the senses, the sixth of which is the mind, they are set in material nature.

15.8

śarīraṁ yad avāpnoti - yac cāpy utkrāmatīśvaraḥ
gṛhītvaitāni saṁyāti - vāyur gandhān ivāśayāt

Acquiring and relinquishing bodies, the lord of the material body carries different conceptions of life from one body to another just as the wind carries different aromas from their sources.

15.9

śrotraṁ cakṣuḥ sparśanaṁ ca - rasanaṁ ghrāṇam eva ca
adhiṣṭhāya manaś cāyaṁ - viṣayān upasevate

Thus, the living being obtains a certain type of hearing, seeing, tasting, smelling, sense of touch, and state of mind through which to pursue the objects of the senses.

15.10

utkrāmantaṁ sthitaṁ vāpi - bhuñjānaṁ vā guṇānvitam
vimūḍhā nānupaśyanti - paśyanti jñāna-cakṣuṣaḥ

Those who are foolish or confused cannot understand how a living being relinquishes their body nor can they understand what sort of body they will acquire due to the influence of material nature; those who see through eyes of knowledge can see all of this.

15.11

yatanto yoginaś cainaṁ - paśyanty ātmany avasthitam
yatanto 'py akṛtātmāno - nainaṁ paśyanty acetasaḥ

Endeavoring transcendentalists see the Self situated within the self. Those whose minds have not developed to the point of self-realization, being unaware, cannot see this, though they may try.

15.12

yad āditya-gataṁ tejo - jagad bhāsayate 'khilam
yac candramasi yac cāgnau - tat tejo viddhi māmakam

Know that the splendor of the sunshine, which illuminates this whole world, as well as the splendor of the moon and the splendor of fire, come from me.

15.13

gām āviśya ca bhūtāni - dhārayāmy aham ojasā
puṣṇāmi cauṣadhīḥ sarvāḥ - somo bhūtvā rasātmakaḥ

I enter into each planet and sustain all living beings. By my energy, the moon supplies the juice of life to all vegetation.

15.14

ahaṁ vaiśvānaro bhūtvā - prāṇināṁ deham āśritaḥ
prāṇāpāna-samāyuktaḥ - pacāmy annaṁ catur-vidham

I am the fire of digestion within the bodies of all living beings, and I am situated within the outflowing and inflowing air of life to balance the digestion of the four kinds of foodstuff.

15.15

sarvasya cāhaṁ hṛdi sanniviṣṭo
mattaḥ smṛtir jñānam apohanaṁ ca
vedaiś ca sarvair aham eva vedyo
vedānta-kṛd veda-vid eva cāham

I am seated deep within everyone's heart and from me come remembrance, knowledge and forgetfulness. By all the Vedas, I alone am to be known. Indeed, I am the author of Vedānta and I alone truly know the Vedas.

15.16

dvāv imau puruṣau loke - kṣaraś cākṣara eva ca
kṣaraḥ sarvāṇi bhūtāni - kūṭa-stho 'kṣara ucyate

There are two classes of beings: the mutable and the imperishable. All living beings in this world are mutable; those who are spiritually situated are imperishable.

15.17

uttamaḥ puruṣas tv anyaḥ - paramātmety udāhṛtaḥ
yo loka-trayam āviśya - bibharty avyaya īśvaraḥ

There is yet another, the Ultimate Person, the Supreme Self, who enters and maintains this three-fold universe as the inexhaustible Lord.

15.18

yasmāt kṣaram atīto 'ham - akṣarād api cottamaḥ
ato 'smi loke vede ca - prathitaḥ puruṣottamaḥ

Because I am transcendental, beyond both the mutable and the imperishable, I am celebrated in both the world and in the Vedas as the Supreme Person.

15.19

yo mām evam asammūḍho - jānāti puruṣottamam
sa sarva-vid bhajati māṁ - sarva-bhāvena bhārata

One who is unbewildered knows me as the Supreme Person. Thus, they are the knower of everything and they offer their devotion to me with the fullness of their being, O son of Bhārata.

15.20

iti guhya-tamaṁ śāstram - idam uktaṁ mayānagha
etad buddhvā buddhimān syāt - kṛta-kṛtyaś ca bhārata

I have now disclosed to you the greatest secret of the revealed scriptures, O sinless one. Wisdom arises in those who understand this, and their actions will be completely perfect.

CHAPTER 16

daivāsura-sampada-yoga

THE YOGA OF DISTINGUISHING BETWEEN DIVINE AND DEMONIC NATURES

Prelude

In the previous chapter, Kṛṣṇa used the metaphor of an indestructible banyan tree to illustrate the inestimable complexity of the material world. He also highlighted the value of attaining freedom from material attachments and once again differentiated himself from all other beings.

Kṛṣṇa begins Chapter 16 by describing the characteristics of people who populate the upper and lower branches of the metaphorical tree he described in Chapter 15, with emphasis given to those who, by virtue of their absorption in the qualities of passion and darkness, become entangled in the lower branches.

It's worth noting that much of what Kṛṣṇa characterizes as "demonic" in this chapter is so common in the modern world that many people would consider these attitudes and behaviors normal or even admirable; further testimony to just how different the Gītā's values are from those of a contemporary materialistic worldview.

Things to look for:

- Kṛṣṇa lists twenty-six qualities of saintly people in verses 1 through 3 and six qualities of demonic people in verse 4. Then, in verse 5, Kṛṣṇa uses the Sanskrit word *abhijātaḥ* to assure Arjuna that he was born with saintly qualities.

  Kṛṣṇa's statement about the nature of Arjuna's birth should not be taken as support for the idea of predestination in the matter of salvation or damnation. On the contrary, Kṛṣṇa has made it abundantly clear in previous chapters, and will indicate again in verses 21 through 24 of this chapter, that anyone who endeavors to relinquish the impetus to demonic behavior and takes shelter of him is eligible for elevation to the highest level of spiritual consciousness.

- The arguments against fighting that Arjuna put forward in Chapter 1 were based on his understanding of scriptural injunctions. In Chapter 2, Kṛṣṇa dismissed the scriptural injunctions Arjuna was basing his arguments on as "flowery language" that he shouldn't get caught up in.

  At the conclusion of this chapter, however, Kṛṣṇa will appear to contradict his previous statements about the value of scripture by emphatically advocating for deference to scripture as a guide to understanding what should or should not be done.

  The explanation for how Kṛṣṇa can both reject and defend scriptural injunctions is that there are two kinds of scriptural injunctions. The kind of scriptural injunctions that Kṛṣṇa rejected earlier in the Gītā were "scriptural solicitations" for temporary material benedictions of little or no lasting value. The kind of scriptural injunctions that Kṛṣṇa will defend in this chapter are those that provide guidance on how to act in "the true self's best interest."

16.1

śrī-bhagavān uvāca
abhayaṁ sattva-saṁśuddhir - jñāna-yoga-vyavasthitiḥ
dānaṁ damaś ca yajñaś ca - svādhyāyas tapa ārjavam

The Blessed Lord said: Fearlessness, purity of body and mind, and persistence in the pursuit of spiritual knowledge; acts of generosity, self-control, sacrifice, introspection guided by scriptural study, austerity, and sincerity; . . .

16.2

ahiṁsā satyam akrodhas - tyāgaḥ śāntir apaiśunam
dayā bhūteṣv aloluptvaṁ - mārdavaṁ hrīr acāpalam

nonviolence, truthfulness, freedom from anger, renunciation, tranquility, being disinclined to find faults in others, having compassion for all beings, freedom from greed, gentleness, modesty, stability, . . .

16.3

tejaḥ kṣamā dhṛtiḥ śaucam - adroho nāti-mānitā
bhavanti sampadaṁ daivīm - abhijātasya bhārata

vitality, leniency, tenacity, cleanliness, freedom from envy and the desire for honor – O son of Bhārata, these are the characteristics of one who is endowed with a godly nature.

16.4

dambho darpo 'bhimānaś ca - krodhaḥ pāruṣyam eva ca
ajñānaṁ cābhijātasya - pārtha sampadam āsurīm

Duplicity, arrogance, conceit, anger, cruelty, and ignorance – these are the characteristics of one who is endowed with a demonic nature, O son of Pṛthā.

16.5

daivī sampad vimokṣāya - nibandhāyāsurī matā
mā śucaḥ sampadaṁ daivīm - abhijāto 'si pāṇḍava

The divine characteristics move one toward liberation whereas the demonic characteristics are understood to move one toward bondage. Have no fear, O son of Pāṇḍu, for your birth has endowed you with divine assets.

16.6

dvau bhūta-sargau loke 'smin - daiva āsura eva ca
daivo vistaraśaḥ prokta - āsuraṁ pārtha me śṛṇu

There are two kinds of created beings in this world: divine and demonic. I have already spoken at great length about the divine. Now, O son of Pṛthā, hear from me about the demonic.

16.7

pravṛttiṁ ca nivṛttiṁ ca - janā na vidur āsurāḥ
na śaucaṁ nāpi cācāro - na satyaṁ teṣu vidyate

People of an ungodly nature do not know what should be done nor what should not be done. Neither cleanliness nor proper behavior nor truth is to be found in them.

16.8

asatyam apratiṣṭhaṁ te - jagad āhur anīśvaram
aparaspara-sambhūtaṁ - kim anyat kāma-haitukam

They say that the world has no truth, no foundation, no Lord in control; that there is no cause other than the interactions of selfish desires.

16.9

etāṁ dṛṣṭim avaṣṭabhya - naṣṭātmāno 'lpa-buddhayaḥ
prabhavanty ugra-karmāṇaḥ - kṣayāya jagato 'hitāḥ

Committed to this vision, such lost and malevolent souls, possessing stunted intelligence, engage in horrible deeds that bring about the world's destruction.

16.10

kāmam āśritya duṣpūraṁ - dambha-māna-madānvitāḥ
mohād gṛhītvāsad-grāhān - pravartante 'śuci-vratāḥ

Clinging to insatiable desires, vanity, and arrogance, the demonic, attracted by the impermanent and deluded by illusion, affirm their commitment to impure actions.

16.11

cintām aparimeyāṁ ca - pralayāntām upāśritāḥ
kāmopabhoga-paramā - etāvad iti niścitāḥ

Convinced that the gratification of selfish desires is the highest goal of life, they are afflicted by immeasurable anxieties that persist until the point of death.

16.12

āśā-pāśa-śatair baddhāḥ - kāma-krodha-parāyaṇāḥ
īhante kāma-bhogārtham - anyāyenārtha-sañcayān

Bound by a hundred chains of hope and propelled by a mentality filled with lust and anger, they strive unjustly to secure wealth for the gratification of their selfish desires.

16.13

idam adya mayā labdham - imaṁ prāpsye manoratham
idam astīdam api me - bhaviṣyati punar dhanam

"I have acquired this today and I shall fulfill my desire to acquire that tomorrow. This wealth is mine and more wealth will be mine in the future."

16.14

asau mayā hataḥ śatrur - haniṣye cāparān api
īśvaro 'ham ahaṁ bhogī - siddho 'haṁ balavān sukhī

"I have killed my enemy and I will kill my other enemies as well. I am in control of everything. I am the enjoyer. I am perfect, powerful and happy."

16.15

āḍhyo 'bhijanavān asmi - ko 'nyo 'sti sadṛśo mayā
yakṣye dāsyāmi modiṣya - ity ajñāna-vimohitāḥ

"I am wealthy and aristocratic. Who else compares with me? I shall perform sacrifices, give charitable gifts, and celebrate," say those who are deluded by ignorance.

16.16

aneka-citta-vibhrāntā - moha-jāla-samāvṛtāḥ
prasaktāḥ kāma-bhogeṣu - patanti narake 'śucau

Swept away by a multitude of such thoughts, entangled in a net of illusions, clinging to the idea of enjoying the objects of their desire, they plummet into a befouled state of misery.

16.17

ātma-sambhāvitāḥ stabdhā - dhana-māna-madānvitāḥ
yajante nāma-yajñais te - dambhenāvidhi-pūrvakam

Self-absorbed, stubborn, filled with pride and the arrogance of wealth, their sacrificial performances are suffused with hypocrisy, without regard for established codes of proper conduct.

16.18

ahaṅkāraṁ balaṁ darpaṁ - kāmaṁ krodhaṁ ca saṁśritāḥ
mām ātma-para-deheṣu - pradviṣanto 'bhyasūyakāḥ

Thinking "I am making things happen" and seeking shelter in their own power, pride, lust, and anger, such envious people despise me, the one who resides within their own bodies and in the bodies of others.

16.19

tān ahaṁ dviṣataḥ krūrān - saṁsāreṣu narādhamān
kṣipāmy ajasram aśubhān - āsurīṣv eva yoniṣu

Hate-filled, cruel, the lowest of humanity; again and again I hurl such people, who are bound to the cycle of transmigration, into the wombs of the ungodly.

16.20

āsurīṁ yonim āpannā - mūḍhā janmani janmani
mām aprāpyaiva kaunteya - tato yānty adhamāṁ gatim

Taking birth after birth from demonic wombs without ever attaining me, such fools surely go to the lowest destination.

16.21

tri-vidhaṁ narakasyedaṁ - dvāraṁ nāśanam ātmanaḥ
kāmaḥ krodhas tathā lobhas - tasmād etat trayaṁ tyajet

The three-fold gateway into this soul-destroying hell consists of lust, anger, and greed. Therefore, one should relinquish these three.

16.22

etair vimuktaḥ kaunteya - tamo-dvārais tribhir naraḥ
ācaraty ātmanaḥ śreyas - tato yāti parāṁ gatim

Upon attaining complete freedom from these three gates of darkness, O son of Kuntī, one acts in the true self's best interest. Thus one proceeds to the supreme destination.

16.23

yaḥ śāstra-vidhim utsṛjya - vartate kāma-kārataḥ
na sa siddhim avāpnoti - na sukhaṁ na parāṁ gatim

One who disregards scriptural injunctions and acts according to their own selfish desires attains neither perfection, nor happiness, nor the supreme destination.

16.24

tasmāc chāstraṁ pramāṇaṁ te - kāryākārya-vyavasthitau
jñātvā śāstra-vidhānoktaṁ - karma kartum ihārhasi

Therefore, let scripture be your evidence in determining what you should do and what you should not do. Knowing such scriptural injunctions, you should engage with the world accordingly.

CHAPTER 17

śraddha-traya-vibhāga-yoga

THE YOGA OF UNDERSTANDING THE THREEFOLD DIVISIONS OF FAITH

Prelude

At the end of Chapter 16, Kṛṣṇa's encouraging statements about our potential to rise above demonic inclinations came with the stipulation that any such aspiration should be guided by scriptural education. Now, in Chapter 17, Arjuna inquires about the position of those who seek to elevate their consciousness without taking guidance from an authoritative source of spiritual knowledge.

In the course of replying to Arjuna's inquiry, Kṛṣṇa demonstrates how analysis informed by knowledge about how the three qualities of material nature influence thinking and behavior provides us with a structured approach to critical thinking about the nature of the world and everyone in it. Of particular interest in this chapter is how analyzing different forms of faith in terms of the three qualities compares with the popular notion that all expressions of faith ultimately point to the same Truth or lead to the same destination.

In this connection, two previous verses are particularly noteworthy: in Chapter 4, verse 11, Kṛṣṇa said that however one approaches him, he will "respond accordingly" and in Chapter 7, verse 21, Kṛṣṇa said that he provides "the conviction required for faithful worship of whatever conception of divinity" someone chooses.

It's reasonable to conclude from these two statements that Kṛṣṇa responds to someone who wishes to distance themselves from him by providing them with conviction in a form of faith that will create the distance they seek, even if alienation from divinity is the result.

We can further conclude that Kṛṣṇa's invitation to engage in a personal relationship with him is being offered on the level of acknowledging our free will rather than on the level of predestination or as a "do it or else" commandment.

Things to look for:

- In verse 14, "the twice born" (*dvija*) refers to people who, under qualified guidance, have undergone a process that both awakens one's knowledge of their spiritual nature and subdues reactions to any unrighteous actions they may have performed in the past. This process is signified by a formal initiation, which includes the reception of sacred mantras from one's preceptor. The purpose of this initiation is to begin the process of changing one's sense of identity, from material to spiritual, and is therefore understood to be akin to a second birth; the first being one's physical birth and the second being one's "spiritual" birth. In Vedic society, such "twice born" people are known as *brāhmaṇas* or, more commonly, Brahmins. It's worth remembering that Kṛṣṇa previously indicated in Chapter 4, verse 13, that a person's social position, as a *brāhmaṇa* or otherwise, is determined by "the qualities people acquire and the actions they perform," not by birth.

- In verses 23 through 27, Kṛṣṇa will propose that consecrating our actions with an invocation of transcendental sound is an effective affirmation of our spiritual intentions. The idea that language can have a spiritual character, an associated spiritual purpose, and an uplifting spiritual effect was introduced in Chapter 8, verse 11, with the word *akṣaraṁ* (indicating the syllable *oṁ*), contextualized in Chapter 9, verse 14, with the words *satataṁ kīrtayanto mām* – "always glorifying me," and amplified in Chapter 10, verse 9, with the words *bodhayantaḥ parasparam - kathayantaś ca māṁ nityaṁ - tuṣyanti ca ramanti ca* – "those who are devoted to me experience complete satisfaction and transcendental bliss by continually enlightening one another and speaking about me."

17.1

arjuna uvāca
ye śāstra-vidhim utsṛjya - yajante śraddhayānvitāḥ
teṣāṁ niṣṭhā tu kā kṛṣṇa - sattvam āho rajas tamaḥ

Arjuna said: O Kṛṣṇa, what is the position of those whose worship is endowed with faith but who do not follow the authoritative principles of scripture? Are they situated in luminance, in passion, or in darkness?

17.2

śrī-bhagavān uvāca
tri-vidhā bhavati śraddhā - dehināṁ sā svabhāva-jā
sāttvikī rājasī caiva - tāmasī ceti tāṁ śṛṇu

The Blessed Lord said: Three kinds of faith arise in an embodied soul according their state of being: the state of luminance, the state of passion, or the state of darkness. Now hear from me about this.

17.3

sattvānurūpā sarvasya - śraddhā bhavati bhārata
śraddhā-mayo 'yaṁ puruṣo - yo yac-chraddhaḥ sa eva saḥ

Everyone's faith manifests according to where they place their heart. A person is made of their faith; one is whatever one's faith is.

17.4

yajante sāttvikā devān - yakṣa-rakṣāṁsi rājasāḥ
pretān bhūta-gaṇāṁś cānye - yajante tāmasā janāḥ

Those who are influenced by the mode of luminance offer their worship to the demigods; those in the mode of passion make offerings to the demons; and those in the mode of darkness make offerings to nature spirits and hordes of ghosts.

17.5

aśāstra-vihitaṁ ghoraṁ - tapyante ye tapo janāḥ
dambhāhaṅkāra-saṁyuktāḥ - kāma-rāga-balānvitāḥ

Those who perform horrible austerities not prescribed in the scriptures, who are fully invested in hypocrisy and egoism and are forcefully driven by desire and attachment; . . .

17.6

karṣayantaḥ śarīra-sthaṁ - bhūta-grāmam acetasaḥ
māṁ caivāntaḥ śarīra-sthaṁ - tān viddhy āsura-niścayān

who are mindless tormentors of the totality of material elements that constitute the body, and thus of me, who dwells within the body, know them to be of an ungodly disposition.

17.7

āhāras tv api sarvasya - tri-vidho bhavati priyaḥ
yajñas tapas tathā dānaṁ - teṣāṁ bhedam imaṁ śṛṇu

Even culinary tastes differ among people in this three-fold fashion, as do offerings, austerities, and charity. Now hear of these distinctions.

17.8

āyuḥ-sattva-balārogya- - sukha-prīti-vivardhanāḥ
rasyāḥ snigdhāḥ sthirā hṛdyā - āhārāḥ sāttvika-priyāḥ

Foods that expand the duration of one's life, that purify one's existence, and give strength, health, happiness, and satisfaction; that are succulent, flavorful, wholesome, and pleasing are dear to those who are influenced by the quality of luminance.

17.9

kaṭv-amla-lavaṇāty-uṣṇa- - tīkṣṇa-rūkṣa-vidāhinaḥ
āhārā rājasasyeṣṭā - duḥkha-śokāmaya-pradāḥ

Foods that are excessively bitter, sour, salty, hot, pungent, dry, and burning are dear to those who are influenced by the quality of passion. Such foods give rise to distress, misery, and disease.

17.10

yāta-yāmaṁ gata-rasaṁ - pūti paryuṣitaṁ ca yat
ucchiṣṭam api cāmedhyaṁ - bhojanaṁ tāmasa-priyam

Foods that are spoiled, tasteless, rancid, and stale, consisting of rejected remnants and that which is impure are dear to those who are influenced by the quality of darkness.

17.11

aphalākāṅkṣibhir yajño - vidhi-diṣṭo ya ijyate
yaṣṭavyam eveti manaḥ - samādhāya sa sāttvikaḥ

An offering that is made in accordance with scriptural directives by one who is free from the desire to enjoy the fruits of their offering, with full concentration, and the attitude that such offerings are to be performed for their own sake, is an offering in the mode of luminance.

17.12

abhisandhāya tu phalaṁ - dambhārtham api caiva yat
ijyate bharata-śreṣṭha - taṁ yajñaṁ viddhi rajasam

An offering performed as a prideful show of religiosity for the sake of gaining a material benefit, however, should be understood to be an offering in the mode of passion.

17.13

vidhi-hīnam asṛṣṭānnaṁ - mantra-hīnam adakṣiṇam
śraddhā-virahitaṁ yajñaṁ - tāmasaṁ paricakṣate

An offering made without any basis in scriptural directives, with neither the distribution of sanctified food nor the recitation of mystical sounds nor any donations to spiritual leaders, and devoid of faith is understood to be an offering in the mode of darkness.

17.14

deva-dvija-guru-prājña- - pūjanaṁ śaucam ārjavam
brahmacaryam ahiṁsā ca - śārīraṁ tapa ucyate

Honoring divinities, the twice born, the spiritual master, and those who are wise; purity, sincerity, celibacy and nonviolence; these are known as austerities of the body.

17.15

anudvega-karaṁ vākyaṁ - satyaṁ priya-hitaṁ ca yat
svādhyāyābhyasanaṁ caiva - vāṅ-mayaṁ tapa ucyate

Speaking in a manner that is not disturbing, that is truthful, pleasing, and beneficial, as well as the practice of scriptural recitation; these are known as austerities of speech.

17.16

manaḥ-prasādaḥ saumyatvaṁ - maunam ātma-vinigrahaḥ
bhāva-saṁśuddhir ity etat - tapo mānasam ucyate

Serenity of mind, gentleness, silence, self-control, and purity of being; these are known as austerities of the mind.

17.17

śraddhayā parayā taptaṁ - tapas tat tri-vidhaṁ naraiḥ
aphalākāṅkṣibhir yuktaiḥ - sāttvikaṁ paricakṣate

This threefold austerity, when performed by people with the highest faith who are linked to the Supreme and free from the desire for mundane rewards, is said to be in the mode of luminance.

17.18

satkāra-māna-pūjārthaṁ - tapo dambhena caiva yat
kriyate tad iha proktaṁ - rājasaṁ calam adhruvam

Austerity that is performed pretentiously, for the sake of praise, honor, and worship, is said to be in the mode of passion. It is erratic and uncertain.

17.19

mūḍha-grāheṇātmano yat - pīḍayā kriyate tapaḥ
parasyotsādanārthaṁ vā - tat tāmasam udāhṛtam

Austerity that is performed with foolish intentions, comprised of self-inflicted suffering or with the objective of bringing harm to others is said to be in the mode of darkness.

17.20

dātavyam iti yad dānaṁ - dīyate 'nupakāriṇe
deśe kāle ca pātre ca - tad dānaṁ sāttvikaṁ smṛtam

Charity that is given with an attitude of "this is simply the right thing to do," without any expectation of getting something in return, in an appropriate time and place, and to a worthy recipient, is understood to be charity in the mode of luminance.

17.21

yat tu pratyupakārārthaṁ - phalam uddiśya vā punaḥ
dīyate ca parikliṣṭaṁ - tad dānaṁ rājasaṁ smṛtam

But charity that is given reluctantly, with the expectation of getting something in return from the recipient, or with a desire for a reward, is understood to be charity in the mode of passion.

17.22

adeśa-kāle yad dānam - apātrebhyaś ca dīyate
asat-kṛtam avajñātaṁ - tat tāmasam udāhṛtam

And charity that is given at an improper time and place to those who are unworthy, or that is given disrespectfully as an insult, is understood to be charity in the mode of darkness.

17.23

oṁ tat sad iti nirdeśo - brahmaṇas tri-vidhaḥ smṛtaḥ
brāhmaṇās tena vedāś ca - yajñāś ca vihitāḥ purā

The words *oṁ tat sat* are known as the threefold indication of the Absolute Truth. At the dawn of creation, knowers of the Truth, of the Vedas, and of ritualistic sacrifices for the satisfaction of the Supreme were sanctified by these three words.

17.24

tasmād oṁ ity udāhṛtya - yajña-dāna-tapaḥ-kriyāḥ
pravartante vidhānoktāḥ - satataṁ brahma-vādinām

Therefore, expert followers of Vedic principles always begin performances of sacrifice, charity, and penance that are prescribed in authoritative scriptures by invoking the Absolute with the sound *oṁ*.

17.25

tad ity anabhisandhāya - phalaṁ yajña-tapaḥ-kriyāḥ
dāna-kriyāś ca vividhāḥ - kriyante mokṣa-kāṅkṣibhiḥ

Sounding the word *tat*, those who are free from the desire to obtain the results of actions and eager to achieve liberation from material existence perform sacrifices and austerities and offer various kinds of charity.

17.26

sad-bhāve sādhu-bhāve ca - sad ity etat prayujyate
praśaste karmaṇi tathā - sac-chabdaḥ pārtha yujyate

Eternal truth, the seeker of eternal truth, and praiseworthy action are all indicated by the word *sat*, O son of Pṛthā.

17.27

yajñe tapasi dāne ca - sthitiḥ sad iti cocyate
karma caiva tad-arthīyaṁ - sad ity evābhidhīyate

The eternal nature of sacrifice, austerity, and charity, as well as action undertaken in pursuance of eternal truth are also indicated by the word *sat*.

17.28

aśraddhayā hutaṁ dattaṁ - tapas taptaṁ kṛtaṁ ca yat
asad ity ucyate pārtha - na ca tat pretya no iha

O son of Pṛthā, without faith [in the Absolute Truth], any act of sacrifice, charity, or austerity one performs is not what it appears to be. It is understood to be disconnected from that which is eternally true and therefore has no real value either during one's life or after one's death.

CHAPTER 18

mokṣa-yoga

THE YOGA OF LIBERATION

Prelude

At the end of Chapter 17, Kṛṣṇa proposed that the real value of an action is found in the strength of its connection to that which is eternally true. Now, in Chapter 18, Kṛṣṇa summarizes the entirety of his teachings and then makes his closing argument.

This chapter begins with Arjuna's final questions, which are posed as a request for clarification about the purpose of renunciation and the activities of a renunciant. At this point, Arjuna is already convinced that he should fight. His inquiry is therefore about the specific mindset that he should take into the battle and how fighting can be compatible with renunciation.

Things to look for:

- In verse 1, Arjuna, having realized that his illusion arose out of a false sense of identity, addresses Kṛṣṇa once again as "the slayer of false pride." He also addresses Kṛṣṇa as the "master of the senses," an indication that Arjuna is ready to allow his senses to be directed by Kṛṣṇa rather than by his false ego. Finally, Arjuna addresses Kṛṣṇa as "mighty-armed" to indicate his confidence that he will be victorious as a result of becoming an instrument of Kṛṣṇa's will.

- Verses 13 through 16 are a callback to a very significant verse spoken earlier in the text: Chapter 3, verse 27.
- In verse 19, "the science of enumeration" refers to Sāṅkhya philosophy, as indicated by the Sanskrit word *saṅkhyāne*, which was the category of knowledge that Kṛṣṇa began his teachings with in Chapter 2.
- In verse 34, the Sanskrit phrase *dharma-kāmārthān*, rendered as "religiosity, the pursuit of wealth, and the gratification of the senses," refers to acts of material piety performed in accordance with Vedic directives (*dharma*) that are rewarded with material prosperity (*artha*), which provides the means for material pleasure (*kāma*). In previous chapters, Kṛṣṇa has repeatedly indicated that the pursuit of material prosperity and pleasure, even when sought in accordance with Vedic directives, is a lesser form of *dharma* that Arjuna should strive to transcend.
- Verse 47 is especially significant: it's the reiteration of Kṛṣṇa's exhortation in Chapter 3, verse 35, that it is better to fail in the course of performing one's own prescribed duty than to succeed in the performance of a duty that's prescribed for someone else.
- Verses 49 through 56 summarize how the respective perfections of *jñāna-yoga* and *dhyāna-yoga*, though complete within their own contexts, can be extended even further to find their ultimate fulfillment in *bhakti-yoga*.
- Verse 57 marks the beginning of Kṛṣṇa's conclusive instructions.

- In verses 61 through 66, Kṛṣṇa alternates between speaking about himself in the third person as the aspect of himself who is situated within the hearts of all beings and in the first person as the personal form of God who is standing before and speaking directly to Arjuna.
- Verse 65 is the crescendo of Kṛṣṇa's teachings: an encore of the verse that appears at the end of Chapter 9, repeated here verbatim but for the final phrase, which reframes Kṛṣṇa's ultimate instruction as a request coupled with a promise that's motivated by the most confidential secret of all: the contents of Kṛṣṇa's heart.
- Verse 66 is the conclusive exclamation point that emphatically confirms the overarching theme of the Bhagavad-gītā and proclaims the Gītā's ultimate philosophical conclusion.

18.1

arjuna uvāca
sannyāsasya mahā-bāho - tattvam icchāmi veditum
tyāgasya ca hṛṣīkeśa - pṛthak keśi-niṣūdana

Arjuna said: O mighty-armed, I wish to know the truth about the distinction between the renunciation of action and the renunciation of the fruits of action, O master of the senses, slayer of false pride.

18.2

śrī-bhagavān uvāca
kāmyānāṁ karmaṇāṁ nyāsaṁ - sannyāsaṁ kavayo viduḥ
sarva-karma-phala-tyāgaṁ - prāhus tyāgaṁ vicakṣaṇāḥ

The Blessed Lord said: To relinquish activities that arise from material desires is what the wise call the renunciation of action. To relinquish the results of all activities is what the wise call renunciation of the fruits of action.

18.3

tyājyaṁ doṣa-vad ity eke - karma prāhur manīṣiṇaḥ
yajña-dāna-tapaḥ-karma - na tyājyam iti cāpare

Some sages say that action itself is inherently flawed and should therefore be renounced. Others maintain that acts of sacrifice, charity, and austerity should never be forsaken.

18.4

niścayaṁ śṛṇu me tatra - tyāge bharata-sattama
tyāgo hi puruṣa-vyāghra - tri-vidhaḥ samprakīrtitaḥ

O best of the Bhāratas, hear now my conclusive judgment about the renunciation of the fruits of action. O tiger among men, such renunciation is proclaimed to be of three types.

18.5

yajña-dāna-tapaḥ-karma - na tyājyaṁ kāryam eva tat
yajño dānaṁ tapaś caiva - pāvanāni manīṣiṇām

Acts of sacrifice, charity, and austerity are not to be forsaken; indeed, they must be performed, for sacrifice, charity, and austerity surely purify even those who are wise.

18.6

etāny api tu karmāṇi - saṅgaṁ tyaktvā phalāni ca
kartavyānīti me pārtha - niścitaṁ matam uttamam

All these activities should certainly be performed, but without attachment or any desire for result, O son of Pṛthā. This is definitely my ultimate opinion.

18.7

niyatasya tu sannyāsaḥ - karmaṇo nopapadyate
mohāt tasya parityāgas - tāmasaḥ parikīrtitaḥ

Prescribed action should not be renounced. Renunciation of such duties due to the influence of illusion is said to be renunciation in the mode of darkness.

18.8

duḥkham ity eva yat karma - kāya-kleśa-bhayāt tyajet
sa kṛtvā rājasaṁ tyāgaṁ - naiva tyāga-phalaṁ labhet

The renunciation of those who abandon prescribed action on the basis of it being troublesome or due to fear of physical suffering is merely in the mode of passion. Thus, they never obtain the rewards of renunciation.

18.9

kāryam ity eva yat karma - niyataṁ kriyate 'rjuna
saṅgaṁ tyaktvā phalaṁ caiva - sa tyāgaḥ sāttviko mataḥ

O Arjuna, one who performs prescribed actions simply because they ought to be performed, renouncing all attachment to both the action and its fruits, is, in my opinion, acting in the mode of luminance.

18.10

na dveṣṭy akuśalaṁ karma - kuśale nānuṣajjate
tyāgī sattva-samāviṣṭo - medhāvī chinna-saṁśayaḥ

The intelligent renunciate, whose doubts have been severed, who is situated in the mode of luminance, has neither an aversion to disagreeable actions nor any attachment to agreeable actions.

18.11

na hi deha-bhṛtā śakyaṁ - tyaktuṁ karmāṇy aśeṣataḥ
yas tu karma-phala-tyāgī - sa tyāgīty abhidhīyate

To entirely abstain from action is indisputably impossible for those who are embodied. One who renounces the fruits of action, however, is said to be a genuine renunciate.

18.12

niṣṭam iṣṭaṁ miśraṁ ca - tri-vidhaṁ karmaṇaḥ phalam
bhavaty atyāgināṁ pretya - na tu sannyāsināṁ kvacit

Even after death, the threefold fruits of action – desirable, undesirable, and mixed – come to those who are not renounced; those who are renounced experience no such results at any time.

18.13

pañcaitāni mahā-bāho - kāraṇāni nibodha me
sāṅkhye kṛtānte proktāni - siddhaye sarva-karmaṇām

Learn from me, O mighty-armed, about the five factors that the conclusive philosophy of enumeration has declared to be the cause of success in all actions.

18.14

adhiṣṭhānaṁ tathā kartā - karaṇaṁ ca pṛthag-vidham
vividhāś ca pṛthak ceṣṭā - daivaṁ caivātra pañcamam

[They are] the place of action, the actor, the different instruments of action, the various methods of action, and the fifth, the divine will of providence.

18.15

śarīra-vāṅ-manobhir yat - karma prārabhate naraḥ
nyāyyaṁ vā viparītaṁ vā - pañcaite tasya hetavaḥ

These five factors are the cause of whatever right or wrong action a human being performs by means of their body, their speech, or their mind.

18.16

tatraivaṁ sati kartāram - ātmānaṁ kevalaṁ tu yaḥ
paśyaty akṛta-buddhitvān - na sa paśyati durmatiḥ

This being so, one who, due to undeveloped intelligence, foolishly thinks of one's self as the only cause of action does not see things as they truly are.

18.17

yasya nāhaṅkṛto bhāvo - buddhir yasya na lipyate
hatvāpi sa imāl̲ lokān - na hanti na nibadhyate

One whose state of being is not influenced by the false belief that they alone are the cause of action and whose power of reason is untainted neither kills nor is bound by the reactions to their actions even if they were to kill all those who are here.

18.18

jñānaṁ jñeyaṁ parijñātā - tri-vidhā karma-codanā
karaṇaṁ karma karteti - tri-vidhaḥ karma-saṅgrahaḥ

The three driving factors of action are knowledge, the object of knowledge, and the knower. Action itself is also comprised of three factors: the instruments of action, the action, and the performer of action.

18.19

jñānaṁ karma ca kartā ca - tridhaiva guṇa-bhedataḥ
procyate guṇa-saṅkhyāne - yathāvac chṛṇu tāny api

According to the science of enumeration, knowledge, action, and the actor are each said to be of three kinds in terms of the different qualities of material nature. Now hear of these from me as well.

18.20

sarva-bhūteṣu yenaikaṁ - bhāvam avyayam īkṣate
avibhaktaṁ vibhakteṣu - taj jñānaṁ viddhi sāttvikam

That knowledge by which one sees the undivided and imperishable within all living beings, though they be innumerably divided, is known as knowledge in the mode of luminance.

18.21

pṛthaktvena tu yaj jñānaṁ - nānā-bhāvān pṛthag-vidhān
vetti sarveṣu bhūteṣu - taj jñānaṁ viddhi rājasam

That knowledge by which one sees a different type of living being in every different type of body is known as knowledge in the mode of passion.

18.22

yat tu kṛtsna-vad ekasmin - kārye saktam ahaitukam
atattvārtha-vad alpaṁ ca - tat tāmasam udāhṛtam

And that knowledge by which one remains irrationally invested in a singular activity as if it were all-inclusive, that is fixated on the trivial and estranged from reality, is known as knowledge in the mode of darkness.

18.23

niyataṁ saṅga-rahitam - arāga-dveṣataḥ kṛtam
aphala-prepsunā karma - yat tat sāttvikam ucyate

Disciplined action that is performed without attachment, free from attraction or repulsion, and without any desire for the fruits of action, is said to be in the mode of luminance.

18.24

yat tu kāmepsunā karma - sāhaṅkāreṇa vā punaḥ
kriyate bahulāyāsaṁ - tad rājasam udāhṛtam

But action performed with great effort by one whose ego is invested in the pursuit of selfish desires is called action in the mode of passion.

18.25

anubandhaṁ kṣayaṁ hiṁsām - anapekṣya ca pauruṣam
mohād ārabhyate karma - yat tat tāmasam ucyate

Action performed under the influence of illusion, without regard for binding consequences, loss, harm to others, or personal limits, is said to be in the mode of darkness.

18.26

mukta-saṅgo 'nahaṁ-vādī - dhṛty-utsāha-samanvitaḥ
siddhy-asiddhyor nirvikāraḥ - kartā sāttvika ucyate

One who is liberated from material attachments, free from the propensity for self-promotion, fully endowed with determination and enthusiasm, and unwavering in success or failure is said to be an actor in the mode of luminance.

18.27

rāgī karma-phala-prepsur - lubdho hiṁsātmako 'śuciḥ
harṣa-śokānvitaḥ kartā - rājasaḥ parikīrtitaḥ

One who is intensely attached to acquiring the fruits of work, driven by the desire to enjoy those fruits, who is greedy, predisposed to aggression, impure, and who vacillates between joy and sorrow is said to be an actor in the mode of passion.

18.28

ayuktaḥ prākṛtaḥ stabdhaḥ - śaṭho naiṣkṛtiko 'lasaḥ
viṣādī dīrgha-sūtrī ca - kartā tāmasa ucyate

One who is unhinged, vulgar, obstinate, deceitful, and adept at insulting others, who is lazy, morose, and prone to procrastination, is said to be an actor in the mode of darkness.

18.29

buddher bhedaṁ dhṛteś caiva - guṇatas tri-vidhaṁ śṛṇu
procyamānam aśeṣeṇa - pṛthaktvena dhanañ-jaya

Hear now, O winner of wealth, as I comprehensively describe the different kinds of discernment and determination according to the three modes of material nature.

18.30

pravṛttiṁ ca nivṛttiṁ ca - kāryākārye bhayābhaye
bandhaṁ mokṣaṁ ca yā vetti - buddhiḥ sā pārtha sāttvikī

O son of Pṛthā, discernment by which one can distinguish between constructive engagement and disengagement, what should be done and what should not to be done, what is to be feared and what is not to be feared, what is binding and what is liberating, is discernment in the mode of luminance.

18.31

yayā dharmam adharmaṁ ca - kāryaṁ cākāryam eva ca
ayathāvat prajānāti - buddhiḥ sā pārtha rājasī

O son of Pṛthā, discernment by which one cannot correctly distinguish between principles of religion and principles of irreligion, between action that should be taken and action that should not be taken, is discernment in the mode of passion.

18.32

adharmaṁ dharmam iti yā - manyate tamasāvṛtā
sarvārthān viparītāṁś ca - buddhiḥ sā pārtha tāmasī

O son of Pṛthā, discernment by which one considers irreligious principles to be religious principles and religious principles to be irreligious principles, that is encased by a shroud of illusion, and that sees things as the opposite of what they really are, is discernment in the mode of darkness.

18.33

dhṛtyā yayā dhārayate - manaḥ-prāṇendriya-kriyāḥ
yogenāvyabhicāriṇyā - dhṛtiḥ sā pārtha sāttvikī

O son of Pṛthā, that determination by which control of the activities of the mind, the life force, and the senses is sustained by an unwavering yoga practice is determination in the mode of luminance.

18.34

yayā tu dharma-kāmārthān - dhṛtyā dhārayate 'rjuna
prasaṅgena phalākāṅkṣī - dhṛtiḥ sā pārtha rājasī

But determination by which the desire for the fruits of action is sustained by attachment to religiosity, the pursuit of wealth, and the gratification of the senses is determination in the mode of passion, O son of Pṛthā.

18.35

yayā svapnaṁ bhayaṁ śokaṁ - viṣādaṁ madam eva ca
na vimuñcati durmedhā - dhṛtiḥ sā pārtha tāmasī

And determination by which a foolish person cannot relinquish fantasy, fear, lamentation, depression, and illusion; that determination, O son of Pṛthā, is in the mode of darkness.

18.36

sukhaṁ tv idānīṁ tri-vidhaṁ - śṛṇu me bharatarṣabha
abhyāsād ramate yatra - duḥkhāntaṁ ca nigacchati

But now hear from me, O best of the Bhāratas, about the three kinds of happiness by which one experiences enjoyment through regular practice and by which one may also attain the end of all sorrows.

18.37

yat tad agre viṣam iva - pariṇāme 'mṛtopamam
tat sukhaṁ sāttvikaṁ proktam - ātma-buddhi-prasāda-jam

That which feels like poison at the start but tastes like nectar in the end is said to be happiness in the mode of luminance, which arises from the serenity of self-knowledge.

18.38

viṣayendriya-saṁyogād - yat tad agre 'mṛtopamam
pariṇāme viṣam iva - tat sukhaṁ rājasaṁ smṛtam

That which arises from connecting the senses with objects of sensual pleasure, and which tastes like nectar in the beginning but feels like poison in the end, is said to be in the mode of passion.

18.39

yad agre cānubandhe ca - sukhaṁ mohanam ātmanaḥ
nidrālasya-pramādotthaṁ - tat tāmasam udāhṛtam

And that which bewilders the self from beginning to end, which arises from sleep, sloth, and madness, is said to be happiness in the mode of darkness.

18.40

na tad asti pṛthivyāṁ vā - divi deveṣu vā punaḥ
sattvaṁ prakṛti-jair muktaṁ - yad ebhiḥ syāt tribhir guṇaiḥ

There is no being in existence, here on this earth or among the gods in the celestial realm, that is free from the influence of these three qualities, which are born of material nature.

18.41

brāhmaṇa-kṣatriya-viśāṁ - śūdrāṇāṁ ca paran-tapa
karmāṇi pravibhaktāni - svabhāva-prabhavair guṇaiḥ

O scorcher of foes, the activities of spiritually enlightened teachers, rulers and warriors, traders and entrepreneurs, as well as those of skilled workers and artisans, are all distinguished by qualities arising from material nature that appear as their own particular natures.

18.42

śamo damas tapaḥ śaucaṁ - kṣāntir ārjavam eva ca
jñānaṁ vijñānam āstikyaṁ - brahma-karma svabhāva-jam

Tranquility, self-discipline, austerity, purity, patience, integrity, knowledge, wisdom, and faith in the principles of religion are the naturally occurring qualities associated with the work of a spiritually enlightened intellectual [a *brāhmaṇa*].

18.43

śauryaṁ tejo dhṛtir dākṣyaṁ - yuddhe cāpy apalāyanam
dānam īśvara-bhāvaś ca - kṣātraṁ karma svabhāva-jam

Heroism, vitality, determination, resourcefulness, not fleeing from battle, generosity, and leadership are the naturally occurring qualities associated with the work of rulers and warriors [a *kṣatriya*].

18.44

kṛṣi-go-rakṣya-vāṇijyaṁ - vaiśya-karma svabhāva-jam
paricaryātmakaṁ karma - śūdrasyāpi svabhāva-jam

Cultivating fields, protecting cows, and engaging in commerce are the natural work for traders and entrepreneurs [a *vaiśya*], and the natural work of skilled workers and artisans [a *śūdra*] consists of service to others.

18.45

sve sve karmaṇy abhirataḥ - saṁsiddhiṁ labhate naraḥ
sva-karma-nirataḥ siddhiṁ - yathā vindati tac chṛṇu

By dedication to one's own work, one can attain complete perfection. Now please hear how one attains perfection through dedication to one's own work.

18.46

yataḥ pravṛttir bhūtānāṁ - yena sarvam idaṁ tatam
sva-karmaṇā tam abhyarcya - siddhiṁ vindati mānavaḥ

By performing one's own work as an act of worship of the Supreme Lord from whom all living beings emanate and by whom all this is pervaded, a human being attains perfection.

18.47

śreyān sva-dharmo viguṇaḥ - para-dharmāt sv-anuṣṭhitāt
svabhāva-niyataṁ karma - kurvan nāpnoti kilbiṣam

Acting in accordance with your own nature, even when such actions appear riddled with fault, is better than accepting the occupation of another and performing it perfectly. One does not invite misfortune by acting in a manner that corresponds to one's nature.

18.48

saha-jaṁ karma kaunteya - sa-doṣam api na tyajet
sarvārambhā hi doṣeṇa - dhūmenāgnir ivāvṛtāḥ

O son of Kuntī, every endeavor is covered by fault, just as fire is covered by smoke. Therefore, one should not relinquish work born of one's nature, even if such work is riddled with flaws.

18.49

asakta-buddhiḥ sarvatra - jitātmā vigata-spṛhaḥ
naiṣkarmya-siddhiṁ paramāṁ - sannyāsenādhigacchati

One whose intelligence is unattached in all circumstances, who retains control of the mind, and who disregards all material desires, can obtain the highest perfection of freedom from reactions to actions by the practice of renunciation.

18.50

siddhiṁ prāpto yathā brahma - tathāpnoti nibodha me
samāsenaiva kaunteya - niṣṭhā jñānasya yā parā

O son of Kuntī, now learn from me as I summarize how, having attained this perfection, one can attain the highest stage of knowledge; the transcendental state of supreme perfection.

18.51

buddhyā viśuddhayā yukto - dhṛtyātmānaṁ niyamya ca
śabdādīn viṣayāṁs tyaktvā - rāga-dveṣau vyudasya ca

Fixed in yoga with purified intelligence; resolute in self-regulation; letting go of sources of sense enjoyment such as mundane sound and the like; giving up attachments and aversions; . . .

18.52

vivikta-sevī laghv-āśī - yata-vāk-kāya-mānasaḥ
dhyāna-yoga-paro nityaṁ - vairāgyaṁ samupāśritaḥ

living in a secluded place; eating in small quantities; controlling speech, the body, and the mind; perpetually absorbed in the yoga of meditation; having taken shelter of detachment; . . .

18.53

ahaṅkāraṁ balaṁ darpaṁ - kāmaṁ krodhaṁ parigraham
vimucya nirmamaḥ śānto - brahma-bhūyāya kalpate

free from the conception of being "the doer," from aggressive demonstrations of power, from pride, lust, anger, possessiveness, and a false sense of proprietorship; peacefully situated – such a person is qualified to attain the supreme spiritual perfection.

18.54

brahma-bhūtaḥ prasannātmā - na śocati na kāṅkṣati
samaḥ sarveṣu bhūteṣu - mad-bhaktiṁ labhate parām

One who is thus united with Absolute Reality, whose self is serene, who neither despairs nor desires, and who is equally disposed toward all living beings; in that state of being, one attains supreme devotion to me.

18.55

bhaktyā mām abhijānāti - yāvān yaś cāsmi tattvataḥ
tato māṁ tattvato jñātvā - viśate tad-anantaram

By offering one's love to me one can recognize me and know the full measure of who I truly am. Upon knowing me in truth, one immediately returns to me.

18.56

sarva-karmāṇy api sadā - kurvāṇo mad-vyapāśrayaḥ
mat-prasādād avāpnoti - śāśvataṁ padam avyayam

Though continually engaged in all manner of activities, under my protection and by my grace, one attains my eternal and imperishable abode.

18.57

cetasā sarva-karmāṇi - mayi sannyasya mat-paraḥ
buddhi-yogam upāśritya - mac-cittaḥ satataṁ bhava

Thinking of all activities as an offering to me, being completely devoted to me, and taking shelter of spiritual intelligence, always be conscious of me.

18.58

mac-cittaḥ sarva-durgāṇi - mat-prasādāt tariṣyasi
atha cet tvam ahaṅkārān - na śroṣyasi vinaṅkṣyasi

By being conscious of me, you will overcome all obstacles by my grace. If, however, you do not hear me due to thinking of yourself as the cause of action, then you will be lost.

18.59

yad ahaṅkāram āśritya - na yotsya iti manyase
mithyaiṣa vyavasāyas te - prakṛtis tvāṁ niyokṣyati

Seeking shelter within the conception of "I am the doer," you are thinking, "I shall not fight." This is all incorrect: your determination not to fight is in vain because the forces of material nature will compel you to do so.

18.60

svabhāva-jena kaunteya - nibaddhaḥ svena karmaṇā
kartuṁ necchasi yan mohāt - kariṣyasy avaśo 'pi tat

O son of Kuntī, being bound by the mode of action that is born of your nature, you will be compelled, even against your will, to do that which, due to illusion, you wish not to do.

18.61

īśvaraḥ sarva-bhūtānāṁ - hṛd-deśe 'rjuna tiṣṭhati
bhrāmayan sarva-bhūtāni - yantrārūḍhāni māyayā

O Arjuna, the Supreme Lord resides within everyone's heart and directs the wanderings of all living beings, who travel as if riding on a mystical machine that's composed of my illusory material energy.

18.62

tam eva śaraṇaṁ gaccha - sarva-bhāvena bhārata
tat-prasādāt parāṁ śāntiṁ - sthānaṁ prāpsyasi śāśvatam

O descendent of Bhārata, take complete shelter in him alone. By his grace you will attain supreme peace and the eternal abode.

18.63

iti te jñānam ākhyātaṁ - guhyād guhya-taraṁ mayā
vimṛśyaitad aśeṣeṇa - yathecchasi tathā kuru

Thus, I have revealed to you a secret that is even greater than the secrets I described before. Carefully consider everything that I have said and then do as you wish.

18.64

sarva-guhyatamaṁ bhūyaḥ - śṛṇu me paramaṁ vacaḥ
iṣṭo 'si me dṛḍham iti - tato vakṣyāmi te hitam

Hear once more my ultimate message, the greatest of all secrets. Because you are so very dear to me, I am speaking for the sake of your well-being.

18.65

man-manā bhava mad-bhakto - mad-yājī māṁ namaskuru
mām evaiṣyasi satyaṁ te - pratijāne priyo 'si me

Direct your mind toward me, become my devotee, offer your sacrifices to me, and act in reverence for me. Thus, you will surely come to me. I promise you this because you are so very dear to me.

18.66

sarva-dharmān parityajya - mām ekaṁ śaraṇaṁ vraja
ahaṁ tvāṁ sarva-pāpebhyo - mokṣayiṣyāmi mā śucaḥ

Abandon all varieties of religious principles and just come to me alone for shelter. I shall free you from all misfortune. You have no reason to grieve.

18.67

idaṁ te nātapaskāya - nābhaktāya kadācana
na cāśuśrūṣave vācyaṁ - na ca māṁ yo 'bhyasūyati

You should never speak about this [great secret] to those who are undisciplined, nor to those who are not endowed with any devotional inclination, nor to those who have no interest in acting on what they hear, nor to those who are envious of me.

18.68

ya idaṁ paramaṁ guhyaṁ - mad-bhakteṣv abhidhāsyati
bhaktiṁ mayi parāṁ kṛtvā - mām evaiṣyaty asaṁśayaḥ

One who reveals this supreme secret of mine to those who are endowed with devotion will surely come to me, for they are engaged in the greatest offering of love to me.

18.69

na ca tasmān manuṣyeṣu - kaścin me priya-kṛttamaḥ
bhavitā na ca me tasmād - anyaḥ priya-taro bhuvi

No human being is as dear to me as one such as this, nor will there ever be anyone on earth whom I will love so dearly.

18.70

adhyeṣyate ca ya imaṁ - dharmyaṁ saṁvādam āvayoḥ
jñāna-yajñena tenāham - iṣṭaḥ syām iti me matiḥ

And I declare that anyone who studies this sacred conversation of ours concerning the principles of religion engages in loving worship of me by performing a sacrifice composed of knowledge.

18.71

śraddhāvān anasūyaś ca - śṛṇuyād api yo naraḥ
so 'pi muktaḥ śubhāl̲ lokān - prāpnuyāt puṇya-karmaṇām

Even those who simply hear with faith, being free from envy, will also attain liberation and dwell in a world of abundance amongst those whose deeds are pure.

18.72

kaccid etac chrutaṁ pārtha - tvayaikāgreṇa cetasā
kaccid ajñāna-sammohaḥ - praṇaṣṭas te dhanañ-jaya

O son of Pṛthā, conqueror of wealth, have you heard all of this with your mind fixed in one-pointed attention? And has the confusion that arose in you due to the absence of knowledge been completely dispelled?

18.73

arjuna uvāca
naṣṭo mohaḥ smṛtir labdhā - tvat-prasādān mayācyuta
sthito 'smi gata-sandehaḥ - kariṣye vacanaṁ tava

Arjuna said: By your grace, O infallible Kṛṣṇa, my illusion has been dispelled and my memory has been restored. I now stand firm, free from doubt, and will act according to your words.

18.74

sañjaya uvāca
ity ahaṁ vāsudevasya - pārthasya ca mahātmanaḥ
saṁvādam imam aśrauṣam - adbhutaṁ roma-harṣaṇam

Sañjaya said: Thus have I heard these two great souls, the son of Vasudeva and the son of Pṛtha, engage in this wondrous conversation that has made my hair stand on end.

18.75

vyāsa-prasādāc chrutavān - etad guhyam ahaṁ param
yogaṁ yogeśvarāt kṛṣṇāt - sākṣāt kathayataḥ svayam

By the mercy of Vyāsa, I have heard this supreme secret of yoga spoken directly by Kṛṣṇa, the Supreme Lord of yoga, himself!

18.76

rājan saṁsmṛtya saṁsmṛtya - saṁvādam imam adbhutam
keśavārjunayoḥ puṇyaṁ - hṛṣyāmi ca muhur muhuḥ

O King, as I remember this wondrous and sacred dialogue between Keśava and Arjuna over and over again, I feel euphoric at every moment.

18.77

tac ca saṁsmṛtya saṁsmṛtya - rūpam aty-adbhutaṁ hareḥ
vismayo me mahān rājan - hṛṣyāmi ca punaḥ punaḥ

And as I remember that most wonderful form of Lord Hari over and over again, O King, my astonishment knows no bounds and I feel ecstatic bliss again and again.

18.78

yatra yogeśvaraḥ kṛṣṇo - yatra pārtho dhanur-dharaḥ
tatra śrīr vijayo bhūtir - dhruvā nītir matir mama

Wherever Kṛṣṇa, the Supreme Lord of mystic yoga, is and wherever the son of Pṛthā, holder of the bow, is, fortune, victory, exceptional power, and righteous conduct will also surely be there. This is my conclusion.

CHAPTER SUMMARIES

Chapter 1
The Yoga of Despair

The blind king, Dhṛtarāṣṭra, asks his secretary, Sañjaya, to describe what is happening on the battlefield where Dhṛtarāṣṭra's sons and the sons of his late brother, Pāṇḍu, have assembled with their respective armies. Dhṛtarāṣṭra's question establishes that the Bhagavad-gītā is a book about how to understand *dharma*: universal principles of righteous action (verse 1).

The principal combatants on the battlefield are identified and the respective armies take their positions in preparation for the start of a monumental war (verses 1-19).

Just as the battle is about to commence, Arjuna asks his chariot driver, Kṛṣṇa, to place his chariot at the center of the battlefield so that he may see everyone who has assembled there. Kṛṣṇa intentionally places the chariot directly in front of the people for whom Arjuna has the greatest respect and affection (verses 20-26).

Foreseeing the tragic aftermath of the war, Arjuna has an emotional breakdown and gives four reasons why it would be better for him to leave the battlefield rather than fight:

1. Compassion for the combatants, whom Arjuna doesn't wish to harm (verses 27-29).

2. There will be no happiness for him in either victory or defeat (verses 30-35).
3. Killing his superiors, such as his teacher and grandfather, as well as members of his own family, is inherently sinful (verse 36).
4. If the chivalrous men who are assembled on the battlefield are killed then women will be left unprotected and will subsequently be exploited by unscrupulous men, resulting in a progressive disintegration of families and social discord (verses 37-43).

Convinced that he has become the perpetrator of a great evil, Arjuna loses his will to fight (verses 44-46).

Chapter 2
The Yoga of Analysis

Arjuna, in the paralyzing throes of an emotional breakdown, drops his weapon and declares that he will not fight. However, he has no idea what he *should* do. Confused about how he should respond to what looks like a hopeless situation, he turns to Kṛṣṇa for help (verses 1-9).

Kṛṣṇa counters Arjuna's first reason for not fighting – compassion for the combatants – by establishing a distinction between the eternal individual self and the temporary material body (verses 10-30).

Kṛṣṇa counters Arjuna's second and third reasons for not fighting – the absence of happiness and the inherent sinfulness of killing – by reframing Arjuna's predicament as a win-win situation rather than a lose-lose situation, and proposes that Arjuna should fight as a matter of duty rather than for the sake of achieving happiness (verses 31-38).

An introduction to the nature and benefits of action that is informed by spiritual intelligence (verses 39-41).

The inadequacy of action that is not informed by spiritual intelligence; Kṛṣṇa's criticism of materialistic religion (verses 42-46).

The results of action that is informed by spiritual intelligence; an overview of *karma-yoga* (verses 47-53).

Arjuna asks Kṛṣṇa to describe the characteristics of a person whose actions are informed by spiritual intelligence. Kṛṣṇa's reply provides us with the criteria by which we can recognize a person whose intelligence has been purified by transcendental knowledge (verses 54-72).

Chapter 3
The Yoga of Action

Arjuna asks Kṛṣṇa to clarify whether he's recommending that Arjuna pursue the path of knowledge or the path of action (verses 1-2).

Kṛṣṇa explains that he is offering a both/and solution to Arjuna's dilemma, not an either/or choice (verses 3-4).

Abstaining from action altogether is not only insufficient for liberation from the reactions to one's actions, it's impossible: everyone is compelled to act according to one's nature. Action imbued with devotion, however, puts one on the path to liberation (verses 5-8).

The perfection of action is to offer all of one's actions to the Supreme Person (Viṣṇu). Such actions result in liberation from karmic reactions whereas to act otherwise ensures one's continued captivity in material existence (verse 9).

There is a natural cycle of life that requires acts of sacrifice as an expression of gratitude for nature's gifts. Participating in the perpetuation of this cycle is the basic activity that lifts consciousness above the propensity to satisfy the senses without a sense of appreciation for the source of one's blessings (verses 10-16).

Leaders of society have a responsibility to set an example of dutiful action without attachment to the fruits of action (verses 17-26).

Under the influence of egoism or "false ego" a person thinks, "I am the doer of activities." The true self is not actually the cause of effects: the interactions of the three qualities of material nature create the appearance of the self being the cause of effects (verse 27).

Acting in ways that conform to one's natural inclinations while working within the parameters of regulative principles that help one cultivate freedom from attachment and envy are far better than trying to perform actions for which one isn't ideally suited (verses 28-35).

Selfish desire is the foremost enemy of those who seek transcendental knowledge (verses 36-43).

Chapter 4
The Yoga of Knowledge

Transcendental knowledge is transmitted through a chain of disciplic succession, from a qualified teacher to a qualified student, who in turn becomes a qualified teacher (verses 1-3).

Kṛṣṇa periodically appears in this world for the purpose of re-establishing universal principles of religion as well as for the sake of pleasing his devotees and protecting them from the wicked (verses 4-8).

Understanding the transcendental nature of Kṛṣṇa's appearance and activities is all that is necessary to achieve liberation from the cycle of repeated birth and death in the material world (verses 9-10).

Kṛṣṇa reciprocates with everyone in ways that are perfectly appropriate to whatever way one feels inspired to relate to him. People can also approach celestial beings (demigods) in order to quickly fulfill their material desires (verses 11-12).

The four divisions of society – spiritually enlightened intellectuals, administrators and protectors, entrepreneurs, and physical laborers such as artists, artisans, engineers, and employees in general – are naturally occurring social divisions of divine origin. These divisions are based on people's natural aptitudes and inclinations rather than being assigned by birth. Arjuna is advised to follow in the footsteps of sages who have achieved liberation by acting with the understanding that Kṛṣṇa, the creator of these divisions, is transcendental to the qualities of material nature that determine one's position within these social divisions (verses 13-15).

Understanding the distinction between moral action, immoral action, and transcendental action is challenging even for those who are wise (verses 16-17).

There are significant differences between actions that bring about favorable reactions, those that bring about unfavorable reactions, and liberating actions that do not generate any reaction at all (verses 18-24).

Different types of people are attracted to different types of sacrifices but everyone engages in sacrifice of one kind or another (verses 25-33).

The best way to learn how to implement the principle of sacrifice is to approach a "seer of the truth" who knows the art and science of matching different kinds of sacrifices to different kinds of people (verse 34).

Transcendental knowledge has the power to purify the heart of anyone who sincerely aspires to it and can inspire anyone in possession of it to fearlessly take dynamic action (verses 35-42).

Chapter 5
The Yoga of Renunciation of Action

Our advancement along the path of self-realization is made faster and easier when our renunciation of material activity is complimented by engagement in spiritual activity (verses 1-12).

Although a person may desire to act and the Supreme Person within may sanction their actions, the actual cause of people's actions is neither the individual person (*ātmā*) nor the universal Supreme Person (*Paramātmā*) but the movements of material nature that create the appearance of people being the causes of their actions (verses 13-15).

Those whose ignorance has been vanquished by transcendental knowledge are freed from both the inclination for impious action and the obligation to experience future births (verses 16-17).

A person in possession of true knowledge sees all beings as spiritual equals and is thus able to remain equipoised in all of their relationships. They experience an inner happiness that isn't dependent on external circumstances (verses 18-21).

Indulging in that which is temporarily pleasing to the senses plants the seed of future suffering (verse 22).

By contrast, tolerating the outward-turning urges of the senses for the sake of turning inward toward the true self gives rise to sustainable happiness and freedom from the "forest fire of material existence" (verses 23-28).

Real and lasting peace, individually and socially, is attained by accepting Kṛṣṇa's position as the "beneficiary of all sacrifices and austerities, the Supreme Lord of all worlds, and the most benevolent friend within the heart of all beings" (verse 29).

Chapter 6
The Yoga of Meditation

Renunciation and yoga are, for all practical purposes, synonymous, because the path of meditative yoga and the path of material enjoyment are mutually exclusive. The pursuit of happiness through the appeasement of the mind and the gratification of the senses precludes the possibility of spiritual awakening (verses 1-4).

To reach the state of meditative absorption, one has to control the mind and senses. Thus, the uncontrolled mind is the enemy of the *yogī* who aspires for self-realization. Equanimity and equal vision are attained by controlling the mind (verses 5-9).

The basics of yogic meditation are finding an appropriate setting, adopting a proper physical posture, controlling the mind by regulating the senses, and practicing meditative yoga with faith and determination (verses 10-17).

The characteristics of a *yogī* who has achieved perfection in meditation (verses 18-23).

In the eightfold path of mystic yoga, the ultimate object of meditation is the Supreme Self who resides within the heart of the practitioner. The perfection of meditation on the Supreme Self results in ultimate freedom and infinite joy (verses 24-28).

One who attains perfection in yogic meditation sees the Supreme Self, Kṛṣṇa, everywhere, sees everything as existing within that same Supreme Self, and feels spiritually connected to all beings (verses 29-32).

Arjuna, after having initially suggested that he should leave the battlefield and go to the forest to practice yoga, now rejects the practice of yogic meditation as unsuitable for him (verses 33-36).

Kṛṣṇa addresses Arjuna's doubts, assuring him that success is possible and that there is no loss for anyone who takes up the practice of yogic meditation. Even if the practitioner doesn't achieve perfection in this life, they'll get the opportunity to pick up where they left off in a future life (verses 37-46).

In Kṛṣṇa's opinion, the *yogī* who experiences themselves as existing within Kṛṣṇa, always thinks of Kṛṣṇa as existing within themselves, and faithfully engages in devotional service to Kṛṣṇa, is situated in the highest position of yoga (verse 47).

Chapter 7

The Yoga of Knowledge and Realization

The sum total of reality consists of Kṛṣṇa and Kṛṣṇa's energies: the five physical elements (earth, water, fire, air, and ether) plus the three metaphysical elements (mind, intelligence, and false ego) constitute Kṛṣṇa's separated and inferior material energy, conscious living beings constitute Kṛṣṇa's superior spiritual energy, and Kṛṣṇa himself is the source, sum, and substance of both the material and spiritual energies (verses 1-7).

The essential aspect of everything we experience in the world is a representation of Kṛṣṇa, giving us an indication of how Kṛṣṇa is present in the world and how the world is within Kṛṣṇa (verses 8-12).

Although it is characterized as inferior, Kṛṣṇa's material energy has a bewildering power that's almost impossible for an embodied being to overcome. However, Kṛṣṇa makes it easy for those who are devoted to him to overcome this bewildering power (verses 13-14).

Four kinds of people – those who are foolish, who are of low character, whose intelligence has been diverted by illusion, and who have surrendered to an ungodly nature – tend to be disinterested in devotion to Kṛṣṇa. Kṛṣṇa is therefore disinclined to reveal himself to such people (verse 15).

Four other kinds of people – those who are distressed, who seek knowledge, who seek wealth, and who have obtained knowledge

– tend to be inclined toward devotion to Kṛṣṇa. Kṛṣṇa is therefore inclined to reveal himself to such people (verse 16-19).

Some people, whose intelligence has been diverted by illusion, devote themselves to demigods whom they hope will fulfill their material desires. Although all such desires are actually fulfilled by Kṛṣṇa, Kṛṣṇa facilitates such a person's faith in the deity of their choice while he himself remains hidden (verses 20-26).

The original cause of our imprisonment by the illusory energy of this material world – inexplicable envy and animosity toward Kṛṣṇa – is echoed as the duality of attraction and aversion that characterizes the impulses of a person under the influence of illusion (verse 27).

The cure for the dualities of attraction and aversion and the key to our liberation from the clutches of illusion is to recognize Kṛṣṇa's position as the "highest principle of divinity" (verses 28-30).

Chapter 8
The Yoga of Attaining the Absolute Truth

Arjuna asks eight questions: what is *Brahman*, what is the nature of the self, what is the nature of *karma*, what is the governing principle of the material world, what is the governing principle of the demigods, what is the governing principle of sacrifice, how is the governing principle of sacrifice present within one's body, and how can one who has attained self-mastery remember Kṛṣṇa at the time of death (verses 1-2).

Kṛṣṇa defines *Brahman* as "the imperishable transcendence, which is the eternal nature of the self" and *karma* as "action that creates the succession of future material bodies for a living being" (verse 3).

Kṛṣṇa describes perpetual change as the governing principle of the material world, the Universal Form of the Lord as the governing principle of the demigods, and the Supreme Self within the hearts of all beings as the governing principle of sacrifice (verse 4).

Having answered the first seven questions, Kṛṣṇa begins his answer to the eighth question by explaining that the consciousness we cultivate during the course of our lives determines our state of mind at the time of our death, which in turn determines the state of being we attain in our next life (verses 5-6).

We can go to Kṛṣṇa, or achieve Kṛṣṇa's qualitative state of being, by leveraging the many ways that Kṛṣṇa appears in or is represented in the world as a way to constantly direct the mind toward Kṛṣṇa (verses 7-15).

The material world, in its entirety, is not designed to be a place of sustainable happiness. On the contrary, the material world, by its very nature, is a place where misery is inevitable (verses 16-19).

By contrast, Kṛṣṇa's personal atmosphere, which is unseen from the vantage point of the material world and attainable only by pure devotion to him, is eternal and, by its very nature, a place of limitless joy (verse 20-22).

A mystic *yogī* who has gained control of their life force can choose the time at which they leave their body. The timing of a *yogī*'s departure from their physical body influences their next destination (verses 23-26).

The *yogī* who has a complete understanding of the process and ultimate goal of yoga transcends the material benefits of knowledge, sacrifice, austerity, and charity en route to the supreme destination (verses 27-28).

Chapter 9
The Yoga of the King of Secrets

Arjuna's qualification for receiving the most confidential knowledge that Kṛṣṇa has to offer is that he is not envious of Kṛṣṇa (verse 1).

Kṛṣṇa characterizes the greatest and most secret knowledge he is revealing as the perfection of religious principles, which can be experienced by direct perception rather than having to be accepted as a matter of blind faith (verses 2-3).

The great theological paradox of the Gītā: Kṛṣṇa is everything but not everything is Kṛṣṇa; everything is Kṛṣṇa in the sense that Kṛṣṇa is the complete and all-inclusive sum and substance of reality *in toto* and yet nothing is Kṛṣṇa save and except for Kṛṣṇa himself (verses 4-10).

Due to his appearance in a human-like form, some people, whom Kṛṣṇa regards as fools, don't realize that Kṛṣṇa is the Supreme Being (verses 11-12).

By contrast, Kṛṣṇa describes those who realize that he is the Supreme Being as "great souls" who are constantly orienting their thoughts and activities toward him (verses 13-14).

Still others engage with Kṛṣṇa in his other forms; as *Brahman* – the undifferentiated Oneness of Ultimate Reality; as *Paramātmā* – the omnipresent and omniscient Supersoul or Supreme Self; and as the *viśva-rūpa* – the Universal Form (verse 15).

Although Kṛṣṇa is present as the essential feature of all forms of religious observances, there are significant differences between worshiping him directly and worshiping him indirectly (verses 16-25).

Kṛṣṇa accepts offerings of food, if they are offered in a mood of devotion, from four general categories, none of which require any harm to be done to any living being (verse 26).

Anyone, irrespective of their past actions, can turn directly to Kṛṣṇa for shelter from the storm of material existence by making every activity an offering to him (verses 27-33).

These four essential instructions on the practice of *bhakti-yoga* that assure one of attaining Kṛṣṇa's grace are the most important of Kṛṣṇa's instructions in the Bhagavad-gītā, as evidenced by their appearance here at the mid-point of the text and the fact that Kṛṣṇa will repeat this verse almost verbatim near the conclusion of Chapter 18 (verse 34).

Chapter 10
The Yoga of Divine Manifestations

Kṛṣṇa declares himself to be the original and incomprehensible source of the world (verses 1-7).

The four key verses around which the rest of the Bhagavad-gītā revolves: Kṛṣṇa reiterates his position as the origin of everything and describes how he dispels the darkness of ignorance from within the hearts of those who have cultivated a mood of love for him (verses 8-11).

Arjuna expresses his acceptance of Kṛṣṇa's declaration and asks Kṛṣṇa to speak further about his divine qualities for the sake of facilitating Arjuna's ability to constantly meditate on Kṛṣṇa (verses 12-18).

Kṛṣṇa uses a series of associations to illustrate how he may be seen in the world in the forms of his being the best of all people, places, and things in any given category as well as being the essential feature or element of excellence in any given experience or state of being (verses 19-38).

Kṛṣṇa summarizes how existence itself is dependent on him, how the most glorious elements of the world are just a microscopic indication of his own glorious nature, and how he effortlessly maintains the entirety of creation (verses 39-42).

Chapter 11
The Yoga of Seeing the Universal Form

Declaring his illusion to have been dispelled, Arjuna asks Kṛṣṇa to show him his Universal Form; the form of divine majesty by which Kṛṣṇa encompasses the entire universe (verses 1-4).

Kṛṣṇa acquiesces to Arjuna's request and gives him the power of divine vision by which he can see Kṛṣṇa's Universal Form (verses 8-11).

Sañjaya, who is narrating the conversation between Kṛṣṇa and Arjuna, has been indirectly empowered to see the same Universal Form that Arjuna is seeing. Sañjaya thus describes what Arjuna sees and Arjuna's symptoms of astonishment as he tries to comprehend what he sees (verse 9-14).

Arjuna tries as best he can to describe the dazzling and immeasurable display of divine power and majesty that he is seeing (verses 15-18).

Arjuna notes the blazing fire roaring out of the mouths of the Universal Form, which indicates that he is beginning to see the Universal Form as all-consuming time. As he sees all of the powerful demigods within the Universal Form adopt positions of submission and supplication and sees the fire of death blazing in all directions, Arjuna's mood changes from astonishment to fear (verses 19-25).

Kṛṣṇa shows Arjuna what the future holds for almost all of the great warriors who are assembled on the battlefield (verses 26-30).

Overwhelmed by the vision that Kṛṣṇa has given him, Arjuna asks for an explanation of who and what he is seeing. Kṛṣṇa replies by telling Arjuna that he is time itself, the great destroyer of the world, and that all of Arjuna's opponents are destined to die on the battlefield as a consequence of divine will, irrespective of what Arjuna does or does not do. Therefore, if Arjuna fights, he is sure to be victorious (verses 31-34).

Sañjaya begins his narration of Arjuna's prayers to Kṛṣṇa in response to Kṛṣṇa's revelation, which begin with a reverential glorification of the appealing and the fear-inducing features of the Universal Form (verses 35-40).

As he continues his prayers, Arjuna asks Kṛṣṇa to forgive him for the nonchalant way he acted toward Kṛṣṇa during their friendly exchanges, which he now regards as having been inappropriate given the fact that, in addition to being his friend, Kṛṣṇa is God (verses 41-44).

Arjuna expresses his gratitude for being allowed to see Kṛṣṇa's Universal Form and requests the benediction that he may see Kṛṣṇa's four-armed Viṣṇu form (verses 45-46).

Kṛṣṇa withdraws his Universal Form and assumes the four-armed Viṣṇu form that Arjuna has asked to see. As he does so, Kṛṣṇa reassures Arjuna and Arjuna regains his composure when Kṛṣṇa returns to his human-like two-armed form (verses 47-51).

Kṛṣṇa closes this chapter by telling Arjuna that his personal form cannot be seen or understood by anyone other than those who exclusively engage in pure devotional service to him, emphasizing once again that *bhakti-yoga* alone can bring one to the ultimate goal of God-realization (verses 52-55).

Chapter 12
The Yoga of Devotional Service

Having regained his composure, Arjuna now seeks to know which kind of spiritual practitioner is better situated: the *bhakti-yogī* who pursues a personal relationship with Kṛṣṇa or the *jñāna-yogī* who pursues impersonal *Brahman* realization. Kṛṣṇa replies that those who faithfully engage in devotional service to him, in his personal form, are approaching the highest truth in the best possible way. By contrast, he characterizes the path of impersonalism as a route to him that entails a higher degree of difficulty over a longer period of time (verses 1-7).

Kṛṣṇa describes a series of devotional opportunities in descending order to indicate that he is always available to us from whatever level of devotion we are currently on (verses 8-12).

Kṛṣṇa closes the chapter and the middle portion of the Bhagavad-gītā by describing thirty-five qualities that he finds especially endearing in those who are devoted to him (verses 13-20).

Chapter 13
The Yoga of Differentiating Material Nature from the Spiritual Person

Arjuna asks Kṛṣṇa to speak on three pairs of topics: material nature and the person who seeks to enjoy material nature, the "field of activities" and the "knower" of the field, and knowledge and the object of knowledge. Some translations of the Gītā omit this verse (verse 1).

Kṛṣṇa speaks on the second pair of topics first, replying that the "field" is a euphemism for the material body, the "knower" is the person within the body, and that he, Kṛṣṇa, is the knower within all bodies (verses 2-3).

Kṛṣṇa summarizes the teachings about the "field of activities" that are found in the Vedānta-sūtra, describing it as consisting of the physical and metaphysical elements, the senses, and the objects of the senses. Kṛṣṇa also summarizes the interactions of the elements that make up the "field" (verses 4-7).

Kṛṣṇa then addresses the third pair of topics by describing the states of being that constitute knowledge, the process through which knowledge is acquired, and the object of knowledge (verses 8-19).

In addressing the third topic that Arjuna has asked him to speak about, Kṛṣṇa describes how a person's interactions with material nature set off chain reactions of cause and effect, how he, the Supersoul, is never affected by the interactions of material nature, and how anyone who understands the nature of the Supersoul can be liberated from the cycle of cause and effect (verses 20-24).

Kṛṣṇa describes the means by which one can attain experiential knowledge of the Supersoul and the characteristics of those who have attained such knowledge (verses 25-35).

Chapter 14
The Yoga of Seeing the Three Qualities of Material Nature

Kṛṣṇa glorifies the knowledge that he's offering a further explanation of as having the power to give the highest perfection to anyone who takes shelter of it (verses 1-2).

We're given a brief explanation of how all living beings enter the material world and of the origin of life as we know it (verses 3-4).

Kṛṣṇa gives a detailed explanation of what the three qualities of material nature are, how they bind a person to different aspects of material existence, and specific symptoms by which each quality may be recognized (verses 5-13).

Kṛṣṇa then describes how the quality of material nature that's wielding the greatest influence over a person at the time of their death will subsequently influence the quality of their next birth (verses 14-18).

By contrast, someone who understands how material nature is working is assured of achieving liberation from the influence of the qualities of material nature (verses 19-20).

Kṛṣṇa confirms the scientific nature of the knowledge he's sharing by providing an objective set of characteristics by which those who have attained liberation from the influence of the qualities of material nature may be recognized (verses 21-25).

Kṛṣṇa further confirms that those who engage in devotional service to him also transcend the qualities of material nature and attain *Brahman* realization (verse 26).

Kṛṣṇa concludes this chapter with an unequivocal declaration that he is the foundation of Ultimate Reality (*Brahman*), of *dharma*, and of incomparable transcendental happiness (verse 27).

Chapter 15
The Yoga of the Supreme Person

Kṛṣṇa uses an upside-down banyan tree, with its branches extending to various levels, as a metaphor for the material world and its various "fields of activities," which must be "cut down" by those who want to disentangle themselves from it (verses 1-3).

Kṛṣṇa gives a set of instructions for the spiritual practitioner who aspires to reside in Kṛṣṇa's own eternal spiritual environment, along with a description of that environment (verses 4-6).

We hear about the position of the Supreme Self in relationship to the infinitesimal selves who transmigrate from body to body, lifetime after lifetime, and the difference between those who see through the lens of transcendental knowledge and those who do not (verses 7-11).

Kṛṣṇa offers even more ways by which we can see and appreciate his presence in the world (verses 12-15).

Erasing any doubts about the validity of spiritual individuality, Kṛṣṇa summarizes the teachings of Vedānta by elaborating even further on the distinction between an infinitesimal individual person and the "Ultimate Person" (verses 16-20).

Chapter 16
The Yoga of Distinguishing Between Divine and Demonic Natures

Kṛṣṇa lists 26 qualities that symptomize a saintly state of being that, if cultivated, can lead to the elevation of consciousness (verses 1-3).

Having already spoken at length about saintly characteristics, Kṛṣṇa summarizes the characteristics that symptomize a demonic state of being that, if cultivated, can lead to the degradation of consciousness (verses 4-6).

Kṛṣṇa follows his summary of unsaintly characteristics with a detailed description of the nature of wickedness and the fate that awaits those who are possessed of such demonic qualities (verses 7-20).

Anticipating that an intelligent and self-reflective person might recognize unsaintly qualities within themselves and comprehend the implications of the presence of those qualities, Kṛṣṇa offers instructions on how to free oneself from demonic propensities (verses 21-24).

Chapter 17
The Yoga of Understanding the Threefold Divisions of Faith

Arjuna asks Kṛṣṇa to describe the status of people who ignore scriptural directives in terms of how the three qualities of material nature are influencing them (verse 1).

Kṛṣṇa replies by describing how a person is defined by their faith and can be categorized according to the general nature of their expressions of faith (verses 2-4).

Kṛṣṇa follows this general description with a specific condemnation of excessive ascetism (verses 5-6).

Illustrating how every aspect of life can be understood through the lens of the three qualities of material nature, Kṛṣṇa proceeds to describe:

- How to understand food according to the three qualities of material nature (verses 7-10),
- How to understand sacrificial offerings according to the three qualities of material nature (verses 11-13),
- How to understand austerity according to the three qualities of material nature (verses 14-19), and
- How to understand charity according to the three qualities of material nature (verses 20-22).

Kṛṣṇa concludes this chapter with an explanation of the transcendental nature and purpose of the Sanskrit phrase *Oṁ Tat Sat* (verses 23-28).

Chapter 18
The Yoga of Liberation

Arjuna circles back to the beginning of the Gītā with his request for a final clarification about the distinction between the renunciation of action and the renunciation of the fruits of action. Kṛṣṇa begins his reply with conclusive summary of *karma-yoga* and the true meaning of renunciation (verses 1-12).

Kṛṣṇa describes five factors of action and the results of action: the place, the person who identifies as the cause of actions and their results, the senses, the effort that a person puts into action, and divine will (verses 13-15).

Kṛṣṇa continues by contrasting how action is experienced by those with a poor fund of knowledge and how action is experienced by those with a rich fund of knowledge (verses 16-17).

Next, we hear about the three constituent elements that comprise the impetus for action and the three constituent elements that comprise action itself (verse 18).

Kṛṣṇa follows his breakdown of the elements of action with an explanation of how knowledge of the three qualities of material nature can be applied to making meaningful differentiations within six different sets of experiences:

1. How to understand knowledge according to the three qualities of material nature (verses 19-22).
2. How to understand action according to the three qualities of material nature (verses 23-25).
3. How to understand the way people act according to the three qualities of material nature (verses 26-28).
4. How to understand knowledge of distinguishing between right and wrong; discernment in relationship to principles of religion (*dharma*) according to the three qualities of material nature (verses 29-32).
5. How to understand determination according to the three qualities of material nature (verses 33-35).
6. How to understand happiness according to the three qualities of material nature (verses 36-39).

Returning to a more general understanding of the underlying mechanics of the material world, Kṛṣṇa describes the universal influence of the three qualities of material nature within the realm of matter (verse 40).

Turning to the social significance of his teachings, Kṛṣṇa describes how we can understand the four social divisions according to the three qualities of material nature (verses 41-44, of which verses 18-44 comprise Kṛṣṇa's conclusive summary of *jñāna-yoga*).

After describing the types of work that each social division is attracted to and responsible for, Kṛṣṇa connects our engagement with the world to the various paths of yoga by describing:

- How to attain perfection by the practice of *karma-yoga* (verses 45-48).
- How to attain perfection by the practice of *jñāna-yoga* (verses 49-53).
- How to attain perfection by the synthesis of *karma-yoga* and *jñāna-yoga* in the context of *bhakti-yoga* (verses 54-56).

Kṛṣṇa's conclusive advice to Arjuna and his request for Arjuna to take the secrets that Kṛṣṇa has revealed to him into account as he decides what to do (verses 57-63).

Kṛṣṇa reiterates his ultimate secret and delivers his conclusive instruction to Arjuna (verses 64-66).

Kṛṣṇa reveals his thoughts and feelings about who is qualified to hear his teachings, those who share his teachings, and those who study his teachings (verses 67-71).

Arjuna expresses his acceptance of Kṛṣṇa's instructions and his intention to act accordingly (verses 72-73).

Sañjaya concludes the Bhagavad-gītā by glorifying Kṛṣṇa and Arjuna, expressing his gratitude and euphoria at having witnessed their conversation, and declares that fortune, victory, exceptional power, and righteous conduct are sure to be found wherever Kṛṣṇa and Arjuna are present (verses 74-78).

PART THREE

Integrating The Bhagavad-gītā Into Your Life

About This Section

The Bhagavad-gītā is not a book for armchair philosophers; it's a manual for the practical application of spiritual wisdom. The knowledge contained in the Gītā comes alive for us when we actively apply that knowledge.

Part Three of this book is a first-person approach to exploring some of the ways in which everyday activities can be transformed into spiritual experiences. In this section, I'll share personal reflections that illustrate how the Gītā's teachings have transformed my way of seeing and being in the world. I'll also recap some of the Gītā's most important philosophical themes and highlight passages from the Gītā that are worthy of special consideration.

You'll also find questions that can serve as jumping off points for conversations, group discussions, or individual contemplation, as well as journaling prompts and personal experiments that you can perform to see if the Gītā's theoretical propositions, when practically applied, correspond to your lived experience.

Here are a few things you might want to keep in mind to get the most out of this part of the book:

1. Before you begin any discussion, journaling, or personal experiment, take a few deep breaths to settle your mind and body. Then, set an intention for your session. Reciting an affirmation or chanting an invocation mantra is a nice way to confirm your intention and invite a divine presence into your session.
2. If you're doing this work on your own, set aside little slices of time by making an appointment with yourself. You can mark your calendar or set an alarm to remind yourself of the commitment you made to increase your knowledge and transform your intellectual comprehension into personal realizations.
3. When it's time to focus on exploring some of these ideas or trying out some of the recommended practices, give yourself a set period of time when no distractions are allowed.
4. Working through these discussions and exercises can be messy and challenging. Have faith in the process and let the results take care of themselves.
5. Don't forget to congratulate yourself for doing these exercises: when you're finished, take a minute to observe a closing ritual to bring a sense of completion to your session.
6. Look for opportunities to share your understanding of Kṛṣṇa's teachings with others. Remember that you are the world's foremost expert on your own experience; you don't have to be an "expert" on the Bhagavad-gītā in order to share your personal realizations with other people. Talking about the Gītā, hearing from others, comparing your insights, exploring questions, and testing ideas through group discussions or one-on-one conversations are very powerful ways to deepen your relationship with the Gītā.

It's also an opportunity to cultivate relationships within a spiritual community.

I want to emphasize the importance and value of sharing your experience of the Bhagavad-gītā with other people. Even if you feel like you've barely scratched the surface of what the Gītā has to offer, don't wait to share your experience of what it's like to see the world from the Gītā's perspective. This is a great way to find out if people you know have been pondering the same questions that brought you to the Gītā and have been anxiously waiting for the opportunity to talk with a kindred spirit about them. You'll also find that your own comprehension of the Gītā's teachings will increase simply by looking for the words you need to articulate your understanding and share your experience. Deepening my own understanding of the Bhagavad-gītā is one reason why I teach courses on it . . . and why I wrote this book.

If you're not already participating in a training or some other forum that's meant to facilitate group discussion, seek out opportunities for small group or one-on-one conversations with people who share your interest in the pursuit of spiritual wisdom.

....

The Bhagavad-gītā is a message of hope that offers us spiritual ideas about how we can find lasting peace in a transient world of inevitable sorrows. It's up to us to apply those spiritual ideas in such a way as to invite their actualization as a lived experience.

Having a Conversation with God

"A real conversation always contains an invitation. You are inviting another person to reveal herself or himself to you, to tell you who they are or what they want."
~ David Whyte

"What do you *really* believe?"

Somehow my date had decided that there was more to me than what met her eye. What I was showing her of myself up to that point appeared to be working pretty well. And I wanted to keep it that way, so I really wasn't interested in answering her question.

I thought that if I answered her honestly then she might think I was nuts. And if I answered dishonestly then I'd be . . . lying. Either way, I felt like I was in a lose-lose situation.

I'd become a *bhakti-yogī* long before I met this woman. As such, I accepted the idea that trading my material desires in for spiritual ones was in my ultimate best interest. Unfortunately, there have been times when my mind had other ideas, my senses had other desires, and I let both overrule my intelligence. My date had appeared in my life during one of these times of vacillation between what I knew I believed and what I thought I wanted.

What I knew I *didn't* want was for her to see the disconnect between my beliefs and my lifestyle. But she'd asked me a reasonable question so now I had to come up with a reasonable answer. I wasn't sure how I would do that.

I thought, "maybe I can dodge this question by giving her an answer that's both honest and incomprehensible" . . . a tactic that reflected the fact that I didn't really want her to understand the answer because I didn't want her to dump me, which was a distinct possibility if she thought that my beliefs were ridiculous or if she didn't want to date a guy who was so discombobulated that he lived in conflict with his core beliefs.

I took a moment to think about it and then replied in such a way as to make what I was saying as unintelligible as possible. For about five carefully-worded minutes I presented my philosophical beliefs in the most truthful yet impenetrable way I could come up with.

It didn't work.

As it turned out, when my date was a youthful punk rocker living in Washington, DC, she and her friends regularly scored cheap lunches at the Krishna House near Dupont Circle. In addition to a nominal donation, the price she had to pay for lunch at Krishna House was having to listen to the devotees talk to her about *bhakti-yoga*.

The result: she saw right through my carefully-worded camouflage and knew exactly what I was talking about. And, as I found out later, she thought, "OMG, this guy is already the strangest person I've ever met and now I find out that he's a closet Hare Krishna?! How much weirder can this get?"

Fortunately, she was attracted to weirdness rather than repelled by it so my revelation didn't scare her away. But she did ask me the obvious follow up question:

"So if that's what you really believe, then how can you live the way you're living?"

There must have been a long silence after she spoke. Although I have absolutely no recollection of how I responded, I clearly remember the two thoughts that popped into my head at that moment.

The first thought was, "I'm on a fool's errand; I need to realign the way I live with what I really believe."

The second thought was, "I need to make sure that I keep this woman in my life."

And I did both.

....

Revealing our vulnerabilities to another person can feel risky, but it can also have huge rewards. And if an honest conversation with another person can change the course of our lives for the better, just imagine how we can benefit from having honest conversations with the Supreme Person.

Arjuna's conversation with Kṛṣṇa is a wonderful example of this. Just as Arjuna shares his innermost thoughts, feelings, and fears with Kṛṣṇa without worrying about being judged, shunned, or shamed, so can we. We can offer Kṛṣṇa prayers of glorification and supplication, but we can also ask questions and express doubts without fear of rejection or reprisal.

In the Gītā, we're presented with a God who welcomes all inquiries, responds to our requests, and enjoys casual conversation in a mood of mutual trust and affection. We can speak just as freely with Kṛṣṇa as we would with our best friend. Kṛṣṇa makes it unmistakably clear that he welcomes our approach.

Having a conversation with God may not always feel like the most comfortable thing to do. We may not think of God as a person we can talk to or as someone who's interested in talking to us. We might think that if God already knows everything then there's no point in telling God anything. We might not want to risk being disappointed if we don't get what we want from God or, worse, if we get something that we don't want.

Approaching God in a mood of awe and reverence is natural, but it also preserves our distance from God. A conversation with God in a mood of friendship and trust closes that distance. And best of all, a conversation with God in a mood of love eliminates our distance from God altogether.

If you could talk to God about anything, what would you want to talk about?

....

Passages to Contemplate

2.7

[Arjuna said] My thoughts are in disarray as I try to ascertain which path is virtuous. Therefore, I am asking you to tell me with certainty what course of action would serve the greatest good.

4.3

Because you are my devotee as well as my friend, I am revealing this transcendental mystery to you.

4.11

However one approaches me, I respond accordingly.

Questions for Conversation or Group Discussion

1. Do you think Arjuna felt judged by Kṛṣṇa after he told Kṛṣṇa he wasn't going to fight? Why or why not?
2. Imagine yourself in Arjuna's position at the beginning of the Bhagavad-gītā: called to fight a battle that, win or lose, will bring about the deaths of people you love and have catastrophic social consequences. What would you think? How would you feel? What would you want to do?
3. Do you think there is any significance to Kṛṣṇa's accepting the

position of being Arjuna's chariot driver? Why or why not?

Questions for Personal Contemplation / Journaling

1. Do you feel judged by whatever Higher Power you believe in? If so, how and why?
2. Do you feel comfortable asking the highest power you can conceive of for guidance? Why or why not?
3. Did you hear anything in the conversation between Kṛṣṇa and Arjuna that reminded you of your own conversations with a higher power?
4. Arjuna doesn't want to fight because he's afraid that he'll lose everything, even if he wins the battle.
    a. What was the biggest loss for you in the past year? How did you get through it?
    b. Have you ever won the battle but lost the war, so to speak? If so, what was that like?
    c. Did anything you read in the Gītā cast these experiences in a new or different light? If so, how so?

Personal Experiments

1. Kṛṣṇa is compassionately offering his guidance to Arjuna at the lowest moment in Arjuna's life. What was the lowest moment in your life? What were you doing, thinking, and feeling?
    a. Take a moment to remember that version of yourself; the person who was going through the worst time of your life. Capture the essence of that version of yourself in your mind.
    b. Imagine that you're Kṛṣṇa and write a letter of compassionate guidance to the version of yourself that was experiencing the lowest moment in your

life. When you're done, try reading it out loud to yourself.

2. In a notebook or journal, complete the following sentences:

   I'm angry about...

   I'm afraid of...

   I'm sad about...

   I'm ashamed of...

   I feel guilty about...

   Then:

   1. Put yourself in Arjuna's position:
      a. How would you speak to Kṛṣṇa about the things you feel angry about, afraid of, sad about, etc.?
      b. How do you think Kṛṣṇa would reply to you?

Becoming Fearless

"A man that flies from his fear may find that he has only taken a short cut to meet it."
~ J.R.R. Tolkien

Anton looked at the table. He saw a short, sharp knife. He picked up the knife, held it close to his face, looked up at me, and, with all the gravity that an 8-year-old boy can summon, he said, "Do you want to see me face my fears?"

Having children in our home when my wife and I entertain guests is usually the exception rather than the rule. Anton's presence was one such exception. Obliged to endure the company of grown-ups without any other children to play with, Anton amused himself for most of the evening by hiding in the bedroom and making spooky noises whenever someone walked in to drop off a coat or get something from their handbag.

After a while, curiosity or boredom got the better of him so he ventured out to see what the adults were doing. I had just taken some vegetables, a cutting board, and the knife out to the dining room table when Anton appeared.

I'm sure there must be some good healthy reason why adults should help children learn to face their fears but, even if I had thought of one, this clearly wasn't the time for me to do so. Besides, I could tell by the sly expression on his face that Anton's query had more to do with pushing my buttons than with testing his own limits. I wasn't going to take the bait. Dissuasion was the obvious choice. I beamed a benevolent smile that masked my inner discomfort with the possibility that our friend's child might be willing to tempt death in our dining room just for the sake of messing with my head and calmly replied: "Perhaps another time, Anton. Right now I have to cut up these vegetables. May I please have that knife?"

Thankfully, Anton complied and went back to haunting the bedroom.

As he disappeared down the hall, I thought about how fortunate he was to be at such a magical age; a time when so many children see the world as a place of wonder that offers adventure to those willing to accept the risks. It appeared that Anton had become aware of the ultimate risk associated with the adventure of life and was willing, even eager, to demonstrate his acceptance of it.

Whether it's fear of heights, fear of failure, fear of public speaking, fear of sharp objects, or fear of children holding sharp objects, all fears ultimately roll back to fear of death.

The Bhagavad-gītā is a book about how to become fearless.

....

In the Gītā's Chapter 2, Kṛṣṇa begins his teachings by declaring that a wise person doesn't lament for anyone, either living or dead, because the soul, the *ātmā*, is eternal. Our material bodies are temporary; they come and go like winter and summer seasons. The spiritual person within the material body, however, is eternal.

The proposition that we've always been and that there's no possibility of us ever not being is a very radical, even subversive idea that undercuts the conventional understanding that we're created beings who come into being at a point in time. Therefore, we have no reason to fear death.

Confidence in the proposition that the soul is indestructible can make a huge difference in how much courage a person who finds themselves on a battlefield can summon.

....

Passages to Contemplate

2.20

The self is never born and never dies, has never come into being and shall never cease to be. Unborn, eternal, everlasting, and primeval, the self is not slain when the body is slain.

2.56

One whose mind is free from attachment, fear, and anger, who is undisturbed by the arrival of sources of misery nor euphoric at the arrival of causes for happiness, is called a sage of steady mind.

18.30

O son of Pṛthā, discernment by which one can distinguish between constructive engagement and disengagement, what should be done and what should not to be done, what is to be feared and what is not to be feared, what is binding and what is liberating, is discernment in the mode of luminance.

Questions for Conversation or Group Discussion

1. Does the idea of being an eternal spiritual person ring true to you? Do you currently identify as an eternal spiritual being? Why or why not?
2. If you were able to experience yourself as an eternal spiritual person whose existence didn't depend on having a body made of matter, how would that change your life?
3. If we're all eternal spiritual beings rather than our temporary material bodies, does that mean that we're all

spiritually equal? How might the idea of "spiritual equality" influence the way we see and respond to issues of social justice?

Questions for Personal Contemplation / Journaling

What's your biggest fear?

Why is it your biggest fear?

- Write a short description of your biggest fear.
- Ask yourself, "Why am I afraid of this?"
- When you have the answer, write it out and then ask the same question about what you've just written: "Why am I afraid of *this*?"

Personal Experiment

Follow this link - https://hari-kirtana.com/eternal-self-meditation - to download a 5-minute guided meditation that will help you to experience the distinction between all that you're conscious of and yourself, the person who is conscious.

Responding to the Concept of Karma

"Begin to be now what you will be hereafter."
~ William James

Everything was chilly and gray: the sky, the skyscrapers, the street, the sidewalk. I was walking toward the East River on the south side of 42nd Street between 6th and 5th Avenues. To my right, the stone wall that defined the northern edge of Bryant Park parted to accommodate an entrance to the New York City subway system.

That's where I stopped.

Once upon a time there was no Internet. Hard to believe but it's true. Forget about sending an attached file to the other side of the world with the tap of a finger: in the olden days, the only way to get a document from an office building on one side of midtown Manhattan to an office building on the other side of midtown Manhattan was to put it in an envelope and hand the envelope to someone who would personally take the document to wherever it needed to go.

That someone was me. I was a foot messenger. Bereft of marketable skills, I chose to squeak out a living by doing the one thing

I could do that someone would pay me for: walk around midtown with a package under my arm.

In addition to earning me just enough money to survive on a steady diet of mercifully cheap West Village falafels, my job also doubled as free time to practice walking meditation. I'd been cultivating a meditation practice since I was 16 years old. My first meditation practice consisted of sitting silently in the basement of my family home on Long Island. I became intimately familiar with the sequence of little pings and padoinks that led up to the "Ka-Chummm" of the boiler going on, but I didn't get any closer to becoming one with the universe.

I'd also tried mantra meditation: I chanted a Buddhist mantra, I chanted *Oṃ*, and I chanted Śiva mantras in the hopes of sanctifying the contents of my hash pipe. Five years later, when I started my job as a messenger, I still had faith in the idea of mantras. One mantra that I knew about but hadn't really tried yet was the Hare Krishna mantra:

hare kṛṣṇa hare kṛṣṇa - kṛṣṇa kṛṣṇa hare hare
hare rāma hare rāma - rāma rāma hare hare

I thought, "it's a symmetrical mantra that's good for chanting while walking and I have a job that's nothing but walking, so . . ."

For the next several weeks I spent about 8 hours of every weekday mentally chanting my way from office building to office building, repeating the mantra to the rhythm of my breathing and matching my breathing to the pace of my stride, my body and mind aligned in moving meditation.

Late one cold and gloomy afternoon as I was chanting my way to a grand neo-gothic skyscraper near Grand Central Station, I stopped. I had to. Somehow, I'd stepped into a different dimension of time-space. My inner world slowed down while the people and the cars around me sped up to a blur. The sounds around me receded as the sound within me took center stage. It wasn't exactly the sound of someone else's voice but what I was hearing in my mind's ear was not of my own making. It was as if I was talking to myself from a script that someone else had written for me.

Wherever the message was coming from, it hit me like a thunderbolt. The message was, "You're accountable for all of the *karma* you've accumulated over innumerable past lifetimes and you're not doing anything about it!"

I was already convinced that I was an eternal spiritual being in a temporary material body and that I therefore must have had past lives even though I couldn't remember them. And I definitely understood that the law of *karma* essentially said "what goes around comes around," which was why I had adopted a vegetarian diet years earlier when I first started my meditation practice.

But what about all the years before I stopped eating animals? And all the lifetimes before this one when who knows what I was eating? Or doing? The law of averages said that there had to be plenty of bad *karma* that I was accountable for mixed in with any good *karma* that I might have generated for myself.

Although I understood the concept of *karma*, I realized that I hadn't fully accepted it until this moment, when I was suddenly seized by a sense of urgency about it. The idea of being accountable for unknown actions I'd performed in previous lives that had unknowable implications for my future lives suddenly seemed less theoretical and more like an all-hands-on-deck emergency. The conditions of my next life, and who knew how many more, depended on my finding a way to circumvent the consequences of my past actions, or at least finding a way to stop acquiring any more karmic reactions.

As my internal reality gradually re-joined my external reality, I slowly started walking again and, as was now my habit, started mentally chanting again. As I pondered where this show-stopping thought about *karma* came from it occurred to me that this mantra I'd been chanting all day every day for the past several weeks might have opened the door to this unexpected insight. This sort of thing had never happened with any other mantra I'd chanted.

The idea that there was a connection between my realization and the incessant mantra meditation I'd been doing felt so solid that, right then and there, I made a commitment to learn more about this mantra to see if there was a logical explanation for how it inspired such a powerful realization.

A month later, I was living in an ashram as a full-time student of the art and science of *bhakti-yoga.*

....

Of course, we're not all cut out for an ashram lifestyle. In fact, most of us don't really have that as an option. Fortunately, it's not necessary; one of the lessons I learned while I was living in the ashram is that we can pull the plug on our *karma* from wherever we're at.

When we consider the possibility that this life isn't the only life we've ever had or will have, it drastically changes the context for how we think about our current life. According to the Gītā, our past *karma* created the blueprint for our current lives and the *karma* we're generating through our actions right now is creating the blueprint for our future lives.

The act of thinking or meditating on something also produces a reaction in the form of moving us in the direction of the object of our meditation. We go where our minds take us. If you want to know what your next life might be like, all you have to do is think about what you think about.

This is why Kṛṣṇa emphasizes the importance of controlling the mind through the practice of yoga so early in his conversation with Arjuna: we want our minds to take us in the direction of actions that free us from karmic reactions.

What do you think your next life will look like?

....

Passages to Contemplate

8.3

Karma is action that creates the succession of future material bodies for a living being.

8.6

O son of Kuntī, whatever state of being one remembers at the end of one's life is the state of being they will carry into their next life, for one is certain to attain whatever state of being one's mind is absorbed in.

3.9

Act only for the sake of offering your actions to Viṣṇu, free from attachment, O son of Kuntī, for by such perfect action you will be liberated from all reactions associated with your deeds. Otherwise, your actions will bind you to this material world.

Questions for Conversation or Group Discussion

1. Does the idea of *karma* make sense to you? Why or why not?
2. The law of *karma* tells us that no matter what we may have done in the past we have the power to change our future. How can we balance a constructive acceptance of the present with a proactive approach to creating the future we want for ourselves and for others?
3. Assuming that the beauty, wealth, fame, or power that a person might have in their current life have come about on account of actions that they performed in previous lives, what are the potential downsides of being blessed with such "good" *karma*?
4. When we see someone who's experiencing misfortune, how do we balance the idea of *karma* with compassion for people who are suffering?

Questions for Personal Contemplation / Journaling

1. Do you think that the actions you perform in this life will generate reactions that you'll experience in a future life? Looking back over the course of your life, what's the one thing that you've done that's likely to have the biggest impact on you in a future life?
2. Are you ultimately responsible for all of your life experiences or are there other factors beyond your control that also have to be taken into account?
3. Would accepting responsibility for your life experiences empower you to respond constructively to negative life experiences or does this just sound like a "blame the victim" rationalization for not holding other people in your life responsible for how their hurtful actions have affected you? Is there a way to combine your responsibility and others' responsibility that makes sense in light of the law of *karma*?
4. Can you accept the idea of *karma* and still feel compassionate toward yourself when you experience misfortune?
5. What impact might divine intervention have on your *karma*? Would you consider inviting such divine intervention? Why or why not?

Personal Experiment

Think about how different you are today from the person you were 10 years ago. Write down the most significant differences.

Then, try to imagine how different you'll be 10 years from now. Write down the most significant changes that you would like to see in yourself 10 years from now and what benefit you'll realize by making this transformation.

Next, start talking about your future self in the first-person present tense, such as "I am (desired change) and I'm experiencing (desired benefit)."

Follow up this self-talk by acting as if you are already the person you want to be in 10 years. If you find yourself acting otherwise, look at what you're doing instead of what your future self would be doing and ask yourself, "Why am I doing (x) instead of (y)? What assumption am I holding onto, consciously or unconsciously, that moves me to hold onto a behavior I want to let go of? Is that assumption true? If not, what new and true assumption should I replace the false assumption with?"

Another approach to the same challenge: Have a conversation with the part of yourself that's resistant to change and ask it what it wants. By treating parts of ourselves as persons unto themselves, we can get valuable insights into the hidden motivations behind acts of self-sabotage that undermine our attempts at personal growth.

Recognizing the Three Qualities of Material Nature

"Some people walk in the rain; others just get wet."
~ Roger Miller

The air was crisp and clean and delicately tinged with the scent of happy cows. The afternoons were so quiet that you could hear the wind whispering across the fields from an acre away. The night sky was so clear that you could watch meteors streak through the earth's atmosphere beneath a glittering sea of stars. As dawn approached, oval silhouettes of sleeping peacocks, perched on the branches of trees that lined the path to a small temple set back in the woods just beyond the pasturing grounds, faded into the foreground.

It was peaceful and spacious, pure and simple; an ideal place for cultivating contentment. It was everything I never wanted. I couldn't wait to get the hell out of there.

I'd never lived on a farm before. My reason for being there had nothing to do with farming, though; my spiritual master had withdrawn to this back of beyond patch of Pennsylvania's Tuscarora Valley because it provided the kind of tranquility that was conducive for writing. I was there to assist him. My service was to help organize the correspondence, transcripts, memoranda, and other documents he had collected for the purpose of composing a biography of his guru.

My problem had nothing to do with the work I was doing; it was interesting, and I felt that I was making a meaningful contribution to a worthwhile project. Nor did it have anything to do with the community; everyone there was congenial and kind.

The problem was that I just couldn't get comfortable in a place that was so quiet, so peaceful, so . . . dull. Sure, there was that time when the nuclear reactor just down the river had a partial core meltdown that nearly turned central Pennsylvania into a radioactive wasteland but, other than that, nothing ever happened.

Seven months was as much as I could take. I asked my spiritual master for permission to return to New York City. Thankfully, permission was granted, and someone was nice enough to drive me to the train station in Harrisburg. Five hours later, I stepped onto the platform at New York's Penn Station, trundled up the steps, dodged my way through the customary riot of dashing commuters, and rode the escalator up to an exit that spit me out at the corner of 8th Avenue and 31st Street.

Black sky. Glaring lights. Roaring traffic. Blaring horns. Stinky smells. Organized chaos rampaging atop a churning undercurrent of commotion multiplied by the psychic impact of millions of people.

Ahh, home sweet home.

As I strolled through the nightly hullabaloo of midtown Manhattan, I realized that the comfort I took in the sensory overload that was bouncing off the walls around me bore witness to the fact that I clearly preferred the modes of passion and darkness to the quality of luminance.

The pastoral setting I'd left behind was exceptionally *sattvic*, situated in the mode of goodness and light. And I was so *rajasic* and *tamasic*, influenced by the qualities of passion and darkness, that I felt totally out of place there and right at home here.

If the process of yoga is meant to free us from the influence of the lower qualities of material nature and lift our consciousness into higher ones, then my fish-back-in-water response to concrete and cacophony made it clear that I still had plenty of work to do.

This is not to say, however, that there is nothing of spiritual value to be gained by living in an urban environment. The intensity of an environment that's bursting at the seams with people from every walk of life moving en masse at breakneck speed simply provides a very different mood of spiritual engagement than the placidly uniform pace of country life. Perhaps this is why the intellectual elite of Vedantic scholarship have historically gravitated toward cosmopolitan settings, where sources of knowledge were easily available, as was the opportunity to engage directly with a multitude of philosophical ideas.

Although I certainly felt energized by the prospect of hearing from the many learned devotees in my lineage who resided in or regularly passed through the city that never sleeps, I can also see how my preference for pandemonium over peacefulness revealed which qualities of material nature I was more attracted to. The farm was a much-needed push out of my comfort zone that made it easier for me to think about how I needed to focus on grounding and *sattvic* activities in the middle of a predominantly *rajasic* and *tamasic* environment.

....

In the Bhagavad-gītā, Kṛṣṇa spends a significant amount of time telling Arjuna how to recognize the influence of the three qualities of material nature on individual and social psychology. Kṛṣṇa's characterizations of the three qualities of material nature can be summarized as follows:

- **Luminance:** arises from purity; characterized by knowledge, clarity of thought, and detachment; results in deeper understanding, elevation of consciousness, and happiness.
- **Passion:** arises from hankering; characterized by distorted intelligence, intense endeavor, and attachment; results in greed, anxiety, misery, and stalled spiritual progress.
- **Darkness:** arises from delusion, characterized by insanity, apathy, and sleep; results in illusion, foolishness, violence, destruction, and degradation of consciousness.

The three qualities of material nature are usually invisible until we develop the eyes to see them. They're present everywhere and permeate everything but we don't notice them because of how they're affecting us. It's like trying to see the Matrix when you're *in* the Matrix. But once we know what to look for, we can recognize each of the three modes of material nature when we see them and see how those modes are influencing us.

For example, someone who's absorbed in reading a book early in the morning in a serene pastoral setting is under the influence of the mode of luminance, someone engaged in vigorous activity in the middle of the day in a bustling environment is being influenced by the mode of passion, and someone who's asleep in a dark and quiet room late at night is being influenced by the mode of darkness. Knowledge and serenity are in the mode of luminance, striving and hustle are in the mode of passion, and unconsciousness is in the mode of darkness.

But the modes are not always so one-dimensional. For example, our early morning reader may be reading a book about how to make a bomb; the reader's destructive intention colors the activity toward the quality of darkness even though the activity itself is taking place in the mode of luminance.

A person vigorously engaged in some mid-day activity may be very attached to a desired outcome but may also be selflessly endeavoring for the welfare of others. In that case, there's a mix of both the mode of luminance and the mode of passion. On the other hand, they may be amorally endeavoring for personal gain at the expense of others, in which case the combination of passion and darkness is in play.

And the person who's sleeping may be sleeping in a clean, peaceful environment conducive to restfulness, having retired at sundown with the intention of waking with the first light of day. So even though sleep itself is in the mode of darkness, the intention and environment place the act of sleeping in the context of the mode of luminance.

The three qualities of material nature are all around us all the time. How are they influencing you right now?

....

Passages to Contemplate

3.27

One who is bewildered by the influence of false ego thinks, "I am the doer of activities." The truth is that all activities are carried out by the three qualities of material nature.

13.22

A person thus situated in material nature experiences a mode of being born of that nature. Clinging to an identity that arises from the qualities of material nature, one meets with good and evil in the course of taking birth among various species.

14.5

Material nature is composed of three qualities – luminance, passion, and darkness – that bind the eternal living being to modes of material embodiment, O mighty-armed Arjuna.

Questions for Conversation or Group Discussion

1. Do you think it's possible to literally *see* the qualities of material nature at work in the world? Why or why not?
2. Discuss a current event that's dominating the media landscape in terms of the three qualities of material nature:
    - What elements of the event are indicative of the mode of luminance?
    - What elements of the event are indicative of the mode of passion?
    - What elements of the event are indicative of the mode of darkness?
    - Overall, which quality of material nature does the event lean toward?
3. Do you think the Gītā's teachings can help human society to rise above conflicts that come about due to conceptions of identity that are produced by the interactions of the three qualities of material nature? If so, how? If not, why not?

Questions for Personal Contemplation / Journaling

1. What happens when you look at the people closest to you, such as friends, family, co-workers, your non-human companion, or your intimate partner, through the lens of the three qualities of material nature? Does anything about the way you see them change?
2. In chapter 2, verse 45, Kṛṣṇa encourages Arjuna to rise above the three qualities of material nature and establish himself in "pure spiritual consciousness." In verse 54, Arjuna asks Kṛṣṇa how to recognize a person who is "transcendentally situated." Kṛṣṇa describes such a person in verses 55 to 61.

    Re-read Chapter 2, verses 55- 61, and ask yourself:

- Can I imagine myself as being the kind of person that Kṛṣṇa is describing in these verses?
- Would I want to be this kind of person? Why or why not?
- If the answer is "yes," what would it take for me to become this kind of person?

Personal Experiment

Follow this link – https://hari-kirtana.com/qualities-ratio-calculator – to download a simple worksheet (pdf file) that will help you see how the three qualities of material nature are influencing you.

INSTRUCTIONS:

1. Read the first phrase in the "Activity" column and then choose which phrase in either the "Luminance," "Passion," or "Darkness" column you would use to complete the sentence. Put a checkmark in the "+" cell to the right of whichever phrase you choose to complete the sentence.
2. You can choose more than one phrase if you would complete the sentence differently according to different circumstances.
3. Repeat the process for every phrase that begins in the "Activity" column, putting a checkmark in the "+" cell to the right of whichever phrase you choose to complete the sentence.
4. When you get to the bottom of the worksheet, add up the checkmarks in each "+" column.
5. Your "Score" shows you how the three qualities of material nature are influencing you in terms of the overall ratio of illumination, passion, and darkness currently manifesting in the various aspects of your life.

6. Consider the ratio you came up with and use the Notes section to write out your response to seeing how the qualities of material nature are impacting your life.

Reverse-engineering the Sequence of Illusion

"Truth would quickly cease to be stranger than fiction once we got as used to it."
~ H.L. Mencken

Mount Freedom, a *shtetl* nested in the Shawangunk Mountains, was once the epicenter of New Jersey's Borscht Belt. At its peak in the 1940s, it was a vacation magnet for Orthodox Jews who spent their summers at the bungalow colonies that sprung up within walking distance of a synagogue and a stone's throw from local hotels that featured A-list entertainers.

The mid-1950s was the beginning of the end. New turnpikes started luring vacationers out to the Jersey shore or up to New York's Catskill mountains. New zoning and building regulations beckoned real estate developers who would soon replace the town's hotels and bungalow colonies. When I arrived, in the summer of 1970, Mt. Freedom was well into the twilight of its run as a resort destination.

But time and real estate development hadn't changed the weather. Mt. Freedom's high elevation ensured that summer temperatures rarely rose above 90 degrees. It was still a perfect place for a sleep-away tennis camp.

And tennis camp was what brought me to Mt. Freedom. I was 14-years-old and my family had just moved from our humble starter home to a new and conspicuously more upscale neighborhood, where tennis was the de-facto sport of the country club set. I was reasonably athletic, but I was too small for football, too short for basketball, too slow for track, and too wiry for gymnastics. Process of elimination conspired with the pressures of social conformity to turn me into a tennis player.

My parents didn't send me off to tennis camp with the idea that it would lead to a professional career in the sport; they were thinking that spending one summer of my youth at a top-level tennis camp would give me a strong foundation in a recreational pastime that I might enjoy for the rest of my life.

They were also thinking that I might become like them: aspirational. They figured that sending me off to hobnob with country club kids on tennis courts would be a good first step toward the kind of hobnobbing they hoped would take me in the direction of respectable upward mobility.

Of course, the first thing I did was to make friends with the other kid at the camp who didn't give a *drek* about respectable upward mobility. As it turned out, he lived a short distance from my new neighborhood. We became good friends that summer and remained so for many years.

There was another kid at that camp who I'll never forget, either. At the start of camp, we all played in a tournament to determine our initial rankings within our age groups. Whenever I wasn't playing in the tournament myself, I watched this kid play because everything about his game was so . . . interesting. As in wrong. And not just wrong; way wrong. He held his racket wrong, he held his body wrong, his strokes were loopy and bizarre, and his service motion looked like the frenzied burst of a herky-jerky jack-in-the-box.

His whole game was *farkakte* but he hit the ball hard, he ran down every shot that his opponents sent back over the net, and even though his serve looked like something out of a Monty Python sketch, he could ace you with it. He did everything wrong and he was totally unbeatable.

So, of course, he won the tournament.

But it was what he did after the tournament that really got my attention: he asked the camp coaches to move him to the bottom of the rankings. He knew that his position at the top of the ladder was an illusion, that he was doing everything wrong and that he had to replace all of his bad habits with good ones if he ever wanted to progress beyond his current level. I learned later that this was why he came to tennis camp: to have the camp instructors take apart his unconventional playing style and reconstruct it in a conventional mold.

In accordance with his wishes, his name was moved to the bottom of the ladder. He was clearly determined to reverse-engineer his playing style and over the course of the next six weeks I watched him do it. Bit by bit, the instructors undid and redid everything about his game, working backwards to the physical origin points of his odd performance and re-directing his raw talent into proper technique. Day by day, match by match, he let go of his old way of playing and internalized the new techniques that the coaches were teaching him.

It wasn't long before his wackadoodle playing style was replaced by textbook fundamentals and confidence in a new set of skills.

Six weeks later, he was the top ranked player in our age group.

. . . .

If you think reverse-engineering a handful of awkward tennis habits accumulated over just a few years is challenging, imagine how hard reverse-engineering habits that we've accumulated over the course of millions of past lives could be.

Of all of our habits, the fundamental habit of material consciousness, misidentifying ourselves as being the material minds and bodies we temporarily inhabit, is the most deeply rooted and therefore the most difficult to unlearn. Even if we know material consciousness is an illusory condition, it's our comfort zone. It's familiar territory.

Unlike the kid at the camp who was determined to unlearn his peculiar playing style, we tend to hold on to our sense of mis-identification, often more tightly than we realize until we try to let go of it. A considerable amount of conviction and resolve, along with expert guidance, is required for us to successfully step out of the comfort zone of material consciousness and into the unfamiliar territory of spiritual consciousness.

At first, it may feel as if spiritual truth is stranger than material fiction. Acting on the basis of our true spiritual nature may take some getting used to. But, at least in my experience, the rewards of stepping out of our comfort zone and into the zone of transcendental knowledge are contentment, clarity, and feelings of optimism about the future.

Crossing the bridge that leads from material consciousness to spiritual consciousness is a gradual process. And a magical one: the further you go across the bridge, the easier it becomes to be in two places at once: the material world and the spiritual world. The process of crossing the bridge is not so much one of leaving the material world behind as one of moving through the material world with the benefit of transcendental knowledge.

What we do in the world may change or it may not, but how we see the world will definitely change: the three qualities of material nature, invisible to the untrained eye, will become as plain as the nose on your face; cats and dogs and pigeons and cows will appear to us as people in non-human bodies rather than as simply being the non-human bodies they inhabit; existence itself will appear to be self-evident proof of an ultimate cause upon which the effect of existence depends.

The sequence of illusion begins with the siren's song of the mind and senses and ends with our subordination to them. The result is that we find ourselves being blindly smashed against the rocks of repeated birth and death over and over again. Surrendering to our mind and senses is how we lose sight of our eternal spiritual identity. Regaining our spiritual vision requires that we put an end to this habitual capitulation, which we can do by reversing the sequence.

Do you think you can reverse-engineer the sequence of illusion and turn it into a sequence of self-realization?

....

Passages to Contemplate

2.62

When one's thoughts dwell on objects that attract the senses, attachment to those objects develops. From attachment to such sense objects, the desire to satisfy the senses is born and from the desire to satisfy the senses, anger arises.

2.63

Anger gives rise to bewilderment and with bewilderment comes a loss of memory. When one's memory is lost, the power of discernment is lost with it. As the power of discernment recedes, the self vanishes from view.

2.64

But those who remain free from attractions and aversions, exercising self-control even as the senses engage with their objects, attain the grace of the Lord.

2.65

The miseries of material existence cease for a recipient of such grace and, with a clear mind, their power of discernment is firmly established.

Questions for Conversation or Group Discussion

1. What's the real extent of our free will when it comes to "choosing" what we like or dislike? Do you think *karma* and the qualities of material nature play a role in free will? Why or why not?
2. Look at the sequence of illusion that Kṛṣṇa described in verses 2.62-63 (above) and compare that sequence to the following reverse-engineered version of the same verses:

   "When one's thoughts dwell on objects that AWAKEN the SPIRITUAL senses, attachment to those objects develops. From attachment to those sense objects, the desire to satisfy the SPIRITUAL senses is born. And from the desire to satisfy the SPIRITUAL senses, CONTENTMENT arises.

   CONTENTMENT gives rise to CLARITY and with CLARITY, memory is RESTORED. When one's memory is RESTORED, the power of discernment is RESTORED with it. As the power of discernment RETURNS, WE CAN ONCE AGAIN SEE THE TRUE NATURE OF THE SELF."

Do you think this reverse-engineered process would work? Why or why not?

Questions for Personal Contemplation / Journaling

1. Has there ever been a time in your life when you felt as if you'd lost your way, as if you'd somehow become estranged from who you really are? If so, what did you do to get yourself back on track?
2. Can you think of something you could meditate on that might awaken your spiritual senses?
3. If you developed the ability to see your true spiritual nature, how do you think that would change the way you move through the world?

Personal Experiment

Follow this link – https://hari-kirtana.com/supreme-self-meditation – to download a 12-minute meditation that will guide you toward a visualization of the Supreme Self who's situated within your heart and within the hearts of all beings.

Seeing with Equal Vision

"There is nothing insignificant in the world.
It all depends on how one looks at it."
~ Johann Wolfgang von Goethe

The heat was intense. The smell of smoke filled my nostrils. The room was pitch black; I couldn't see a thing. My mind was sending me an urgent message: "You're going the wrong way! Go the *other* way!"

I ignored my mind and inched my way forward, each blind step taking me closer to the invisible source of the rising heat that was blanketing the front of my body.

Suddenly, thin glowing tendrils of orange and blue twisted angrily right above me, flickering just long enough to whisper, "Here it comes!" before they disappeared. I held my breath.

But not for long. The next thing I knew, a tsunami of flames raced out across the ceiling from the top of the wall in front of me. I was standing beneath a blazing canopy of rippling fire.

I let go of the hose and adjusted the aperture on my video camera as the men in front of me shot quick hits of straight stream at the inferno above us.

In 2005, I was a civilian employee of the New York City Fire Department. My job was to produce training videos. The simulated fire I'd walked into was part of a training exercise in a building at the FDNY Academy on Randall's Island. My responsibility was to record the performance of the Probies (probationary firefighters) for evaluation purposes. It was an interesting job: I got to be a fly on the wall for everything from fire inspections in Chinatown garment factories to interdepartmental drills in preparation for potential terrorist attacks.

I also got to document the development of an escape system that firefighters could use if the only way out of a burning building was through a window on an upper floor. Week after week I went to an assortment of abandoned buildings around the city with a team of firefighters, some with military or rock-climbing experience, who were testing various kinds of rope, carabiners, and hooks, and techniques for exiting through a window. I recorded them as they worked through every scenario they could think of in order to design equipment and an exit strategy that could save a firefighter's life.

And, even though I wasn't a firefighter, they let me try the finished system. I put on some borrowed bunker gear and executed the maneuver exactly as I'd seen it done dozens of times. If I ever have to anchor a rope to a steam pipe, roll head-first out of a fifth-floor window, spin around like a spider, and repel down the side of a building, I know how to do it.

One day, while the escape system training sessions were going on inside the big building at the FDNY Training Facility, I was hanging out with one of the firefighters on the design team. We were standing just inside the entrance to the building. I had my back to a closed garage door.

As we were talking, this brave and selfless firefighter, who wouldn't hesitate to run into a burning building to save a stranger's life, nonchalantly reached his right hand up and over my left shoulder. I turned my head just in time to see him squish a bug that was crawling up the garage door window just behind my ear.

It wasn't a dangerous bug. It was just a garden-variety bug doing its bug thing when, all of a sudden, it was crushed to death by someone who was in the business of saving lives.

I'm sure my expression didn't give it away, but I was kind of horrified. I had long since come to believe that all living beings are spiritually equal. As far as I was concerned, the person who was karmically obligated to inhabit that bug body was, on a spiritual level, no different from me, a person who was karmically privileged to inhabit a human body. There but for the grace of God went I.

I had the utmost respect for all of the firefighters I met during my time at the FDNY. They were courageous, compassionate, generous, and dedicated, especially to one another. They were cheerfully fatalistic, they were both macho and humble, they could be deadly serious one minute and slapstick comedians the next. They were fun to work with. It was an honor to be among them. The firefighter I was hanging out with was no exception.

And yet, killing this hapless little creature for no particular reason seemed perfectly normal to him. I suppose it would've seemed perfectly normal to most people.

I didn't say anything as he wiped the remnants of the bug's body off of his thumb. He kept talking as if nothing had happened.

....

One of the paradoxes of the Bhagavad-gītā is that Kṛṣṇa lists *ahiṁsā*, non-violence, as an element of knowledge (13.8) while making an argument in favor of fighting. In its positive expression, *ahiṁsā* means demonstrating compassion for all beings. Practicing *ahiṁsā* means making a good faith effort to do the least possible harm to any and every living being.

The most obvious contemporary application of *ahiṁsā* is the adoption of a harm-free diet. It's worth noting that the four sources of nourishment that Kṛṣṇa says he'll accept when they're lovingly offered to him can be acquired without doing any harm to any living being, including plants (9.26).

If we accept the proposition that all sentient beings are spiritual beings with the same unalienable rights to life, liberty, and the pursuit of happiness that humans have, adopting, or at least moving in the direction of, a harm-free diet becomes an obvious moral choice. But the idea of spiritual equality has significant implications beyond any personal or environmental benefits that a harm-free diet might offer. If the long arc of history bends toward justice, then the force that's bending that arc is the spiritual equality of all beings. Recognizing the spiritual equality and unalienable rights of all beings is what lifts social activism to the level of spiritual activism. And spiritualizing social activism isn't an option if the pursuit of justice is to have any meaningful basis in the idea of equality.

To understand why this is so, let's consider the meaning of "equal." "Equal" means being the same in quantity, size, degree, value, status, or quality. "Equality" always implies two or more things that share the same "something" but are not the same thing. Logically, something can't be equal to itself because "equal" is a comparison between a multiplicity of things. "Equal" doesn't mean that we're all "One" in any literal sense because "equal" requires two or more things.

So, how are we all equal? Well, certainly not by any empirical measurement. No one's physical body has all the same quantities or qualities as another person's body. We're not equal metaphysically, either; we all have different psychologies and different levels of intelligence. Nor are we equal in terms of our possessions, talents, or accomplishments. Some of us are smarter than others. Some of us are faster than others. Some of us are stronger than others. Some of us are wealthier or more influential or more beautiful than others.

From a purely materialistic perspective, there's no possibility of equality. And if there's no meaning to our lives other than the meaning we create for ourselves then we have no objective measure by which we can substantiate equality. We just have everyone's subjective conception of "equality" which, by definition, is not the same as anyone's else's.

In other words, it's impossible to rationally establish anything we can call "equality" on a material level. The only way to make a rational case for the equality of all people is on a spiritual level. And on a spiritual level, that equality isn't limited to human beings; it extends to all beings.

According to the Gītā, all sentient beings are quantitatively different but qualitatively equal. As Kṛṣṇa puts it, "The living beings in this world of conditioned life are eternal fragments of my very Self" (15.7). If all beings are part and parcel of Kṛṣṇa, the Supreme Spiritual Being, then, from the Gītā's point of view, the spiritual equality of all beings is a self-evident truth.

Without a spiritual context, social activism has no rational basis for equality. Without equality, we don't have a rational basis for justice. Without justice, we don't have a rational foundation upon which to build a peaceful society. Peace requires justice, justice requires equality, and equality requires a spiritual conception of personhood. Therefore, social activism must take place within a spiritual context if the pursuit of justice is to have any meaningful basis in an assertion of equality.

The activation of transcendental knowledge brings about equal vision: the ability to see the spiritual equality of all beings. Equal vision is the basis for spiritual activism: engagement with the world from a transcendental perspective. It's not as if we just go up a ladder and leave the world behind. Transcendental knowledge gives us the ability to be in two places at once: in the world and beyond the world.

....

Passages to Contemplate

5.18

Those who are wise see an elevated soul who is endowed with higher learning and a gentle disposition, a cow, an elephant, a dog, and one who eats dogs, with equal vision.

5.29

Peace is attained by knowing me to be the beneficiary of all sacrifices and austerities, the Supreme Lord of all worlds, and the most benevolent friend within the heart of all beings.

13.28

One who sees the same Supreme Lord residing within all living beings, who sees the imperishable within the perishable, actually sees.

Questions for Conversation or Group Discussion

1. Do you accept the proposition that all beings are spiritually equal? If not, why not? If so, does this idea change the way you relate to other sentient beings? If so, in what way?
2. Consider this passage from the U.S. Declaration of Independence:

   "*We hold these truths to be self-evident, that all men are created equal, that they are endowed by their Creator with certain unalienable Rights, that among these are Life, Liberty and the pursuit of Happiness.*"

   How does this passage apply to the idea of spiritual equality?

   Now, change the word "men" to "living beings." Does this statement still qualify as a "self-evident" truth?
3. Is there a connection between the concept of spiritual equality and the concept of the law of *karma*? If so, what's the connection?

Questions for Personal Contemplation / Journaling

1. When you hear the word "equality," what does that mean to you? Can you think of a way to establish the idea of equality on something other than a spiritual level?
2. How does your sense of personal identity correspond to the social causes you support? Are the causes you support just as aligned with your understanding of your eternal spiritual identity as with your temporary material identity?
3. What's your relationship to people who support the same social or political causes that you support? What's your relationship to people who oppose the social or political causes that you support? Do you think you can apply the principle of "equal vision" as easily to those who share your point of view as those who do not? Why or why not?

Personal Experiment

Be on the look-out for non-human sentient beings in your environment: cats, dogs, birds, squirrels, deer, bugs, etc. When you see them, try reframing your conception of them by thinking of them as people in animal bodies instead of thinking of them as animals. Notice if this changes your perception of them or your feelings about them.

Try the same thing with animals that are commonly thought of as food: cows, pigs, chickens, fish, etc. Notice if this changes your perception of them or your feelings about them.

Learning to Surrender

"Some of us think holding on makes us strong;
but sometimes it is letting go."
~ Hermann Hesse

An eastward swing down Porter Street, a long tree-lined mediary between two busy thoroughfares in the northwest quadrant of Washington, D.C., offers an easy downhill glide to bicyclists with a modicum of common sense.

But am I a sensible cyclist? Nope.

I was coasting down a curve after leaving a friend's house near the top of the hill when I realized that I'd forgotten to roll up my right pant leg to avoid its ruination by the grease from the chain.

An intelligent rider would have just stopped for a moment to safely attend to such sartorial concerns.

But am I an intelligent rider? Nope.

On the assumption that I could easily correct this oversight without interrupting my ride, I bent my knee to bring my foot up toward the seat and reached back for the cuff at my ankle. Glancing over my shoulder was my big mistake: the next thing I knew, my front wheel was perpendicular to my trajectory, and the laws of physics demanded that I be launched out of my seat and up over the handlebars.

As time slowed down to let me fully appreciate the sensation of weightlessness and contemplate what the promise of gravity had in store for me, an inner voice spoke to me. The voice said, "Surrender."

So that's what I did. Somehow or other, I was able to instantly surrender to the inevitable as I catapulted through the air *en route* to a rendezvous with the pavement below. I let go, both literally and figuratively, relaxing my body as I accepted the departure of my hands from the handlebar. I rolled through the air, landed across the backs of my shoulders, and popped up to my feet just in time to see the eyes of the driver in the car behind me nearly pop out of his head as he hit the brakes . . . also just in time.

And so it goes: one moment we're gliding through life, the next moment life gives us a beating. They say the only things in life that are certain are death and taxes. I'm certain that we should add uncertainty to that list.

....

The Sanskrit words *prapadyante,* "to offer oneself to" (appearing in verses 4.11 and 7.14), and *śaraṇaṁ,* "to take shelter of" (appearing in verses 9.18 and 18.66), offer us a way to think about surrender other than as "giving up." In the spiritual philosophy of the Bhagavad-gītā, "surrender" is an act of humility rather than an expression of humiliation, an acknowledgement of reality rather than an admission of defeat. It's the recognition that the basic need for shelter extends beyond the merely physical or psychological but to the spiritual as well.

Psychologists tell us that uncertainty is unhealthy, that we need to have some sense of certainty about the future, some confidence in our ability to control the outcomes of our actions. I think I can, I think I can, I know I can . . . Yet, time after time, the will of providence pulls the rug out from under our feet, repeatedly proving to us that thinking we've got the situation under control is an illusion. Which makes us anxious. And angry. And bewildered.

All of which can serve as a reminder that moving through a sequence of desire, anger, and bewilderment is how we lost sight of our true spiritual nature in the first place.

As I crouched by the side of the road to see if my bicycle had sustained as much damage as I had (it hadn't), I took a moment to reflect on how I had clearly been defeated by the laws of material nature, the will of providence, and my own poor judgment. And I thought about how my choice to surrender to the fate I had created for myself probably saved me from more serious injury.

We don't usually notice how the force of gravity holds us to the earth or how the laws of physics dictate the nature of our experience. Similarly, we're usually unaware of how our attempts to control events in accordance with our desires actually entangles us in a world we can't control. The result is that we continually find ourselves being ejected from comfortable situations and thrown into uncomfortable ones in a perpetual cycle of alternating happiness and distress.

The Bhagavad-gītā tells us that we have an alternative to being thrown hither and thither by the illusory power of material nature: surrender to the source of that power.

....

Passages to Contemplate

2.7

My heart is afflicted by a wretched weakness. My thoughts are in disarray as I try to ascertain which path is virtuous. Therefore, I am asking you to tell me with certainty what course of action would serve the greatest good. Please tell me, for I am now your disciple; a soul surrendered to you.

7.14

My divine power of illusion, composed of the qualities of material nature, is nearly impossible to overcome. But those who offer themselves to me can easily cross beyond this bewildering power.

9.18

I am the goal, the sustainer, the master, and the witness. I am the abode, the shelter, and the most intimate friend. I am the origin and the dissolution, the foundation of existence, the resting place and the imperishable seed.

Questions for Conversation or Group Discussion

1. What comes to mind when you think of "surrender"?
2. How is the idea of surrender in a spiritual context different from the idea of surrender in a material context?
3. How is thinking about spirituality as a process for becoming an instrument of Divine Will different from thinking of spirituality as a strategy for developing a personal sense of contentment?

Questions for Personal Contemplation / Journaling

1. What would an act of surrender to your conception of a Supreme Being consist of?
2. How might surrender to your conception of a Supreme Being be empowering? How might it be intimidating? Or scary?
3. What might you want to give up or renounce as an act of surrender?
4. What might you try to acquire to enable you to surrender?

Personal Experiments

1. Make a list of three simple things that you're in control of. Then, for each item on the list, make a list of three things that you have no control over upon which the thing you *do* have control over depends. For example, if you control when you go out to buy groceries, you could list when the grocery store is open, the presence of the groceries you want or need in the grocery store, and circumstances like the weather or road closures that might impact your ability to get there as three things you *don't* control that need to be in alignment with your desire to go to the grocery store.

   After you make your list, sit with it for a bit and see what comes up for you. What does your list say about the extent of your control over events? What does it say about the degree of your dependence on things that are beyond your control?

2. Reflect back on the emotional arc of the Bhagavad-gītā, from Arjuna's initial condition to Kṛṣṇa's initial response to Arjuna's distress to the central verses and the revelation of the Universal Form all the way to the final chapter. Try to draw a map of both Arjuna's and Kṛṣṇa's journey in terms of the emotional states of being they express throughout the Gītā from beginning to middle to end.

Afterword

"If I find within myself a desire which no experience of this world can fulfill, then I must conclude that I was made for another world."
~ C.S. Lewis

We all share the same ultimate goal: happiness. Any other objective we pursue is a means to that end. You read this book because you hoped it would make you happy or, better still, show you how to become happy.

Over the course of his conversation with Kṛṣṇa, Arjuna's conception of happiness changes. In the beginning, he thinks that getting what he wants will make him happy. His inability to see how to get what he wants is the source of his despair. In the end, Arjuna comes to understand that trying to change the situation in order to get what he wants is, in itself, a strategy for unhappiness.

It usually doesn't occur to us to think that the pursuit of happiness might be the cause of unhappiness. Pursuing happiness seems to be a perfectly normal thing to do. And in one sense, it is: joy is hardwired into our spiritual identity so it's natural for us to gravitate toward whatever we think will bring us joy.

The real problem isn't the pursuit itself; it's the direction that the pursuit takes us in. Most of us are pursuing material happiness because it's the only kind of happiness we know. We don't make a distinction between material happiness, which is fleeting at best, and spiritual happiness, which is lasting by definition, simply for lack of spiritual knowledge.

However, once we have that knowledge, we still have the challenge of adapting to it in order to actualize it. The obstacle here is that our dormant spiritual senses are covered by a thick, wet blanket of material energy. The real obstacle to our happiness, then, isn't a world that refuses to align itself with our desires; it's the absence of knowledge combined with a heavy veil of illusion that covers our spiritual vision.

A thoughtful person will naturally inquire as to how this veil can be lifted and our spiritual vision restored. The Bhagavad-gītā is guidebook for doing just that.

The Gītā tells us that our natural state of being is one of joyful equanimity, that we have the innate capacity for complete self-knowledge, that we're spiritually indestructible, and that someone who's infinitely greater than we are is ready, willing, and able to help us return to that natural state of being.

What if the Gītā is right? What if the technology of yoga really can help us to attain a state of transcendental consciousness? What if there really is a Supreme Person living within our hearts, patiently waiting for the opportunity to guide us home.

What then?

Poverty, climate change, food insecurity, global instability, inadequate healthcare systems, disinformation, extremism, and the many faces of violence that plague our planet are all urgent problems that people of good will are anxious to solve. The acceleration of these problems bears witness to the persistence of short-sightedness, self-centeredness, and delusion, particularly among those who control the levers of power.

We can't solve a problem by using the same kind of thinking that was used to create it. Constraining ourselves to materialistic thinking that ignores the spiritual context within which the world operates won't cut it. What's needed is the introduction, dissemination, and actualization of spiritually enlightened values to provide us with a foundation upon which otherwise intractable real-world problems can be substantively addressed and resolved.

We know that there is something wrong with the world. We may not know exactly what it is, but we know that something's not right. It's not a little thing; it's a million little things that add up to one big thing, an underlying defect in the foundation of the world that can only be seen, understood, and counteracted by a collective transformation of consciousness and a corresponding call to action.

Beyond the problems of the world are the questions we ask about ourselves: questions about what it means to be in the world, to be human, to be; questions about how we'll get through the most trying moments of our lives and how a life that will inevitably end in death can be lived in a way that awakens us to life everlasting. Even when our lives appear to be going reasonably well, we suspect that there's an underlying defect in the foundation of our experience that can only be seen, understood, and counteracted by a personal transformation of consciousness and a corresponding course of action.

The practical application of spiritual solutions to material problems, big and small, personal or social, opens up a path that can lead us to peace, freedom, deeper understanding, and transcendental happiness; a path along which we can change the terms of any personal battle we face, serve something greater than ourselves, and turn inescapable tragedies into glorious victories.

Acknowledgments

I offer my deepest expression of gratitude to my *parama-guru*, A.C. Bhaktivedanta Swami Prabhupāda, who provided the philosophical, theological, and hermeneutical foundation upon which my presentation of the Bhagavad-gītā rests. Śrīla Prabhupāda's personal commitment to the spiritual upliftment of human society profoundly changed the course of my life. I hope that this book contributes something of value to his mission of bringing unity, peace, friendship, and prosperity to the world.

To Śrīla Prabhupāda's disciple and my *dīkṣā-guru*, Satsvarūpa dāsa Goswāmī, thank you for giving me my name and, by the example of your own writing, a license to explore the many ways in which a modern author can faithfully re-present traditional spiritual wisdom.

I owe the substance of my explanations about how to meet the Gītā's challenges and understand its concepts to my many teachers, whose lectures I continually listen to. To Ravindra-svarūpa Prabhu (William H. Deadwyler, Ph.D.) and Hridayananda das Goswami (Howard J. Resnick, Ph.D.), your contributions to my repertoire of elucidations are too numerous to list. I'm very grateful for all of them. To Dhanurdhara Swami, a special thank you for being a consistent source of enlightenment, inspiration, encouragement, and friendship. To Jayādvaita Swami, thank you for your very reassuring assessment of my efforts as well as your helpful correctives. To Bhūrijāna Prabhu, thank you for showing me the ways in which the Gītā's chapters are connected to one another and for your insightful suggestion as we walked together near the Yamunā River that morning many years ago. To Urmilā Devī Dāsī (Dr. Edith Best), thank you for sharing your valuable insights into the science of scriptural exegesis with me, as well as for sharing your expertise on the topic of *dharma*.

I relied on a wide variety of test readers to give me feedback at various points along the way to completing this book. Each of them made valuable and deeply appreciated contributions that helped me to stay focused on what was essential, part ways with what was superfluous, correct everything that was erroneous, and clarify anything that was fuzzy. To Prof. Edwin Bryant, thank you for your thoughtful analysis of my approach to the Gītā and for saving me from a few prefatory faux pas. To Dr. Måns Broo, thank you for so scrutinizingly evaluating my use of Sanskrit, for offering so many constructive points of critical wisdom, and for your excellent interior design suggestion. To Pranada Comtois, thank you for your practical advice, resource recommendations, encouraging words, and inspiring example.

To Jessica Karpiak, thank you for pointing out the blanks I needed to fill in and for stopping me from shooting myself in the foot. To Dr. Trish Tillman, thank you for sharing your knowledge of history, your observations on the allure of urban settings, and for urging me not to tiptoe through the tulips. To Christy Freer, thank you for helping me to keep concepts connected in clear, logical sequences and for making sure I didn't lose track of any loose wires. To Rebecca Freeh, thank you for doing an early round of copy editing and for letting me know what portions of the text were especially illuminating for you. To Vraj Vihari Prabhu, thank you for your helpful feedback on my earliest drafts, and to Tara Mitchell, thank you for taking my renditions of the Gītā's verses for a test drive.

I owe a great debt of gratitude to all of my friends and students who've taken workshops, courses, and trainings with me, the many people who exchanged correspondence with me, and especially those who gave me the honor of allowing me to be their mentor for the past few years. Your questions, comments, doubts, and realizations told me what readers would want to know and need to hear. To Stanley Currier, Be Luecke, Turtle Angelo, Esther Urbano-Thomas, Touré Akela, Kerry Contini, Martha Windhall, Leslie Harrington, David Watt, Thomas Brown, Deborah Teasley, Diane Timmerman, Amanda Roache, Caron Harris, Michelle Henderson, Bill Liger, John LeBlanc, and a host of others whose thoughtful engagement with me has informed my thinking about how to present the Gītā to a modern Western audience, my heartfelt thanks. To Delia Gallegos, a special thank you for so many meaningful conversations and for fine-tuning my conceptual illustrations. To Min Kim, an extra-special thank you for your enthusiastic dedication to scriptural study, for your willingness to dive into the deep end of the pool, and for helping me think through the ways in which readers can get the greatest possible benefit from my tips for contemplative reading.

As I considered the purpose and methodologies of this book, my thinking was influenced by some exceptionally smart and very generous people. To Dr. Zane Gibbs, thank you for helping me identify the obstacles readers might have to overcome in order to experience the Gītā's transformative potential. To Michelle Martello, gadzooks! What would I have done for all these years without you guiding me through every aspect of online entrepreneurship? Thank you so much! To Prof. Ravi Gupta, thank you for dropping such an important missing piece into the puzzle of how the validation of spiritual truth and reasonable faith aren't dependent on the historicity of scriptural content. To Brooke Gladstone, thank you for giving me a different take on the nature of reality, and to Stacey Gladstone, thank you for helping me learn how to describe the unnaturalness of death. To Jen Rak, thank you for making me think about how different I was ten years ago . . . ten years ago; your impromptu visualization has stayed with me all this time, benefitted dozens of students with whom I've shared it since, and, hopefully, will continue to give readers of this book something to think about for many years to come.

I had two great writing coaches. Jocelyn Lindsey, thank you for helping me polish the lens that I've invited my readers to look through when they read the Gītā and take its teachings out of this book and into their lives. Marisa Corcoran, thank you for teaching me about story strip-downs, word closets, sales page structures, and meet-cutes, all of which were more applicable to writing a non-fiction book about spiritual philosophy than you might have imagined.

To all of the Yoga Teacher Training leaders who invited me to be a guest teacher in their programs, thank you for giving me an opportunity to engage with your students, work out my ideas in live settings, and learn more about my audience. To all the students who enrolled in my own yoga teacher trainings, thank you for your enthusiastic participation in all of our discussions.

Among the dozen browser windows that decorate my desktop every day, the one that's dedicated to Bhaktivedanta Vedabase has been the most constant and essential source of information during the course of writing this book. To the great souls who keep this site up and running, especially Prahlād Nṛsiṁha das, all glories to your service.

To my final copy editor, Holli Chmela: by the time you got my manuscript I'd gone through it so many times that I was *sure* you wouldn't have much to do. Ha ha! Thank you for another exquisitely precise and thorough job.

To my dear friend and favorite proofreader, Syamala Priya, thank you for so carefully casting your gaze on every page of my final edited manuscript.

To K4V3R1, thank you for coming up with such an original concept and illustration for the cover, to Jal Keli das, thank you for so generously creating the foundation of the cover's design, and to both of you, thank you for your willingness to collaborate with me and for all the patience and tolerance that entailed.

To Mayapriya Long, thank you for making the time to conceptualize and design the interior of this book, for all the care you took in executing its technical and aesthetic details, for putting the finishing touches on the cover, and for all of your help in preparing this book for publication.

Lastly, and most importantly, this book would never have been written at all were it not for the all-encompassing support and unwavering encouragement I received from my amazing wife, Elizabeth Elson. Beyond just making this book possible, Elizabeth was my indispensable developmental editor who used her story-telling expertise to ensure that each section and the book as a whole flowed smoothly toward a clear conclusion. Hers was the voice of persistence when sections that I thought were almost finished were actually just off to a good start and of perseverance when I felt fed up with the whole project. She's my manager, my patron, my extra brain, the President of my fan club and the Queen of my life. Elizabeth, I just can't thank you enough.

Partial Bibliography and Resources

Prabhupada, A.C. Bhaktivedanta Swami (1986). *Bhagavad-gītā As It Is.* Bhaktivedanta Book Trust.

Goswami, H.D. (2015) *A Comprehensive Guide to Bhagavad-gītā with Literal Translation*. Krishna West, Inc.

Schweig, Graham M. (2007). *Bhagavad-gītā: The Beloved Lord's Secret Love Song.* HarperCollins.

Dasa, Bhurijana (1997). *Surrender Unto Me: An Overview of the Bhagavad-gītā.* VIHE Publications.

Greene, Joshua M. (2008). *Gita Wisdom: An Introduction to India's Essential Yoga Text.* Mandala Publishing.

Dasi, Visakha Devi (2011). *Harmony and the Bhagavad-gita: Lessons from a Life-changing Move to the Wilderness.* Torchlight Publishing, Inc.

Swami, B.V. Tripurari (2001). *The Bhagavad Gita: It's Feeling and Philosophy.* Mandala Publishing Group.

Radhakrishnan, S. (1948 / 2011). *The Bhagavadgita.* George Allen & Unwin / HarperCollins.

Sridhar, Swami B.R. (2006). *Śrīmad Bhagavad-gītā: The Hidden Treasure of the Sweet Absolute.* Vaisnava Seva Society.

Easwaran, Eknath (2000). *The Bhagavad Gita.* Vintage Spiritual Classics / Random House

Mascarò, Juan (1994). *The Bhagavad Gita.* Penguin Classics.

Rama, Swami (1985). *Perennial Psychology of the Bhagavad Gita.* The Himalayan Institute Press.

Davis, Richard H. (2015). *The Bhagavad Gita: A Biography.* Princeton University Press.

Lovejoy, Arthur O. (1976). *The Great Chain of Being: A Study of the History of an Idea.* Harvard University Press

Comtois, Pranada (2022). *Bhakti Shakti: Goddess of Divine Love.* Chandra Media.

Fraenkel, Andy (2013). *Mahabharata: The Eternal Quest.* Flying Mountain Press.

Best, Urmila Edith and Ruchira S. Datta (2023). *Career Dharma: The Natural Art of Work.* Nine Islands Media.

Evans, Rachel Held (2021). *Wholehearted Faith.* HarperCollins.

Gladstone, Brooke (2017). *The Trouble with Reality: A Rumination on Moral Panic in Our Time.* Workman Publishing.

Kegan, Robert and Lisa Laskow Lahey (2009). *Immunity to Change: How to Overcome It and Unlock the Potential in Yourself and Your Organization.* Harvard Business Press.

Williams, Justin Michael (2020). *Stay Woke: A Meditation Guide for the Rest of Us.* Sounds True.

Tippett, Krista (2007). *Speaking of Faith.* Viking Penguin Group.

Śrīmad Bhagavad-gītā (n.d.). Bhagavad-gita.org. https://bhagavad-gita.org/

Bhagavad-gītā As It Is (n.d.). Vedabase.io. https://vedabase.io/en/library/bg/

About the Author

Hari-kirtana das is a yoga teacher and mentor who guides people on journeys of self-discovery, spiritual reconstruction, and personal transformation. He's been practicing various forms of yoga and meditation for almost 50 years, lived in yoga ashrams and intentional communities, worked for Fortune 500 companies and Silicon Valley start-ups, and brings a wide range of spiritual knowledge and life experience to his books, talks, workshops, and courses. His talent for making complex ideas easy to understand, keen sense of humor, enthusiasm for meaningful dialogue, and passion for critical thinking have made him a sought-after yoga teacher training instructor, public speaker, and podcast guest. Hari's articles and essays about the enduring relevance of yoga's ancient wisdom appear in various forums and journals. He lives in Washington, D.C., with his wife, Elizabeth.

Printed in the USA
CPSIA information can be obtained
at www.ICGtesting.com
JSHW081938190424
61543JS00005B/154

9 780998 077314